D1012649

THE BIRTH OF TRAGEDY

AND

THE GENEALOGY OF MORALS

Wilhelm Friedrich Nietzsche was born into a family of clergymen in the Prussian province of Saxony in 1844. He studied at the universities of Bonn and Leipzig and in 1869 was appointed Professor of Philology at the University of Basel, where he taught for ten years. He suffered a nervous collapse in 1889 and died in Weimar in 1900.

His works include *Thus Spake Zarathustra* (Parts 1–3, 1883–84; Part 4, 1891), *Human, All Too Human* (1878), *Joyful Wisdom* (1882), and *Beyond Good and Evil* (1886).

The Birth of Tragedy was first published in 1872 and *The Genealogy of Morals* in 1887. These two works have been translated expressly for the Anchor edition by Francis Golffing.

FRIEDRICH NIETZSCHE

THE BIRTH OF TRAGEDY

AND

THE GENEALOGY OF MORALS

TRANSLATED BY

FRANCIS GOLFFING

Doubleday Anchor Books

DOUBLEDAY & COMPANY, INC.
GARDEN CITY, NEW YORK

LIBRARY OF CONGRESS CATALOG CARD NUMBER 56–7535

The Anchor Books edition is the first publication of this translation of *The Birth of Tragedy* and *The Genealogy of Morals*.

Anchor Books edition: 1956

Cover painting by Chi Kwan Chen
Cover layout by Christopher Simon

CONTENTS

The two works of Nietzsche presented in this volume are perhaps the richest in substance as well as the most connected in form of all the philosopher's abundant productions. They are separated from one another by a span of sixteen years: years of incessant intellectual labor, which saw Nietzsche's growing idolatry and final repudiation of Wagner, his warm espousal of Dr. Rée's trenchant psychology of motivation and his much more lasting endorsement of Taine's sociological theories, whose stress on environmental and racial factors reappears—with both an extraordinary gain in genius and an extraordinary loss in discretion—in the pages of *The Genealogy of Morals.* These same years had witnessed Nietzsche's elaboration of the grand secular myth whose troubling upshot is *Zarathustra:* a book where uncanny insight seems to be constantly at war with a language that is outrageous, that overreaches and thus caricatures its subject, and that achieves the singular feat of being at once acrobatic and stilted. Nietzsche's prose, for all its signal distinction, never numbered sobriety among its virtues; if in some of his earliest compositions the writer maintained a semblance of decorum, that semblance was soon abandoned. Nietzsche's peculiar rhetorical resources developed apace, a function, as has been convincingly argued, of his mounting distraction. The alternate fire and ice of his diction, the obsessive punning, the rapid successive flashes of brilliance degenerating, all too often, into mere flashiness—every reader of our author is familiar with these traits and finds himself by turns appalled and delighted. What makes Nietzsche's style so unique, and so uniquely disconcerting, is the delight it manages to create when, in a sense, it is at its worst: most mannered, or idiosyncratically ill-mannered; and conversely, the distaste it frequently provokes when it appears most plausible, poised, or authoritative. One might well suppose that such a perverse response on the part of the reader is the faithful reflection of a perverseness in the mind of the writer. Nietzsche strikes us as being most forthright, authentic, indeed most engaging, whenever he indulges freely his polemical rage, his tortuous ingenuity or his imaginative extravagance; the minute he tightens the reins and starts to lecture he is apt to sound ponderous, stiff, incredibly self-important and false. (The same may be said of Carlyle and, with certain qualifications, of Ruskin. Nietzsche shared many intellectual dispositions, even a few stylistic devices or crotchets, with Carlyle—a writer whom he detested—while he showed the highest regard for Emerson's sly and suave manner, thinking it somewhat akin to his own.) The trouble with *Zarathustra* lies not in its verbal pyrotechnics, nor in its doctrine, which is centrally sound: it lies in the author's stance, who in this work addresses the crowd from the wrong rostrum, with a fury that is obnoxious only because it is constantly restrained, occulted with biblical echoes, set out in rows of grandiloquent propositions which, instead of fiercely pointing out or persuading, *exhort*. It is mostly when he wishes to exhort, or otherwise edify, that Nietzsche becomes insufferable—witness a good many passages in both *The Genealogy of Morals* and *The Birth of Tragedy;* not enough of them, fortunately, to mar seriously either of these admirable jobs of demolition and, at the same time, of cogent and compelling exposition.

Of the two books in this volume, *The Genealogy of Morals* will doubtless prove the more exciting to contemporary readers: it has lost little of its shock value since the days when it was staged, by its author, as a frontal, all-out attack on the Christian ideal. The issue it propounds with so much genuine brilliance of argument in some places, so much brilliant sophistry in others, is as far from being a closed issue today as it was in 1887. The issue dealt with in the earlier book is certainly no whit less profound, and here Nietzsche's grasp of his material, in all its marvelous complexity, commands even greater respect. The central thesis of *The Birth of Tragedy* anticipates, by sheer intuition, it would seem, what Frazer, Gilbert Murray and Jane Harrison were later to establish quite irrefragably: the ritual origin of Greek tragedy, as well as the interdependence of myth and ritual in all primitive cultures. But the work is equally prophetic of Freud, if we consider its depth-psychological aspects and its insistence, in a different vocabulary to be sure, on the interaction in every individual of an ego, super-ego and id. (Nietzsche's scrutiny in *The Genealogy of Morals* of the phenomena of repression, compensation and sublimation may seem to some readers even more remarkable and at the same time more startlingly Freudian. So far as I know, Nietzsche has never received full credit as a forerunner of psychoanalysis.) But the very fact that both psychoanalysis and the Cambridge school of anthropology have been complacently embraced by our contemporaries—so much so that it almost looks as though today these two persuasions were dividing the entire realm of non-scientific speculation between them— might well rob Nietzsche's audacities of some of their impact; the kind of impact which, at least for the majority of readers, arises either from radical novelty (its charm or shock) or else from the appeal to a continuing, unappeased malaise of the mind. If we add to this limitation certain intrinsic flaws of *The Birth of Tragedy*: prolixity, repetitiousness, an occasional cloudiness of thought or inflation of style, not to mention the frequent lapses of both taste and judgment, then we can readily see why for an unprofessional audience *The Genealogy of Morals* would hold the stronger appeal: here all is sharply profiled, perspicuous, subtle; the style, coruscating, never flags in its brio; a sense of crisis, of extreme urgency, invades us from every page, and that urgency is not of yesterday only but of today and tomorrow; it concerns the confirmed atheist no less than the confirmed believer, and will certainly give pause to the agnostic.

For the rest, both books are major documents of Western thought and so can dispense with my commendation. To analyze them at length here would be inopportune, nor is this the place to engage in the kind of radical criticism which they have fully sustained in the past and which, unless I am much mistaken, they will continue to sustain in the future. I have tried to transpose both works with the minimum loss, but loss there will be, inevitably: let the reader be judge of all that has been lost in the traffic and then go on to consider the gain, however modest, accrued to our own language.

Francis Golffing

THE BIRTH OF TRAGEDY

AND

THE GENEALOGY OF MORALS

THE BIRTH OF TRAGEDY

(1870–71)

A Critical Backward Glance

I

Whatever it was that gave rise to this problematical work, of one thing there can be no question: the issue it propounded must have been supremely important and attractive as well as very personal to its author. The times in which (in spite of which) it was composed bear out that fact. The date is 1870–71, the turbulent period of the Franco-Prussian war. While the thunder of the Battle of Wörth was rumbling over Europe, a lover of subtleties and conundrums—father-to-be of this book—sat down in an alpine recess, much bemused and bedeviled (which is to say, both engrossed and detached) to pen the substance of that odd and forbidding work for which the following pages shall now serve as a belated preface or postscript. A few weeks later he could be discovered beneath the walls of Metz, still wrestling with the question mark which he had put after the alleged "serenity" of the Greeks and of Greek art; until at last, in that month of deep suspense which saw the emergence of peace at Versailles, he too made peace with himself and, still recovering from an ailment brought home from the field, gave final shape to *The Birth of Tragedy from the Spirit of Music.*

—From *music?* Music and tragedy? The Greeks and dramatic music? The Greeks and pessimistic art? The Greeks: this most beautiful and accomplished, this thoroughly sane, universally envied species of man—was it conceivable that they, of all people, should have stood in need of tragedy—or, indeed, of art? Greek art: how did it function, how *could* it?

3

By now the reader will have come to suspect where I had put my mark of interrogation. The question was one of value, the value placed on existence. Is pessimism inevitably a sign of decadence, warp, weakened instincts, as it was once with the ancient Hindus, as it is now with us modern Europeans? Or is there such a thing as a *strong* pessimism? A penchant of the mind for what is hard, terrible, evil, dubious in existence, arising from a plethora of health, plenitude of being? Could it be, perhaps, that the very feeling of superabundance created its own kind of suffering: a temerity of penetration, hankering for the enemy (the worth-while enemy) so as to prove its strength, to experience at last what it means to fear something? What meaning did the tragic myth have for the Greeks during the period of their greatest power and courage? And what of the Dionysiac spirit, so tremendous in its implications? What of the tragedy that grew out of that spirit?

Or one might look at it the other way round. Those agencies that had proved fatal to tragedy: Socratic ethics, dialectics, the temperance and cheerfulness of the pure scholar—couldn't these, rather than their opposites, be viewed as symptoms of decline, fatigue, distemper, of instincts caught in anarchic dissolution? Or the "Greek serenity" of the later period as, simply, the glow of a sun about to set? Or the Epicurean animus against pessimism merely as the sort of precaution a suffering man might use? And as for "disinterested inquiry," so-called: what, in the last analysis, did inquiry come to when judged as a symptom of the life process? What were we to say of the end (or, worse, of the beginning) of all inquiry? Might it be that the "inquiring mind" was simply the human mind terrified by pessimism and trying to escape from it, a clever bulwark erected against the truth? Something craven and false, if one wanted to be moral about it? Or, if one preferred to put it amorally, a dodge? Had this perhaps been your secret, great Socrates? Most secretive of ironists, had *this* been your deepest irony?

11

I was then beginning to take hold of a dangerous problem —taking it by the horns, as it were—not Old Nick himself, perhaps, but something almost as hot to handle: the problem of scholarly investigation. For the first time in history somebody had *come to grips* with scholarship—and what a formidable, perplexing thing it turned out to be! But the book, crystallization of my youthful courage and suspicions, was an impossible book; since the task required fully matured powers it could scarcely be anything else. Built from precocious, purely personal insights, all but incommunicable; conceived in terms of *art* (for the issue of scholarly inquiry cannot be argued on its own terms), this book addressed itself to artists or, rather, to artists with analytical and retrospective leanings: to a special kind of artist who is far to seek and possibly not worth the seeking. It was a book novel in its psychology, brimming with artists' secrets, its background a metaphysics of art; the work of a young man, written with the unstinted courage and melancholy of youth, defiantly independent even in those places where the author was paying homage to revered models. In short, a "first book," also in the worst sense of that term, and one that exhibited, for all the hoariness of its topic, every conceivable fault of adolescence. It was terribly diffuse and full of unpalatable ferment. All the

5

same, if one examines its impact it may certainly be said to have *proved* itself—in the eyes of the few contemporaries who mattered and most signally in the eyes of that great artist, Richard Wagner, whom it addressed as in a dialogue. This fact alone should ensure it a discreet treatment on my part; yet I cannot wholly suppress a feeling of distaste, or strangeness, as I look at it now, after a lapse of sixteen years. I have grown older, to be sure, and a hundred times more exacting, but by no means colder toward the question propounded in that heady work. And the question is still what it was then, how to view scholarship from the vantage of the artist and art from the vantage of life.

III

Once again: as I look at it today my treatise strikes me as quite impossible. It is poorly written, heavy-handed, embarrassing. The imagery is both frantic and confused. In spots it is saccharine to the point of effeminacy; the tempo is erratic; it lacks logical nicety and is so sure of its message that it dispenses with any kind of proof. Worse than that, it suspects the very notion of proof, being a book written for initiates, a "music" for men christened in the name of music and held together by special esthetic experiences, a shibboleth for the highbrow confraternity. An arrogant and extravagant book, which from the very first withdrew even more haughtily from the ruck of the intelligentsia than it did from the acknowledged barbarians; and which yet, as its impact has proved, knew then as it does now how to enlist fellow revelers and to tempt them into secret alleys, onto mysterious dancing grounds. Both the curious and the hostile had to admit that here was an unfamiliar voice, the disciple of an unrecognized god, hiding his identity (for the time being) under the skullcap of the scholar, the ponderousness and broad dialectics of the German, the bad manners of the Wagnerite. Here was a mind with odd, anonymous needs; a memory rife with questions, experiences, secrets, all of which had the name *Dionysos* attached to them like a question mark. People would hint suspiciously that there was a sort of maenadic soul in this book, stammering out laborious, arbitrary phrases in an alien tongue—as though the speaker were not quite sure himself whether he preferred speech to silence. And, indeed, this "new soul" should have *sung*, not spoken. What a pity that I could not tell as a poet what demanded to be told! Or at least as a philologist, seeing that even today philologists tend to shy away from this whole area and especially from the fact that the area contains a *problem*, that the Greeks will continue to remain totally obscure, unimaginable beings until we have found an answer to the question, "What is the meaning of the Dionysiac spirit?"

IV

How, then, are we to define the "Dionysiac spirit"? In my book I answered that question with the authority of the adept or disciple. Talking of the matter today, I would doubtless use more discretion and less eloquence; the origin of Greek tragedy is both too tough and too subtle an issue to wax eloquent over. One of the cardinal questions here is that of the Greek attitude to pain. What kind of sensibility did these people have? Was that sensibility constant, or did it change from generation to generation? Should we attribute the ever increasing desire of the Greeks for beauty, in the form of banquets, ritual ceremonies, new cults, to some fundamental *lack*—a melancholy disposition perhaps or an obsession with pain? If this interpretation is correct—there are several suggestions in Pericles' (or Thucydides') great funeral oration which seem to bear it out—how are we to explain the Greek desire, both prior and contrary to the first, for ugliness, or the strict commitment of the earlier Greeks to a pessimistic doctrine? Or their commitment to the tragic myth, image of all that is awful, evil, perplexing, destructive, ominous in human existence? What, in short, made the Greek mind turn to tragedy? A sense of euphoria maybe—sheer exuberance, reckless health, and power? But in that case, what is the significance, physiologically speaking, of that Dionysiac frenzy which gave rise to tragedy and comedy alike? Can frenzy be viewed as something that is *not* a symptom of decay, disorder, overripeness? Is there such a thing—let alienists answer that question—as a neurosis arising from *health*, from the youthful condition of the race? What does the union of god and goat, expressed in the figure of the satyr, really mean? What was it that prompted the Greeks to embody the Dionysiac reveler—primary man—in a shape like that? Turning next to the origin of the tragic chorus: did those days of superb somatic and psychological health give rise, perhaps, to endemic trances, collective visions, and hallucinations? And are not these the same Greeks who, signally in the early periods, gave every evidence of possessing tragic vision: a will to tragedy, profound pessimism? Was it not Plato who credited frenzy with all the superlative blessings of Greece? Contrariwise, was it not precisely during their period of dissolution and weakness that the Greeks turned to optimism, frivolity, histrionics;

that they began to be mad for logic and rational cosmology; that they grew at once "gayer" and "more scientific"? Why, is it possible to assume—in the face of all the up-to-date notions on that subject, in defiance of all the known prejudices of our democratic age—that the great optimist-rationalist-utilitarian victory, together with democracy, its political contemporary, was at bottom nothing other than a symptom of declining strength, approaching senility, somatic exhaustion—*it*, and not its opposite, pessimism? Could it be that Epicurus was an optimist—precisely because he suffered? . . .

The reader can see now what a heavy pack of questions this book was forced to carry. Let me add here the heaviest question of all, What kind of figure does ethics cut once we decide to view it in the biological perspective?

v

In the preface I addressed to Richard Wagner I claimed that art, rather than ethics, constituted the essential metaphysical activity of man, while in the body of the book I made several suggestive statements to the effect that existence could be justified only in esthetic terms. As a matter of fact, throughout the book I attributed a purely esthetic meaning—whether implied or overt—to all process: a kind of divinity if you like, God as the supreme artist, amoral, recklessly creating and destroying, realizing himself indifferently in whatever he does or undoes, ridding himself by his acts of the embarrassment of his riches and the strain of his internal contradictions. Thus the world was made to appear, at every instant, as a successful *solution* of God's own tensions, as an ever new vision projected by that grand sufferer for whom illusion is the only possible mode of redemption. That whole esthetic metaphysics might be rejected out of hand as so much prattle or rant. Yet in its essential traits it already prefigured that spirit of deep distrust and defiance which, later on, was to resist to the bitter end any moral interpretation of existence whatsoever. It is here that one could find—perhaps for the first time in history—a pessimism situated "beyond good and evil"; a "perversity of stance" of the kind Schopenhauer spent all his life fulminating against; a philosophy which dared place ethics among the phenomena (and so "demote" it) —or, rather, place it not even among the phenomena in the idealistic sense but among the "deceptions." Morality, on this view, became a mere fabrication for purposes of gulling: at best, an artistic fiction; at worst, an outrageous imposture.

The depth of this anti-moral bias may best be gauged by noting the wary and hostile silence I observed on the subject of Christianity—Christianity being the most extravagant set of variations ever produced on the theme of ethics. No doubt, the purely esthetic interpretation and justification of the world I was propounding in those pages placed them at the opposite pole from Christian doctrine, a doctrine entirely moral in purport, using absolute standards: God's absolute truth, for example, which relegates all art to the realm of falsehood and in so doing condemns it. I had always sensed strongly the furious, vindictive hatred of life implicit in that system of ideas and values; and sensed, too, that in order to be consistent with its premises a system of this sort was forced to abominate art. For both art and life depend wholly on the laws of optics, on perspective and illusion; both, to be blunt, depend on the necessity of error. From the very first, Christianity spelled life loathing itself, and that loathing was simply disguised, tricked out, with notions of an "other" and "better" life. A hatred of the "world," a curse on the affective urges, a fear of beauty and sensuality, a transcendence rigged up to slander mortal existence, a yearning for extinction, cessation of all effort until the great "sabbath of sabbaths"—this whole cluster of distortions, together with the intransigent Christian assertion that nothing counts except moral values, had always struck me as being the most dangerous, most sinister form the will to destruction can take; at all events, as a sign of profound sickness, moroseness, exhaustion, biological etiolation. And since according to ethics (specifically Christian, absolute ethics) life will *always* be in the wrong, it followed quite naturally that one must smother it under a load of contempt and constant negation; must view it as an object not only unworthy of our desire but absolutely worthless in itself.

As for morality, on the other hand, could it be anything but a will to deny life, a secret instinct of destruction, a principle of calumny, a reductive agent—the beginning of the end?—and, for that very reason, the Supreme Danger? Thus it happened that in those days, with this problem book, my vital instincts turned against ethics and founded a radical counterdoctrine, slanted esthetically, to oppose the Christian libel on life. But it still wanted a name. Being a philologist, that is to say a man of *words,* I christened it rather arbitrarily—for who can tell the real name of the Antichrist?—with the name of a Greek god, Dionysos.

VI

Have I made it clear what kind of task I proposed myself in this book? What a pity, though, that I did not yet have the courage (or shall I say the immodesty?) to risk a fresh language in keeping with the hazard, the radical novelty of my ideas, that I fumbled along, using terms borrowed from the vocabularies of Kant and Schopenhauer to express value judgments which were in flagrant contradiction to the spirit or taste of these men! Remember what Schopenhauer has to say about tragedy, in the second part of his *World as Will and Idea*. He writes: "The power of transport peculiar to tragedy may be seen to arise from our sudden recognition that life fails to provide any true satisfactions and hence does not deserve our loyalty. Tragedy guides us to the final goal, which is resignation." Dionysos had told me a very different story; his lesson, as I understood it, was anything but defeatist. It certainly is too bad that I had to obscure and spoil Dionysiac hints with formulas borrowed from Schopenhauer, but there is another feature of the book which seems even worse in retrospect: my tendency to sophisticate such insights as I had into the marvelous Greek issue with an alloy of up-to-date matters; my urge to hope where there was nothing left to hope for, all signs pointing unmistakably toward imminent ruin; my foolish prattle, prompted by the latest feats of German music, about the "German temper"—as though that temper had then been on the verge of discovering, or rediscovering, itself! And all this at a time when the German mind, which, not so very long ago, had shown itself capable of European leadership, was definitely ready to relinquish any aspirations of this sort and to effect the transition to mediocrity, democracy, and "modern ideas"—in the pompous guise, to be sure, of empire building. The intervening years have certainly taught me one thing if they have taught me nothing else: to adopt a hopeless and merciless view toward that "German temper," ditto toward German music, which I now recognize for what it really is: a thorough-going romanticism, the least Greek of all art forms and, over and above that, a drug of the worst sort, especially dangerous to a nation given to hard drinking and one that vaunts intellectual ferment for its power both to intoxicate the mind and to befog it. And yet there remains the great Dionysiac question mark, intact, apart from all those rash hopes, those wrong applications to contemporary matters, which tended to spoil my first book; remains even with regard to music. For the question here is (and must continue to be), "What should a music look like which is no longer romantic in inspiration, like the German, but Dionysiac instead?"

VII

—But, my dear chap, where on earth are we to find romanticism if not in *your* book? Can that profound hatred of "contemporariness," "actuality," "modern ideas" be carried any farther than you have carried it in your esthetic metaphysics—a metaphysics which would rather believe in nothingness, indeed in the devil himself, than in the here and now? Do we not hear a ground bass of rage and destructive fury growl through all your ear-beguiling contrapuntal art—a fierce hostility to everything that is happening today, an iron will (not far removed from active

nihilism) which seems to proclaim, "I'd rather that nothing were true than see *you* triumph and *your* truth?" Listen, you high priest of art and pessimism, to one of your
own statements, that eloquent passage full of dragon
killer's bravado and ratcatcher's tricks so appealing to innocent ears; listen to it and tell us, aren't we dealing here
with the confession of a true romantic of the 1830's, disguised as a pessimist of the 1850's? Can't we hear behind
your confession the annunciatory sounds of the usual romantic finale: rupture, collapse, return, and prostration
before an *old* faith, before the *old* God. . . . Come now,
isn't your pessimistic work itself a piece of anti-Hellenism
and romantic moonshine, fit to "befog and intoxicate," a
kind of drug—in fact, a piece of *music,* and German music
to boot? Just listen to this: "Let us imagine a rising generation with undaunted eyes, with a heroic drive towards
the unexplored; let us imagine the bold step of these St.
Georges, their reckless pride as they turn their backs on all
the valetudinarian doctrines of optimism, preparing to
'dwell resolutely in the fullness of being': *would it not be
necessary* for the tragic individual of such a culture,
readied by his discipline for every contingency, every terror, to want as his Helena a novel art of metaphysical
solace and to exclaim as Faust did:

> *And shall not I, by mightiest desire,*
> *In living shape that precious form acquire?"*

"Would it not be necessary?"—no, indeed, my romantic
fledglings, it would *not* be necessary. But it is quite possible that things—that you yourselves—*might* end that
way: "metaphysically solaced" despite all your grueling
self-discipline and, as romantics usually do, in the bosom
of the Church. But I would rather have you learn, first,

the art of terrestrial comfort; teach you how to laugh—if, that is, you really insist on remaining pessimists. And then it may perhaps happen that one fine day you will, with a peal of laughter, send all metaphysical palliatives packing, metaphysics herself leading the great exodus. Or, to speak in the language of that Dionysiac monster, Zarathustra:

Lift up your hearts, my fellows, higher and higher! And the legs—you mustn't forget those! Lift up your legs too, accomplished dancers; or, to top it all, stand on your heads!

This crown of the man who knows laughter, this rose-chaplet crown: I have placed it on my head, I have consecrated laughter. But not a single soul have I found strong enough to join me.

Zarathustra the dancer, the fleet Zarathustra, waving his wings, beckoning with his wings to all birds around him, poised for flight, casual and cavalier—

Zarathustra the soothsayer, Zarathustra the laughing truthsayer, never out of sorts, never *insisting*, lover of leaps and tangents: I myself have put on this crown!

This crown of the laughter-loving, this rose-chaplet crown: to you, my fellows, do I fling this crown! Laughter I declare to be blessed; you who aspire to greatness, learn how to laugh!

Zarathustra
PART IV, "Of Greater Men"

Sils-Maria, Upper Engadine
August 1886

Preface to Richard Wagner

In order to keep at bay all thought of the scruples, excitements, and misunderstandings which this book, considering the peculiar character of our literary scene, is likely to arouse upon publication, and to be able also to write these prefatory remarks with the same contemplative delight to which the text itself—crystallization of rich, inspiring hours—bears witness on every page, I try to picture the moment when this essay reaches your house: how, returning from one of your evening strolls through the winter snow, you will scan the Prometheus Unbound on the title page, read my name and be convinced forthwith that the author has something extremely urgent to say—be the contents of the book what they will; that, furthermore, in all his meditations he has communed with you as with one actually present and thus could write down only what befitted your presence. You will then remember that this book was composed at the same time as your own magnificent homage to Beethoven, which is to say during the stirring and terrible days of the recent war. And yet, anybody judging these pages to be a mere antidote to patriotic frenzy would judge amiss; they are more than a sportive fancy rising airily from a scene dedicated to bloody horror and military virtue. Upon a serious perusal of the essay my readers should become aware, with a sting of surprise, that I have been grappling with a crucial German issue—an issue situated at the very center of our hopes and aspirations. But it may well be that these same readers will feel shocked at seeing an esthetic issue taken so seriously, especially if they are in the habit of looking at art merely as a merry diversion, a light carillon sounding on the edges of earnest pursuits, easily dispensed with—as though they did not know (and quite likely they don't) what such a confrontation with "stark reality" *really* implies. These earnest readers I beg to inform of my conviction that art is the highest human task, the true metaphysical activity such as it is understood by the man to whom, as my great precursor on that path, I now dedicate these pages.

Basel, December 1871

I

Much will have been gained for esthetics once we have succeeded in apprehending directly—rather than merely *ascertaining*—that art owes its continuous evolution to the Apollonian-Dionysiac duality, even as the propagation of the species depends on the duality of the sexes, their constant conflicts and periodic acts of reconciliation. I have borrowed my adjectives from the Greeks, who developed their mystical doctrines of art through plausible *embodiments,* not through purely conceptual means. It is by those two art-sponsoring deities, Apollo and Dionysos, that we are made to recognize the tremendous split, as regards both origins and objectives, between the plastic, Apollonian arts and the non-visual art of music inspired by Dionysos. The two creative tendencies developed alongside one another, usually in fierce opposition, each by its taunts forcing the other to more energetic production, both perpetuating in a discordant concord that agon which the term *art* but feebly denominates: until at last, by the thaumaturgy of an Hellenic act of will, the pair accepted the yoke of marriage and, in this condition, begot Attic tragedy, which exhibits the salient features of both parents.

To reach a closer understanding of both these tendencies, let us begin by viewing them as the separate art realms of *dream* and *intoxication,* two physiological phenomena standing toward one another in much the same relationship as the Apollonian and Dionysiac. It was in a dream, according to Lucretius, that the marvelous gods and goddesses first presented themselves to the minds of men. That great sculptor, Phidias, beheld in a dream the entrancing bodies of more-than-human beings, and likewise, if anyone had asked the Greek poets about the mystery of poetic creation, they too would have referred him to dreams and instructed him much as Hans Sachs instructs us in *Die Meistersinger*:

> *My friend, it is the poet's work*
> *Dreams to interpret and to mark.*
> *Believe me that man's true conceit*
> *In a dream becomes complete:*
> *All poetry we ever read*
> *Is but true dreams interpreted.*

The fair illusion of the dream sphere, in the production of which every man proves himself an accomplished artist, is a precondition not only of all plastic art, but even, as we shall see presently, of a wide range of poetry. Here we enjoy an immediate apprehension of form, all shapes speak to us directly, nothing seems indifferent or redundant. Despite the high intensity with which these dream realities exist for us, we still have a residual sensation that they are illusions; at least such has been my experience—and the frequency, not to say normality, of the experience is borne out in many passages of the poets. Men of philosophical disposition are known for their constant premonition that our everyday reality, too, is an illusion, hiding another, totally different kind of reality. It was Schopenhauer who considered the ability to view at certain times all men and things as mere phantoms or dream images to be the true mark of philosophic talent. The person who is responsive to the stimuli of art behaves toward the reality of dream much the way the philosopher behaves toward the reality of existence: he observes exactly and enjoys his observations, for it is by these images that he interprets life, by these processes that he rehearses it. Nor is it by pleasant images only that such plausible connections are made: the whole divine comedy of life, including its somber aspects, its sudden balkings, impish accidents, anxious expectations, moves past him, not quite like a shadow play—for it is he himself, after all, who lives and suffers through these scenes—yet never without giving a fleeting sense of illusion; and I imagine that many persons have reassured themselves amidst the perils of dream by calling out, "It is a dream! I want it to go on." I have even heard of people spinning out the causality of one and the same dream over three or more successive nights. All these facts clearly bear witness that our innermost being, the common substratum of humanity, experiences dreams with deep delight and a sense of real necessity. This deep and happy sense of the necessity of dream experiences was expressed by the Greeks in the image of Apollo. Apollo is at once the god of all plastic powers and the soothsaying god. He who is etymologically the "lucent" one, the god of light, reigns also over the fair illusion of our inner world of fantasy. The perfection of these conditions in contrast to our imperfectly understood waking reality, as well as our profound awareness of nature's healing powers during the interval of sleep and dream, furnishes a symbolic analogue to the soothsaying faculty and quite generally to the arts, which make life possible and worth living. But the image of Apollo must incorporate that thin line which the dream image may not cross, under penalty of becoming pathological, of imposing itself on us as crass reality: a discreet limitation, a freedom from all extravagant urges, the sapient tranquillity of the plastic god. His eye must be sunlike, in keeping with his origin. Even at those moments when he is angry and ill-tempered there lies upon him the consecration of fair illusion. In an eccentric way one might say of Apollo what Schopenhauer says, in the first part of *The World as Will and Idea,* of man caught in the veil of Maya: "Even as on an immense, raging sea, assailed by huge wave crests, a man sits in a little rowboat trusting his frail craft, so, amidst the furious torments of this world, the individual sits tranquilly, supported by the *principium individuationis* and relying on it." One might say that the unshakable confidence in that principle has received its most magnificent expression in Apollo, and that Apollo himself may be regarded as the marvelous divine image of the *principium individuationis,* whose looks and gestures radiate the full delight, wisdom, and beauty of "illusion."

In the same context Schopenhauer has described for us the tremendous awe which seizes man when he suddenly begins to doubt the cognitive modes of experience, in other words, when in a given instance the law of causation seems to suspend itself. If we add to this awe the glorious transport which arises in man, even from the very depths of nature, at the shattering of the *principium individuationis,* then we are in a position to apprehend the essence of Dionysiac rapture, whose closest analogy is furnished by physical intoxication. Dionysiac stirrings arise either through the influence of those narcotic potions of which all primitive races speak in their hymns, or through the powerful approach of spring, which penetrates with joy the whole frame of nature. So stirred, the individual forgets himself completely. It is the same Dionysiac power which in medieval Germany drove ever increasing crowds of people singing and dancing from place to place; we recognize in these St. John's and St. Vitus' dancers the bacchic choruses of the Greeks, who had their precursors in Asia Minor and as far back as Babylon and the orgiastic Sacaea. There are people who, either from lack of experience or out of sheer stupidity, turn away from such phenomena, and, strong in the sense of their own sanity, label them either mockingly or pityingly "endemic diseases." These benighted souls have no idea how cadaverous and ghostly their "sanity" appears as the intense throng of Dionysiac revelers sweeps past them.

Not only does the bond between man and man come to be forged once more by the magic of the Dionysiac rite, but nature itself, long alienated or subjugated, rises again to celebrate the reconciliation with her prodigal son, man. The earth offers its gifts voluntarily, and the savage beasts of mountain and desert approach in peace. The chariot of Dionysos is bedecked with flowers and garlands; panthers and tigers stride beneath his yoke. If one were to convert Beethoven's "Paean to Joy" into a painting, and refuse to curb the imagination when that multitude prostrates itself reverently in the dust, one might form some apprehension of Dionysiac ritual. Now the slave emerges as a freeman; all the rigid, hostile walls which either necessity or despotism has erected between men are shattered. Now that the gospel of universal harmony is sounded, each individual becomes not only reconciled to his fellow but actually at one with him—as though the veil of Maya had been torn apart and there remained only shreds floating before the vision of mystical Oneness. Man now expresses himself through song and dance as the member of a higher community; he has forgotten how to walk, how to speak, and is on the brink of taking wing as he dances. Each of his gestures betokens enchantment; through him sounds a supernatural power, the same power which makes the animals speak and the earth render up milk and honey.

He feels himself to be godlike and strides with the same elation and ecstasy as the gods he has seen in his dreams. No longer the *artist*, he has himself become a *work of art*: the productive power of the whole universe is now manifest in his transport, to the glorious satisfaction of the primordial One. The finest clay, the most precious marble —man—is here kneaded and hewn, and the chisel blows of the Dionysiac world artist are accompanied by the cry of the Eleusinian mystagogues: "Do you fall on your knees, multitudes, do you divine your creator?"

II

So far we have examined the Apollonian and Dionysiac states as the product of formative forces arising directly from nature without the mediation of the human artist. At this stage artistic urges are satisfied directly, on the one hand through the imagery of dreams, whose perfection is quite independent of the intellectual rank, the artistic development of the individual; on the other hand, through an ecstatic reality which once again takes no account of the individual and may even destroy him, or else redeem him through a mystical experience of the collective. In relation to these immediate creative conditions of nature every artist must appear as "imitator," either as the Apollonian dream artist or the Dionysiac ecstatic artist, or, finally (as in Greek tragedy, for example) as dream and ecstatic artist in one. We might picture to ourselves how the last of these, in a state of Dionysiac intoxication and mystical self-abrogation, wandering apart from the reveling throng, sinks upon the ground, and how there is then revealed to him his own condition—complete oneness with the essence of the universe—in a dream similitude.

Having set down these general premises and distinctions, we now turn to the Greeks in order to realize to what degree the formative forces of nature were developed in them. Such an inquiry will enable us to assess properly the relation of the Greek artist to his prototypes or, to use Aristotle's expression, his "imitation of nature." Of the dreams the Greeks dreamed it is not possible to speak with any certainty, despite the extant dream literature and the large number of dream anecdotes. But considering the incredible accuracy of their eyes, their keen and unabashed delight in colors, one can hardly be wrong in assuming that their dreams too showed a strict consequence of lines and contours, hues and groupings, a progression of scenes similar to their best bas-reliefs. The perfection of these dream scenes might almost tempt us to consider the dreaming Greek as a Homer and Homer as a dreaming Greek; which would be as though the modern man were to compare himself in his dreaming to Shakespeare.

Yet there is another point about which we do not have to conjecture at all: I mean the profound gap separating the Dionysiac Greeks from the Dionysiac barbarians. Throughout the range of ancient civilization (leaving the newer civilizations out of account for the moment) we find evidence of Dionysiac celebrations which stand to the Greek type in much the same relation as the bearded satyr, whose name and attributes are derived from the he-goat, stands to the god Dionysos. The central concern of such celebrations was, almost universally, a complete sexual promiscuity overriding every form of established tribal law; all the savage urges of the mind were unleashed on those occasions until they reached that paroxysm of lust and cruelty which has always struck me as the "witches' cauldron" *par excellence*. It would appear that the Greeks were for a while quite immune from these feverish excesses which must have reached them by every known land or sea route. What kept Greece safe was the proud, imposing image of Apollo, who in holding up the head of the Gorgon to those brutal and grotesque Dionysiac forces subdued them. Doric art has immortalized Apollo's majestic rejection of all license. But resistance became difficult, even impossible, as soon as similar urges began to break forth from the deep substratum of Hellenism itself. Soon the function of the Delphic god developed into something quite different and much more limited: all he could hope to accomplish now was to wrest the destructive weapon, by a timely gesture of pacification, from his opponent's hand. That act of pacification represents the most important event in the history of Greek ritual; every department of life now shows symptoms of a revolutionary change. The two great antagonists have been reconciled. Each feels obliged henceforth to keep to his bounds, each will honor the other by the bestowal of periodic gifts, while the cleavage remains fundamentally the same. And yet, if we examine what happened to the Dionysiac powers under the pressure of that treaty we notice a great difference: in the place of the Babylonian Sacaea, with their throwback of men to the condition of apes and tigers, we now see entirely new rites celebrated: rites of universal redemption, of glorious transfiguration. Only now has it become possible to speak of nature's celebrating an *esthetic* triumph; only now has the abrogation of the *principium individuationis* become an esthetic event. That terrible witches' brew concocted of lust and cruelty has lost all power under the new conditions. Yet the peculiar blending of emotions in the heart of the Dionysiac reveler—his ambiguity if you will—seems still to hark back (as the medicinal drug harks back to the deadly poison) to the days when the infliction of pain was experienced as joy while a sense of supreme triumph elicited cries of anguish from the heart. For now in every exuberant joy there is heard an undertone of terror, or else a wistful lament over an irrecoverable loss. It is as though in these Greek festivals a sentimental trait of nature were coming to the fore, as though nature were bemoaning the fact of her fragmentation, her decomposition into separate individuals. The chants and gestures of these revelers, so ambiguous in their motivation, represented an absolute *novum* in the world of the Homeric Greeks; their Dionysiac music, in especial, spread abroad terror and a deep shudder. It is true: music had long been familiar to the Greeks as an Apollonian art, as a regular beat like that of waves lapping the shore, a plastic rhythm expressly developed for the portrayal of Apollonian conditions. Apollo's music was a Doric architecture of sound—of barely hinted sounds such as are proper to the cithara. Those very elements which characterize Dionysiac music and, after it, music quite generally: the heart-shaking power of tone, the uniform stream of melody, the incomparable resources of harmony—all those elements had been carefully kept at a distance as being inconsonant with the Apollonian norm. In the Dionysiac dithyramb man is incited to strain his symbolic faculties to the utmost; something quite unheard of is now clamoring to be heard: the desire to tear asunder the veil of Maya, to sink back into the original oneness of nature; the desire to express the very essence of nature symbolically. Thus an entirely new set of symbols springs into being. First, all the symbols pertaining to physical features:

mouth, face, the spoken word, the dance movement which coordinates the limbs and bends them to its rhythm. Then suddenly all the rest of the symbolic forces—music and rhythm as such, dynamics, harmony—assert themselves with great energy. In order to comprehend this total emancipation of all the symbolic powers one must have reached the same measure of inner freedom those powers themselves were making manifest; which is to say that the votary of Dionysos could not be understood except by his own kind. It is not difficult to imagine the awed surprise with which the Apollonian Greek must have looked on him. And that surprise would be further increased as the latter realized, with a shudder, that all this was not so alien to him after all, that his Apollonian consciousness was but a thin veil hiding from him the whole Dionysiac realm.

III

In order to comprehend this we must take down the elaborate edifice of Apollonian culture stone by stone until we discover its foundations. At first the eye is struck by the marvelous shapes of the Olympian gods who stand upon its pediments, and whose exploits, in shining bas-relief, adorn its friezes. The fact that among them we find Apollo as one god among many, making no claim to a privileged position, should not mislead us. The same drive that found its most complete representation in Apollo generated the whole Olympian world, and in this sense we may consider Apollo the father of that world. But what was the radical need out of which that illustrious society of Olympian beings sprang?

Whoever approaches the Olympians with a different religion in his heart, seeking moral elevation, sanctity, spirituality, loving-kindness, will presently be forced to turn away from them in ill-humored disappointment. Nothing in these deities reminds us of asceticism, high intellect, or duty: we are confronted by luxuriant, triumphant *existence,* which deifies the good and the bad indifferently. And the beholder may find himself dismayed in the presence of such overflowing life and ask himself what potion these heady people must have drunk in order to behold, in whatever direction they looked, Helen laughing back at them, the beguiling image of their own existence. But we shall call out to this beholder, who has already turned his back: Don't go! Listen first to what the Greeks themselves have to say of this life, which spreads itself before you with such puzzling serenity. An old legend has it that King Midas hunted a long time in the woods for the wise Silenus, companion of Dionysos, without being able to catch him. When he had finally caught him the king asked him what he considered man's greatest good. The daemon remained sullen and uncommunicative until finally, forced by the king, he broke into a shrill laugh and spoke: "Ephemeral wretch, begotten by accident and toil, why do you force me to tell you what it would be your greatest boon not to hear? What would be best for you is quite beyond your reach: not to have been born, not to *be,* to be *nothing.* But the second best is to die soon."

What is the relation of the Olympian gods to this popular wisdom? It is that of the entranced vision of the martyr to his torment.

Now the Olympian magic mountain opens itself before us, showing us its very roots. The Greeks were keenly aware of the terrors and horrors of existence; in order to

be able to live at all they had to place before them the
shining fantasy of the Olympians. Their tremendous distrust of the titanic forces of nature: *Moira,* mercilessly
enthroned beyond the knowable world; the vulture which
fed upon the great philanthropist Prometheus; the terrible
lot drawn by wise Oedipus; the curse on the house of
Atreus which brought Orestes to the murder of his mother:
that whole Panic philosophy, in short, with its mythic examples, by which the gloomy Etruscans perished, the
Greeks conquered—or at least hid from view—again and
again by means of this artificial Olympus. In order to live
at all the Greeks had to construct these deities. The Apollonian need for beauty had to develop the Olympian
hierarchy of joy by slow degrees from the original titanic
hierarchy of terror, as roses are seen to break from a thorny
thicket. How else could life have been borne by a race
so hypersensitive, so emotionally intense, so equipped for
suffering? The same drive which called art into being as a
completion and consummation of existence, and as a
guarantee of further existence, gave rise also to that Olympian realm which acted as a transfiguring mirror to the
Hellenic will. The gods justified human life by living it
themselves—the only satisfactory theodicy ever invented.
To exist in the clear sunlight of such deities was now felt
to be the highest good, and the only real grief suffered
by Homeric man was inspired by the thought of leaving
that sunlight, especially when the departure seemed imminent. Now it became possible to stand the wisdom of
Silenus on its head and proclaim that it was the worst evil
for man to die soon, and second worst for him to die at all.
Such laments as arise now arise over short-lived Achilles,
over the generations ephemeral as leaves, the decline of
the heroic age. It is not unbecoming to even the greatest

hero to yearn for an afterlife, though it be as a day laborer. So impetuously, during the Apollonian phase, does man's will desire to remain on earth, so identified does he become with existence, that even his lament turns to a song of praise.

It should have become apparent by now that the harmony with nature which we late-comers regard with such nostalgia, and for which Schiller has coined the cant term *naïve*, is by no means a simple and inevitable condition to be found at the gateway to every culture, a kind of paradise. Such a belief could have been endorsed only by a period for which Rousseau's Emile was an artist and Homer just such an artist nurtured in the bosom of nature. Whenever we encounter "naïveté" in art, we are face to face with the ripest fruit of Apollonian culture—which must always triumph first over titans, kill monsters, and overcome the somber contemplation of actuality, the intense susceptibility to suffering, by means of illusions strenuously and zestfully entertained. But how rare are the instances of true naïveté, of that complete identification with the beauty of appearance! It is this achievement which makes Homer so magnificent—Homer, who, as a single individual, stood to Apollonian popular culture in the same relation as the individual dream artist to the oneiric capacity of a race and of nature generally. The naïveté of Homer must be viewed as a complete victory of Apollonian illusion. Nature often uses illusions of this sort in order to accomplish its secret purposes. The true goal is covered over by a phantasm. We stretch out our hands to the latter, while nature, aided by our deception, attains the former. In the case of the Greeks it was the will wishing to behold itself in the work of art, in the transcendence of genius; but in order so to behold itself its creatures had first to view themselves as glorious, to transpose themselves to a higher sphere, without having that sphere of pure contemplation either challenge them or upbraid them with insufficiency. It was in that sphere of beauty that the Greeks saw the Olympians as their mirror images; it was by means of that esthetic mirror that the Greek will opposed suffering and the somber wisdom of suffering which always accompanies artistic talent. As a monument to its victory stands Homer, the naïve artist.

IV

We can learn something about that naïve artist through the analogy of dream. We can imagine the dreamer as he calls out to himself, still caught in the illusion of his dream and without disturbing it, "This is a dream, and I want to go on dreaming," and we can infer, on the one hand, that he takes deep delight in the contemplation of his dream, and, on the other, that he must have forgotten the day, with its horrible importunity, so to enjoy his dream. Apollo, the interpreter of dreams, will furnish the clue to what is happening here. Although of the two halves of life—the waking and the dreaming—the former is generally considered not only the more important but the only one which is truly lived, I would, at the risk of sounding paradoxical, propose the opposite view. The more I have come to realize in nature those omnipotent formative tendencies and, with them, an intense longing for illusion, the more I feel inclined to the hypothesis that the original Oneness, the ground of Being, ever-suffering and contradictory, time and again has need of rapt vision and delightful illusion to redeem itself. Since we ourselves are the very stuff of such illusions, we must view ourselves as the truly non-existent, that is to say, as a perpetual unfolding in time, space, and causality—what we label "empiric reality." But if, for the moment, we abstract from our own reality, viewing our empiric existence, as well as the existence of the world at large, as the *idea* of the original Oneness, produced anew each instant, then our dreams will appear to us as illusions of illusions, hence as a still higher form of satisfaction of the original desire for illusion. It is for this reason that the very core of nature takes such a deep delight in the naïve artist and the naïve work of art, which likewise is merely the illusion of an illusion. Raphael, himself one of those immortal "naïve" artists, in a symbolic canvas has illustrated that reduction of illusion to further illusion which is the original act of the naïve artist and at the same time of all Apollonian culture. In the lower half of his "Transfiguration," through the figures of the possessed boy, the despairing bearers, the helpless, terrified disciples, we see a reflection of original pain, the sole ground of being: "illusion" here is a reflection of eternal contradiction, begetter of all things. From this illusion there rises, like the fragrance of ambrosia, a new illusory world, invisible to those enmeshed in the first: a radiant vision of pure delight, a rapt seeing through wide-open eyes. Here we have, in a great symbol of art, both the fair world of Apollo and its substratum, the terrible wisdom of Silenus, and we can comprehend intuitively how they mutually require one another. But Apollo appears to us once again as the apotheosis of the *principium individuationis,* in whom the eternal goal of the original Oneness, namely its redemption through illusion, accomplishes itself. With august gesture the god shows us how there is need for a whole world of torment in order for the individual to produce the redemptive vision and to sit quietly in his rocking rowboat in mid-sea, absorbed in contemplation.

If this apotheosis of individuation is to be read in normative terms, we may infer that there is one norm only: the individual—or, more precisely, the observance of the limits of the individual: *sophrosyne*. As a moral deity Apollo demands self-control from his people and, in order to observe such self-control, a knowledge of self. And so we find that the esthetic necessity of beauty is accompanied by the imperatives, "Know thyself," and "Nothing too much." Conversely, excess and *hubris* come to be regarded as the hostile spirits of the non-Apollonian sphere, hence as properties of the pre-Apollonian era—the age of Titans —and the extra-Apollonian world, that is to say the world of the barbarians. It was because of his Titanic love of man that Prometheus had to be devoured by vultures; it was because of his extravagant wisdom which succeeded in solving the riddle of the Sphinx that Oedipus had to be cast into a whirlpool of crime: in this fashion does the Delphic god interpret the Greek past.

The effects of the Dionysiac spirit struck the Apollonian Greeks as titanic and barbaric; yet they could not disguise from themselves the fact that they were essentially akin to those deposed Titans and heroes. They felt more than that: their whole existence, with its temperate beauty, rested upon a base of suffering and *knowledge* which had been hidden from them until the reinstatement of Dionysos uncovered it once more. And lo and behold! Apollo found it impossible to live without Dionysos. The elements of titanism and barbarism turned out to be quite as fundamental as the Apollonian element. And now let us imagine how the ecstatic sounds of the Dionysiac rites penetrated ever more enticingly into that artificially restrained and discreet world of illusion, how this clamor expressed the whole outrageous gamut of nature—delight, grief, knowledge—even to the most piercing cry; and then let us imagine how the Apollonian artist with his thin, monotonous harp music must have sounded beside the demoniac chant of the multitude! The muses presiding over the illusory arts paled before an art which enthusiastically told the truth, and the wisdom of Silenus cried "Woe!" against the serene Olympians. The individual, with his limits and moderations, forgot himself in the Dionysiac vortex and became oblivious to the laws of Apollo. Indiscreet extravagance revealed itself as truth, and contradiction, a delight born of pain, spoke out of the bosom of nature. Wherever the Dionysiac voice was heard, the Apollonian norm seemed suspended or destroyed. Yet it is equally true that, in those places where the first assault was withstood, the prestige and majesty of the Delphic god appeared more rigid and threatening than before. The only way I am able to view Doric art and the Doric state is as a perpetual military encampment of the Apollonian forces. An art so defiantly austere, so ringed about with fortifications—an education so military and exacting—a polity so ruthlessly cruel—could endure only in a continual state of resistance against the titanic and barbaric menace of Dionysos.

Up to this point I have developed at some length a theme which was sounded at the beginning of this essay: how the Dionysiac and Apollonian elements, in a continuous chain of creations, each enhancing the other, dominated the Hellenic mind; how from the Iron Age, with its battles of Titans and its austere popular philosophy, there developed under the aegis of Apollo the Homeric world of beauty; how this "naïve" splendor was then absorbed

once more by the Dionysiac torrent, and how, face to face
with this new power, the Apollonian code rigidified into
the majesty of Doric art and contemplation. If the earlier
phase of Greek history may justly be broken down into
four major artistic epochs dramatizing the battle between
the two hostile principles, then we must inquire further
(lest Doric art appear to us as the acme and final goal of
all these striving tendencies) what was the true end toward which that evolution moved. And our eyes will come
to rest on the sublime and much lauded achievement of
the dramatic dithyramb and Attic tragedy, as the common
goal of both urges; whose mysterious marriage, after
long discord, ennobled itself with such a child, at once
Antigone and Cassandra.

V

We are now approaching the central concern of our inquiry, which has as its aim an understanding of the Dio-
nysiac-Apollonian spirit, or at least an intuitive compre-
hension of the mystery which made this conjunction
possible. Our first question must be: where in the Greek
world is the new seed first to be found which was later
to develop into tragedy and the dramatic dithyramb? Greek
antiquity gives us a pictorial clue when it represents in
statues, on cameos, etc., Homer and Archilochus side by
side as ancestors and torchbearers of Greek poetry, in the
certainty that only these two are to be regarded as truly
original minds, from whom a stream of fire flowed onto
the entire later Greek world. Homer, the hoary dreamer,
caught in utter abstraction, prototype of the Apollonian
naïve artist, stares in amazement at the passionate head of

Archilochus, soldierly servant of the Muses, knocked about by fortune. All that more recent esthetics has been able to add by way of interpretation is that here the "objective" artist is confronted by the first "subjective" artist. We find this interpretation of little use, since to us the subjective artist is simply the bad artist, and since we demand above all, in every genre and range of art, a triumph over subjectivity, deliverance from the self, the silencing of every personal will and desire; since, in fact, we cannot imagine the smallest genuine art work lacking objectivity and disinterested contemplation. For this reason our esthetic must first solve the following problem: how is the lyrical poet at all possible as artist—he who, according to the experience of all times, always says "I" and recites to us the entire chromatic scale of his passions and appetites? It is this Archilochus who most disturbs us, placed there beside Homer, with the stridor of his hate and mockery, the drunken outbursts of his desire. Isn't he—the first artist to be called subjective—for that reason the veritable non-artist? How, then, are we to explain the reverence in which he was held as a poet, the honor done him by the Delphic oracle, that seat of "objective" art, in a number of very curious sayings?

Schiller has thrown some light on his own manner of composition by a psychological observation which seems inexplicable to himself without, however, giving him pause. Schiller confessed that, prior to composing, he experienced not a logically connected series of images but rather a *musical mood*. "With me emotion is at the beginning without clear and definite ideas; those ideas do not arise until later on. A certain musical disposition of mind comes first, and after follows the poetical idea." If we enlarge on this, taking into account the most important phe-

nomenon of ancient poetry, by which I mean that union—
nay identity—everywhere considered natural, between musician and poet (alongside which our modern poetry appears as the statue of a god without a head), then we may,
on the basis of the esthetics adumbrated earlier, explain
the lyrical poet in the following manner. He is, first and
foremost, a Dionysiac artist, become wholly identified with
the original Oneness, its pain and contradiction, and producing a replica of that Oneness as music, if music may
legitimately be seen as a repetition of the world; however,
this music becomes visible to him again, as in a dream
similitude, through the Apollonian dream influence. That
reflection, without image or idea, of original pain in music,
with its redemption through illusion, now produces a second reflection as a single simile or example. The artist had
abrogated his subjectivity earlier, during the Dionysiac
phase: the image which now reveals to him his oneness
with the heart of the world is a dream scene showing forth
vividly, together with original pain, the original delight of
illusion. The "I" thus sounds out of the depth of being;
what recent writers on esthetics speak of as "subjectivity"
is a mere figment. When Archilochus, the first lyric poet
of the Greeks, hurls both his frantic love and his contempt
at the daughters of Lycambes, it is not his own passion
that we see dancing before us in an orgiastic frenzy: we
see Dionysos and the maenads, we see the drunken reveler
Archilochus, sunk down in sleep—as Euripides describes
him for us in the *Bacchae,* asleep on a high mountain
meadow, in the midday sun—and now Apollo approaches
him and touches him with his laurel. The sleeper's enchantment through Dionysiac music now begins to emit
sparks of imagery, poems which, at their point of highest

evolution, will bear the name of tragedies and dramatic dithyrambs.

The sculptor, as well as his brother, the epic poet, is committed to the pure contemplation of images. The Dionysiac musician, himself imageless, is nothing but original pain and reverberation of the image. Out of this mystical process of un-selving, the poet's spirit feels a whole world of images and similitudes arise, which are quite different in hue, causality, and pace from the images of the sculptor or narrative poet. While the last lives in those images, and only in them, with joyful complacence, and never tires of scanning them down to the most minute features, while even the image of angry Achilles is no more for him than an *image* whose irate countenance he enjoys with a dreamer's delight in appearance—so that this mirror of appearance protects him from complete fusion with his characters—the lyrical poet, on the other hand, himself becomes his images, his images are objectified versions of himself. Being the active center of that world he may boldly speak in the first person, only his "I" is not that of the actual waking man, but the "I" dwelling, truly and eternally, in the ground of being. It is through the reflections of that "I" that the lyric poet beholds the ground of being. Let us imagine, next, how he views himself too among these reflections—as non-genius, that is, as his own subject matter, the whole teeming crowd of his passions and intentions directed toward a definite goal; and when it now appears as though the poet and the non-poet joined to him were one, and as though the former were using the pronoun "I," we are able to see through this appearance, which has deceived those who have attached the label "subjective" to the lyrical poet. The man Archilochus, with his passionate loves and hates, is really only a vision of genius, a genius who is no longer merely Archilochus but the genius of the universe, expressing its pain through the similitude of Archilochus the man. Archilochus, on the other hand, the subjectively willing and desiring human being, can never be a poet. Nor is it at all necessary for the poet to see only the phenomenon of the man Archilochus before him as a reflection of Eternal Being: the world of tragedy shows us to what extent the vision of the poet can remove itself from the urgent, immediate phenomenon.

Schopenhauer, who was fully aware of the difficulties the lyrical poet creates for the speculative esthetician, thought that he had found a solution, which, however, I cannot endorse. It is true that he alone possessed the means, in his profound philosophy of music, for solving this problem; and I think I have honored his achievement in these pages, I hope in his own spirit. Yet in the first part of *The World as Will and Idea* he characterizes the essence of song as follows: "The consciousness of the singer is filled with the subject of will, which is to say with his own willing. That willing may either be a released, satisfied willing (joy), or, as happens more commonly, an inhibited willing (sadness). In either case there is affect here: passion, violent commotion. At the same time, however, the singer is moved by the contemplation of nature surrounding him to experience himself as the subject of pure, un-willing ideation, and the unshakable tranquillity of that ideation becomes contrasted with the urgency of his willing, its limits, and its lacks. It is the experience of this contrast, or tug of war, which he expresses in his song. While we find ourselves in the lyrical condition, pure ideation approaches us, as it were, to deliver us from the urgencies of willing; we obey, yet obey for moments only. Again and again our willing, our memory of personal objectives, distracts us from tranquil contemplation, while, conversely, the next scene of beauty we behold will yield us up once more to pure ideation. For this reason we find in song and in the lyrical mood a curious mixture of willing (our personal interest in *purposes*) and pure contemplation (whose subject matter is furnished by our surroundings); relations are sought and imagined between these two sets of experiences. Subjective mood—the affection of the will—communicates its color to the purely viewed surroundings, and vice versa. All authentic song reflects a state of mind mixed and divided in this manner."

Who can fail to perceive in this description that lyric poetry is presented as an art never completely realized, indeed a hybrid whose essence is made to consist in an uneasy mixture of will and contemplation, i.e., the esthetic and the non-esthetic conditions? We, on our part, maintain that the distinction between subjective and objective, which even Schopenhauer still uses as a sort of measuring stick to distinguish the arts, has no value whatever in esthetics; the reason being that the subject—the striving individual bent on furthering his egoistic purposes—can be thought of only as an enemy to art, never as its source. But to the extent that the subject is an artist he is already delivered from individual will and has become a medium through which the True Subject celebrates His redemption in illusion. For better or worse, one thing should be quite obvious to all of us: the entire comedy of art is not played for our own sakes—for our betterment or education, say—nor can we consider ourselves the true originators of that art realm; while on the other hand we have every right to view ourselves as esthetic projections of the veritable creator and derive such dignity as we possess from our status as art works. Only as an esthetic product can the world be justified to all eternity—although our consciousness of our own significance does scarcely exceed the consciousness a painted soldier might have of the battle in which he takes part. Thus our whole knowledge of art is at bottom illusory, seeing that as mere *knowers* we can never be fused with that essential spirit, at the same time creator and spectator, who has prepared the comedy of art for his own edification. Only as the genius in the act of creation merges with the primal architect of the cosmos can he truly know something of the eternal essence of art. For in that condition he resembles the uncanny fairy tale image which is able to see itself by turning its eyes. He is at once subject and object, poet, actor, and audience.

VI

Scholarship has discovered in respect of Archilochus that he introduced folk song into literature, and that it was this feat which earned him the unique distinction of being placed beside Homer. Yet what does folk song represent in contrast to epic poetry, which is wholly Apollonian? Surely the classical instance of a union between Apollonian and Dionysiac intentions. Its tremendous distribution, as well as its constant proliferation wherever we look, attests the strength of that dual generative motive in nature: a motive which leaves its traces in folk song much the way the orgiastic movements of a nation leave their traces in music. Nor should it be difficult to show by historical evidence that every period which abounded in folk songs has, by the same token, been deeply stirred by Dionysiac currents. Those currents have long been considered the necessary substratum, or precondition, of folk poetry.

But first of all we must regard folk song as a musical mirror of the cosmos, as primordial melody casting about for an analogue and finding that analogue eventually in poetry. Since melody precedes all else, it may have to undergo any number of objectifications, such as a variety of texts presents. But it is always, according to the naïve estimation of the populace, much superior in importance to those texts. Melody gives birth to poetry again and again: this is implied by the strophic form of folk song. For a long time I wondered at this phenomenon, until finally the following explanation offered itself. If we examine any collection of folk poetry—for example, *Des Knaben Wunderhorn*—in this light, we shall find countless examples of melody generating whole series of images, and those images, in their varicolored hues, abrupt transitions, and headlong forward rush, stand in the most marked contrast to the equable movement, the calm illusion, of epic verse. Viewed from the standpoint of the epic the uneven and irregular imagery of folk song becomes quite objectionable. Such must have been the feeling which the solemn rhapsodists of the Apollonian rites, during the age of Terpander, entertained with regard to popular lyric effusions.

In folk poetry we find, moreover, the most intense effort of language to imitate the condition of music. For this reason Archilochus may be claimed to have ushered in an entirely new world of poetry, profoundly at variance with the Homeric; and by this distinction we have hinted at the only possible relation between poetry and music, word and sound. Word, image, and idea, in undergoing the power of music, now seek for a kind of expression that would parallel it. In this sense we may distinguish two main currents in the history of Greek verse, according as language is used to imitate the world of appearance or that of music. To understand more profoundly the significance of this distinction, let the reader ponder the utter dissimilarity of verbal color, syntax and phraseology in the works of Homer and Pindar. He then cannot fail to conjecture that in the interval there must have sounded the orgiastic flute notes of Olympus, which, as late as Aristotle's time, in the midst of an infinitely more complex music, still rouses men to wild enthusiasm, and which at their inception must have challenged all contemporaries to imitate them by every available poetic resource. I wish to instance in this connection a well-known phenomenon of our own era which our modish estheticians consider most exceptionable. We have noticed again and again how a Beethoven symphony compels the individual hearers to use pictorial speech—though it must be granted that a collocation of these various descriptive sequences might appear rather checkered, fantastic, even contradictory. Small wonder, then, that our critics have exercised their feeble wit on these musical images, or else passed over the phenomenon—surely one worthy of further investigation—in complete silence. Even in cases where the composer himself has employed pictorial tags in talking about his work—calling one symphony "Pastoral," one movement "Brook Scene" and another "Jolly Concourse of Peasants"—these tropes are properly reducible to purely musical elements rather than standing for actual objects expressed through music. It is true that such musical representations can neither instruct us much concerning the Dionysiac content of music nor yet lay claim to any distinctive value as images. But once we study this discharge of music through images in a youthful milieu, among a people whose linguistic creativity is unimpaired, we can form some idea of how strophic folk song must have arisen and how a nation's entire store of verbal resources might be mobilized by means of that novel principle, imitation of the language of music.

If we are right in viewing lyric poetry as an efflorescence of music in images and ideas, then our next question will be, "How does music manifest itself in that mirror of images and ideas?" It manifests itself as *will*, using the term in Schopenhauer's sense, that is to say as the opposite of the esthetic, contemplative, un-willing disposition. At this point it becomes necessary to discriminate very clearly between essence and appearance—for it is obviously impossible for music to represent the essential nature of the will; if it did, we would have to banish it from the realm of art altogether, seeing that the will is the non-esthetic element *par excellence*. Rather we should say that music *appears* as the will. In order to express that appearance through images the lyrical poet must employ the whole register of emotions, from the whisper of love to the roar of frenzy; moved by the urge to talk of music in Apollonian similitudes, he must first comprehend the whole range of nature, including himself, as the eternal source of volition, desire, appetite. But to the extent that he interprets music through images he is dwelling on the still sea of Apollonian contemplation, no matter how turbulently all that he beholds through the musical medium may surge about him. And when he looks at himself through that medium he will discover his own image in a state of turmoil: his own willing and desiring, his groans and jubilations, will all appear to him as a similitude by which music is interpreted. Such is the phenomenon of the lyric poet. Being an

Apollonian genius, he interprets music through the image of the will, while he is himself turned into the pure, unshadowed eye of the sun, utterly detached from the will and its greed.

Throughout this inquiry I have maintained the position that lyric poetry is dependent on the spirit of music to the same degree that music itself, in its absolute sovereignty, is independent of either image or concept, though it may tolerate both. The poet cannot tell us anything that was not already contained, with a most universal validity, in such music as prompted him to his figurative discourse. The cosmic symbolism of music resists any adequate treatment by language, for the simple reason that music, in referring to primordial contradiction and pain, symbolizes a sphere which is both earlier than appearance and beyond it. Once we set it over against music, all appearance becomes a mere analogy. So it happens that language, the organ and symbol of appearance, can never succeed in bringing the innermost core of music to the surface. Whenever it engages in the imitation of music, language remains in purely superficial contact with it, and no amount of poetic eloquence will carry us a step closer to the essential secret of that art.

VII

At this point we need to call upon every esthetic principle so far discussed, in order to find our way through the labyrinthine origins of Greek tragedy. I believe I am saying nothing extravagant when I claim that the problem of these origins has never even been posed, much less solved, no matter how often the elusive rags of ancient tradition have been speculatively sewn together and ripped apart. That tradition tells us in no uncertain terms that tragedy arose out of the tragic chorus and was, to begin with, nothing but chorus. We are thus bound to scan the chorus closely as the archetypal drama, disregarding the current explanations of it as the idealized spectator, or as representing the populace over against the noble realm of the set. The latter interpretation, which sounds so grandly edifying to certain politicians (as though the democratic Athenians had represented in the popular chorus the invariable moral law, always right in face of the passionate misdeeds and extravagances of kings) may have been suggested by a phrase in Aristotle, but this lofty notion can have had no influence whatever on the original formation of tragedy, whose purely religious origins would exclude not only the opposition between the people and their rulers but any kind of political or social context. Likewise we would consider it blasphemous, in the light of the classical form of the chorus as we know it from Aeschylus and Sophocles, to speak of a "foreshadowing" of constitutional democracy, though others have not stuck at such blasphemy. No ancient polity ever embodied constitutional democracy, and one dares to hope that ancient tragedy did not even foreshadow it.

Much more famous than this political explanation of the chorus is the notion of A. W. Schlegel, who advises us to regard the chorus as the quintessence of the audience, as the "ideal spectator." If we hold this view against the historical tradition according to which tragedy was, in the beginning, nothing but chorus, it turns out to be a crude, unscholarly, though dazzling hypothesis—dazzling because of the effective formulation, the typically German bias for anything called "ideal," and our momentary wonder at the notion. For we are indeed amazed when we compare our familiar theater audience with the tragic chorus and ask ourselves whether the former could conceivably be construed into something analogous to the latter. We tacitly deny the possibility, and then are brought to wonder both at the boldness of Schlegel's assertion and at what must have been the totally different complexion of the Greek audience. We had supposed all along that the spectator, whoever he might be, would always have to remain conscious of the fact that he had before him a work of art, not empiric reality, whereas the tragic chorus of the Greeks is constrained to view the characters enacted on the stage as veritably existing. The chorus of the Oceanides think that they behold the actual Titan Prometheus, and believe themselves every bit as real as the god. Are we seriously to assume that the highest and purest type of spectator is he who, like the Oceanides, regards the god as physically present and real? That it is characteristic of the ideal spectator to rush on stage and deliver the god from his fetters? We had put our faith in an artistic audience, believing that the more intelligent the individual spectator was, the more capable he was of viewing the work of art as art; and now Schlegel's theory suggests to us that the perfect spectator viewed the world of the stage not at all as art but as reality. "Oh these Greeks!" we moan. "They upset our entire esthetic!" But once we have grown accustomed to it, we repeat Schlegel's pronouncement whenever the question of the chorus comes up.

The emphatic tradition I spoke of militates against Schlegel: chorus as such, without stage—the primitive form of tragedy—is incompatible with that chorus of ideal spectators. What sort of artistic genre would it be that derived from the idea of the spectator and crystallized itself in the mode of the "pure" spectator? A spectator without drama is an absurdity. We suspect that the birth of tragedy can be explained neither by any reverence for the moral intelligence of the multitude nor by the notion of a spectator without drama, and, altogether, we consider the problem much too complex to be touched by such facile interpretations.

An infinitely more valuable insight into the significance of the chorus was furnished by Schiller in the famous preface to his *Bride of Messina,* where the chorus is seen as a living wall which tragedy draws about itself in order to achieve insulation from the actual world, to preserve its ideal ground and its poetic freedom.

Schiller used this view as his main weapon against commonplace naturalism, against the illusionistic demand made upon dramatic poetry. While the day of the stage was conceded to be artificial, the architecture of the set symbolic, the metrical discourse stylized, a larger misconception still prevailed. Schiller was not content to have what constitutes the very essence of poetry merely tolerated as poetic license. He insisted that the introduction of the chorus was the decisive step by which any naturalism in art was openly challenged. This way of looking at art seems to me the one which our present age, thinking itself so superior, has labeled pseudo-idealism. But I very much fear that we, with our idolatry of verisimilitude, have arrived at the opposite pole of all idealism, the realm of the waxworks. This too betrays a kind of art, as do certain popular novels of today. All I ask is that we not be importuned by the pretense that such art has left Goethe's and Schiller's "pseudo-idealism" behind.

It is certainly true, as Schiller saw, that the Greek chorus of satyrs, the chorus of primitive tragedy, moved on ideal ground, a ground raised high above the common path of mortals. The Greek has built for his chorus the scaffolding of a fictive chthonic realm and placed thereon fictive nature spirits. Tragedy developed on this foundation, and so has been exempt since its beginning from the embarrassing task of copying actuality. All the same, the world of tragedy is by no means a world arbitrarily projected between heaven and earth; rather it is a world having the same reality and credibility as Olympus possessed for the devout Greek. The satyr, as the Dionysiac chorist, dwells in a reality sanctioned by myth and ritual. That tragedy should begin with him, that the Dionysiac wisdom of tragedy should speak through him, is as puzzling a phenomenon as, more generally, the origin of tragedy from the chorus. Perhaps we can gain a starting point for this inquiry by claiming that the satyr, that fictive nature sprite, stands to cultured man in the same relation as Dionysiac music does to civilization. Richard Wagner has said of the latter that it is absorbed by music as lamplight by daylight. In the same manner, I believe, the cultured Greek felt himself absorbed into the satyr chorus, and in the next development of Greek tragedy state and society, in fact all that separated man from man, gave way before an overwhelming sense of unity which led back into the heart of nature. The metaphysical solace (with which, I wish to say at once, all true tragedy sends us away) that, despite every phenomenal change, life is at bottom indestructibly joyful and powerful, was expressed most concretely in the chorus of satyrs, nature beings who dwell behind all civilization and preserve their identity through every change of generations and historical movement.

With this chorus the profound Greek, so uniquely susceptible to the subtlest and deepest suffering, who had penetrated the destructive agencies of both nature and history, solaced himself. Though he had been in danger of craving a Buddhistic denial of the will, he was saved by art, and through art life reclaimed him.

While the transport of the Dionysiac state, with its suspension of all the ordinary barriers of existence, lasts, it carries with it a Lethean element in which everything that has been experienced by the individual is drowned. This chasm of oblivion separates the quotidian reality from the Dionysiac. But as soon as that quotidian reality enters consciousness once more it is viewed with loathing, and the consequence is an ascetic, abulic state of mind. In this sense Dionysiac man might be said to resemble Hamlet: both have looked deeply into the true nature of things, they have *understood* and are now loath to act. They realize that no action of theirs can work any change in the eternal condition of things, and they regard the imputation as ludicrous or debasing that they should set right the time which is out of joint. Understanding kills action, for in order to act we require the veil of illusion; such is Hamlet's doctrine, not to be confounded with the cheap wisdom of John-a-Dreams, who through too much reflection, as it were a surplus of possibilities, never arrives at action. What, both in the case of Hamlet and of Dionysiac man, overbalances any motive leading to action, is not reflection but understanding, the apprehension of truth and its terror. Now no comfort any longer avails, desire reaches beyond the transcendental world, beyond the gods themselves, and existence, together with its gulling reflection in the gods and an immortal Beyond, is denied. The truth once seen, man is aware everywhere of the ghastly absurdity of existence, comprehends the symbolism of Ophelia's fate and the wisdom of the wood sprite Silenus: nausea invades him.

Then, in this supreme jeopardy of the will, art, that sorceress expert in healing, approaches him; only she can turn his fits of nausea into imaginations with which it is possible to live. These are on the one hand the spirit of the *sublime,* which subjugates terror by means of art; on the other hand the *comic* spirit, which releases us, through art, from the tedium of absurdity. The satyr chorus of the dithyramb was the salvation of Greek art; the threatening paroxysms I have mentioned were contained by the intermediary of those Dionysiac attendants.

VIII

The satyr and the idyllic shepherd of later times have both been products of a desire for naturalness and simplicity. But how firmly the Greek shaped his wood sprite, and how self-consciously and mawkishly the modern dallies with his tender, fluting shepherd! For the Greek the satyr expressed nature in a rude, uncultivated state: he did not, for that reason, confound him with the monkey. Quite the contrary, the satyr was man's true prototype, an expression of his highest and strongest aspirations. He was an enthusiastic reveler, filled with transport by the approach of the god; a compassionate companion re-enacting the sufferings of the god; a prophet of wisdom born out of nature's womb; a symbol of the sexual omnipotence of nature, which the Greek was accustomed to view with reverent wonder. The satyr was sublime and divine—so he must have looked to the traumatically wounded vision of Dionysiac man. Our tricked-out, contrived shepherd would have offended him, but his eyes rested with sublime satisfaction on the open, undistorted limnings of nature. Here archetypal man was cleansed of the illusion of culture, and what revealed itself was authentic man, the bearded satyr jubilantly greeting his god. Before him cultured man dwindled to a false cartoon. Schiller is also correct as regards these beginnings of the tragic art: the chorus is a living wall against the onset of reality because it depicts reality more truthfully and more completely than does civilized man, who ordinarily considers himself the only reality. Poetry does not lie outside the world as a fantastic impossibility begotten of the poet's brain; it seeks to be the exact opposite, an unvarnished expression of truth, and for this reason must cast away the trumpery garments worn by the supposed reality of civilized man. The contrast between this truth of nature and the pretentious lie of civilization is quite similar to that between the eternal core of things and the entire phenomenal world. Even as tragedy, with its metaphysical solace, points to the eternity of true being surviving every phenomenal change, so does the symbolism of the satyr chorus express analogically the primordial relation between the thing in itself and appearance. The idyllic shepherd of modern man is but a replica of the sum of cultural illusions which he mistakes for nature. The Dionysiac Greek, desiring truth and nature at their highest power, sees himself metamorphosed into the satyr.

Such are the dispositions and insights of the reveling throng of Dionysos; and the power of these dispositions and insights transforms them in their own eyes, until they behold themselves restored to the condition of genii, of satyrs. Later the tragic chorus came to be an esthetic imitation of that natural phenomenon; which then necessitated a distinction between Dionysiac spectators and votaries actually spellbound by the god. What must be kept in mind in all these investigations is that the audience of Attic tragedy discovered *itself* in the chorus of the orchestra. Audience and chorus were never fundamentally set over against each other: all was one grand chorus of dancing, singing satyrs, and of those who let themselves be represented by them. This granted, Schlegel's dictum assumes a profounder meaning. The chorus is the "ideal spectator" inasmuch as it is the only *seer*—seer of the visionary world of the proscenium. An audience of spectators, such as we know it, was unknown to the Greeks. Given the terraced structure of the Greek theater, rising in concentric arcs, each spectator could quite literally survey the entire cultural world about him and imagine himself, in the fullness of seeing, as a chorist. Thus we are enabled to view the chorus of primitive prototragedy as the projected image of Dionysiac man. The clearest illustration of this phenomenon is the experience of the actor, who, if he is truly gifted, has before his eyes the vivid image of the role he is to play. The satyr chorus is, above all, a vision of the Dionysiac multitude, just as the world of the stage is a vision of that satyr chorus—a vision so powerful that it blurs the actors' sense of the "reality" of cultured spectators ranged row on row about him. The structure of the Greek theater reminds us of a lonely mountain valley: the architecture of the stage resembles a luminous cloud configuration which the Bacchae behold as they swarm down from the mountaintops; a marvelous frame in the center of which Dionysos manifests himself to them.

Our scholarly ideas of elementary artistic process are likely to be offended by the primitive events which I have adduced here to explain the tragic chorus. And yet nothing can be more evident than the fact that the poet is poet only insofar as he sees himself surrounded by living, acting shapes into whose innermost being he penetrates. It is our peculiar modern weakness to see all primitive esthetic phenomena in too complicated and abstract a way. Metaphor, for the authentic poet, is not a figure of rhetoric but a representative image standing concretely before him in lieu of a concept. A character, to him, is not an assemblage of individual traits laboriously pieced together, but a personage beheld as insistently living before his eyes, differing from the image of the painter only in its capacity to continue living and acting. What is it that makes Homer so much more vivid and concrete in his descriptions than any other poet? His lively eye, with which he discerns so much more. We all talk about poetry so abstractly because we all tend to be indifferent poets. At bottom the esthetic phenomenon is quite simple: all one needs in order to be a poet is the ability to have a lively action going on before one continually, to live surrounded by hosts of spirits. To be a dramatist all one needs is the urge to transform oneself and speak out of strange bodies and souls.

Dionysiac excitation is capable of communicating to a whole multitude this artistic power to feel itself surrounded by, and one with, a host of spirits. What happens in the dramatic chorus is the primary *dramatic* phenomenon: projecting oneself outside oneself and then acting as though one had really entered another body, another character. This constitutes the first step in the evolution of drama. This art is no longer that of the rhapsodist, who does not merge with his images but, like the painter, contemplates them as something outside himself; what we have here is the individual effacing himself through entering a strange being. It should be made clear that this phenomenon is not singular but epidemic: a whole crowd becomes rapt in this manner. It is for this reason that the dithyramb differs essentially from any other kind of chorus. The virgins who, carrying laurel branches and singing a processional chant, move solemnly toward the temple of Apollo, retain their identities and their civic names. The dithyrambic chorus on the other hand is a chorus of the transformed, who have forgotten their civic past and social rank, who have become timeless servants of their god and live outside all social spheres. While all the other types of Greek choric verse are simply the highest intensification of the Apollonian musician, in the dithyramb we see a community of unconscious actors all of whom see one another as enchanted.

Enchantment is the precondition of all dramatic art. In this enchantment the Dionysiac reveler sees himself as satyr, and as satyr, in turn, he sees the god. In his transformation he sees a new vision, which is the Apollonian completion of his state. And by the same token this new vision completes the dramatic act.

Thus we have come to interpret Greek tragedy as a Dionysiac chorus which again and again discharges itself in Apollonian images. Those choric portions with which the tragedy is interlaced constitute, as it were, the matrix of the *dialogue*, that is to say, of the entire stage-world of the actual drama. This substratum of tragedy irradiates, in several consecutive discharges, the vision of the drama—a vision on the one hand completely of the nature of Apollonian dream-illusion and therefore epic, but on the other hand, as the objectification of a Dionysiac condition, tending toward the shattering of the individual and his fusion with the original Oneness. Tragedy is an Apollonian embodiment of Dionysiac insights and powers, and for that reason separated by a tremendous gulf from the epic.

On this view the chorus of Greek tragedy, symbol of an entire multitude agitated by Dionysos, can be fully explained. Whereas we who are accustomed to the role of the chorus in modern theater, especially opera, find it hard to conceive how the chorus of the Greeks should have been older, more central than the dramatic action proper (although we have clear testimony to this effect); and whereas we have never been quite able to reconcile with this position of importance the fact that the chorus was composed of such lowly beings as—originally—goatlike satyrs; and whereas, further, the orchestra in front of the stage has always seemed a riddle to us—we now realize that the stage with its action was originally conceived as pure vision and that the only reality was the chorus, who created that vision out of itself and proclaimed it through the medium of dance, music, and spoken word. Since, in this vision, the chorus beholds its lord and master Dionysos, it remains forever an *attending* chorus; it sees how the god suffers and transforms himself, and it has, for that reason, no need to act. But, notwithstanding its subordination to the god, the chorus remains the highest expression of nature, and, like nature, utters in its enthusiasm oracular words of wisdom. Being compassionate as well as wise, it proclaims a truth that issues from the heart of the world. Thus we see how that fantastic and at first sight embarrassing figure arises, the wise and enthusiastic satyr who is at the same time the "simpleton" as opposed to the god. The satyr is a replica of nature in its strongest tendencies and at the same time a herald of its wisdom and art. He combines in his person the roles of musician, poet, dancer and visionary.

It is in keeping both with this insight and with general tradition that in the earliest tragedy Dionysos was not actually present but merely imagined. Original tragedy is only chorus and not drama at all. Later an attempt was made to demonstrate the god as real and to bring the visionary figure, together with the transfiguring frame, vividly before the eyes of every spectator. This marks the beginning of drama in the strict sense of the word. It then became the task of the dithyrambic chorus so to excite the mood of the listeners that when the tragic hero appeared they would behold not the awkwardly masked man but a figure born of their own rapt vision. If we imagine Admetus brooding on the memory of his recently departed wife, consuming himself in a spiritual contemplation of her form, and how a figure of similar shape and gait is led toward him in deep disguise; if we then imagine his tremor of excitement, his impetuous comparisons, his instinctive conviction—then we have an analogue for the excitement of the spectator beholding the god, with whose sufferings he has already identified himself, stride onto the stage. Instinctively he would project the shape of the god that was magically present to his mind onto that masked figure of a man, dissolving the latter's reality into a ghostly unreality. This is the Apollonian dream state, in which the daylight world is veiled and a new world—clearer, more comprehensible, more affecting than the first, and at the same time more shadowy—falls upon the eye in ever changing shapes. Thus we may recognize a drastic stylistic opposition: language, color, pace, dynamics of speech are polarized into the Dionysiac poetry of the chorus, on the one hand, and the Apollonian dream world of the scene on the other. The result is two completely separate spheres of expression. The Apollonian embodiments in which Dionysos assumes objective shape are very different from the continual inter-play of shifting forces in the music of the chorus, from those powers deeply felt by the enthusiast, but which he is incapable of condensing into a clear image. The adept no longer obscurely senses the approach of the god: the god now speaks to him from the proscenium with the clarity and firmness of epic, as an epic hero, almost in the language of Homer.

IX

Everything that rises to the surface in the Apollonian por-tion of Greek tragedy (in the dialogue) looks simple, trans-parent, beautiful. In this sense the dialogue is a mirror of the Greek mind, whose nature manifests itself in dance, since in dance the maximum power is only potentially present, betraying itself in the suppleness and opulence of movement. The language of the Sophoclean heroes sur-prises us by its Apollonian determinacy and lucidity. It seems to us that we can fathom their innermost being, and we are somewhat surprised that we had such a short way to go. However, once we abstract from the character of the hero as it rises to the surface and becomes visible (a charac-ter at bottom no more than a luminous shape projected onto a dark wall, that is to say, *appearance* through and through) and instead penetrate into the myth which is projected in these luminous reflections, we suddenly come up against a phenomenon which is the exact opposite of a familiar optical one. After an energetic attempt to focus on the sun, we have, by way of remedy almost, dark spots before our eyes when we turn away. Conversely, the lu-minous images of the Sophoclean heroes—those Apollonian masks—are the necessary productions of a deep look into the horror of nature; luminous spots, as it were, designed to cure an eye hurt by the ghastly night. Only in this way can we form an adequate notion of the seriousness of Greek "serenity"; whereas we find that serenity generally misinterpreted nowadays as a condition of undisturbed complacence.

Sophocles conceived doomed Oedipus, the greatest sufferer of the Greek stage, as a pattern of nobility, destined to error and misery despite his wisdom, yet exercising a beneficent influence upon his environment in virtue of his boundless grief. The profound poet tells us that a man who is truly noble is incapable of sin; though every law, every natural order, indeed the entire canon of ethics, perish by his actions, those very actions will create a circle of higher consequences able to found a new world on the ruins of the old. This is the poet's message, insofar as he is at the same time a religious thinker. In his capacity as poet, he presents us in the beginning with a complicated legal knot, in the slow unraveling of which the judge brings about his own destruction. The typically Greek delight in this dialectical solution is so great that it imparts an element of triumphant serenity to the work, and thus removes the sting lurking in the ghastly premises of the plot. In *Oedipus at Colonus* we meet this same serenity, but utterly transfigured. In contrast to the aged hero, stricken with excess of grief and passively undergoing his many misfortunes, we have here a transcendent serenity issuing from above and hinting that by his passive endurance the hero may yet gain a consummate energy of action. This activity (so different from his earlier conscious striving, which had resulted in pure passivity) will extend far beyond the limited experience of his own life. Thus the legal knot of the Oedipus fable, which had seemed to mortal eyes incapable of being disentangled, is slowly loosened. And we experience the most profound human joy as we witness this divine counterpart of dialectics. If this explanation has done the poet justice, it may yet be asked whether it has exhausted the implications of the myth; and now we see that the poet's entire conception was nothing more nor less than the luminous afterimage which kind nature provides our eyes after a look into the abyss. Oedipus, his father's murderer, his mother's lover, solver of the Sphinx's riddle! What is the meaning of this triple fate? An ancient popular belief, especially strong in Persia, holds that a wise *magus* must be incestuously begotten. If we examine Oedipus, the solver of riddles and liberator of his mother, in the light of this Parsee belief, we may conclude that wherever soothsaying and magical powers have broken the spell of present and future, the rigid law of individuation, the magic circle of nature, extreme unnaturalness—in this case incest—is the necessary antecedent; for how should man force nature to yield up her secrets but by successfully resisting her, that is to say, by unnatural acts? This is the recognition I find expressed in the terrible triad of Oedipean fates: the same man who solved the riddle of nature (the ambiguous Sphinx) must also, as murderer of his father and husband of his mother, break the consecrated tables of the natural order. It is as though the myth whispered to us that wisdom, and especially Dionysiac wisdom, is an unnatural crime, and that whoever, in pride of knowledge, hurls nature into the abyss of destruction, must himself experience nature's disintegration. "The edge of wisdom is turned against the wise man; wisdom is a crime committed on nature": such are the terrible words addressed to us by myth. Yet the Greek poet, like a sunbeam, touches the terrible and austere Memnon's Column of myth, which proceeds to give forth Sophoclean melodies. Now I wish to contrast to the glory of passivity the glory of action, as it irradiates the *Prometheus* of Aeschylus. Young Goethe has revealed to us, in the bold words his Prometheus addresses to Zeus, what the thinker Aeschylus meant to say, but what, as poet, he merely gave us to divine in symbol:

> *Here I sit, kneading men*
> *In my image,*
> *A race like myself,*
> *Made to suffer, weep,*
> *Laugh and delight,*
> *And forget all about you—*
> *As I have forgotten.*

Man, raised to titanic proportions, conquers his own civilization and compels the gods to join forces with him, since by his autonomous wisdom he commands both their existence and the limitations of their sway. What appears most wonderful, however, in the Prometheus poem—ostensibly a hymn in praise of impiety—is its profound Aeschylean longing for *justice*. The immense suffering of the bold individual, on the one hand, and on the other the extreme jeopardy of the gods, prefiguring a "twilight of the gods"—the two together pointing to a reconciliation, a merger of their universes of suffering—all this reminds one vividly of the central tenet of Aeschylean speculation in which Moira, as eternal justice, is seen enthroned above men and gods alike. In considering the extraordinary boldness with which Aeschylus places the Olympian world on his scales of justice, we must remember that the profound Greek had an absolutely stable basis of metaphysical thought in his mystery cults and that he was free to discharge all his sceptical velleities on the Olympians. The Greek artist, especially, experienced in respect of these divinities an obscure sense of mutual dependency, a feeling which has been perfectly symbolized in the *Prometheus* of Aeschylus. The titanic artist was strong in his defiant belief that he could create men and, at the least, destroy Olympian gods; this he was able to do by virtue of his superior wisdom, which, to be sure, he must atone for by eternal suffering. The glorious power to *do,* which is possessed by great genius, and for which even eternal suffering is not too high a price to pay—the *artist's* austere pride—is of the very essence of Aeschylean poetry, while Sophocles in his *Oedipus* intones a paean to the *saint.* But even Aeschylus' interpretation of the myth fails to exhaust its extraordinary depth of terror. Once again, we may see the artist's buoyancy and creative joy as a luminous cloud shape reflected upon the dark surface of a lake of sorrow. The legend of Prometheus is indigenous to the entire community of Aryan races and attests to their prevailing talent for profound and tragic vision. In fact, it is not improbable that this myth has the same characteristic importance for the Aryan mind as the myth of the Fall has for the Semitic, and that the two myths are related as brother and sister. The presupposition of the Prometheus myth is primitive man's belief in the supreme value of fire as the true palladium of every rising civilization. But for man to dispose of fire freely, and not receive it as a gift from heaven in the kindling thunderbolt and the warming sunlight, seemed a crime to thoughtful primitive man, a despoiling of divine nature. Thus this original philosophical problem poses at once an insoluble conflict between men and the gods, which lies like a huge boulder at the gateway to every culture. Man's highest good must be bought with a crime and paid for by the flood of grief and suffering which the offended divinities visit upon the human race in its noble ambition. An austere notion, this, which by the dignity it confers on crime presents a strange contrast to the Semitic myth of the Fall—a myth that exhibits curiosity, deception, suggestibility, concupiscence, in short a whole series of principally feminine frailties, as the root of all evil. What distinguishes the Aryan conception is an exalted notion of active sin as the properly Promethean virtue; this notion provides us with the ethical substratum of pessimistic tragedy, which comes to be seen as a justification of human ills, that is to say of human guilt as well as the suffering purchased by that guilt. The tragedy at the heart of things, which the thoughtful Aryan is not disposed to quibble away, the contrariety at the center of the universe, is seen by him as an interpenetration of several worlds, as for instance a divine and a human, each individually in the right but each, as it encroaches upon the other, having to suffer for its individuality. The individual, in the course of his heroic striving towards universality, de-individuation, comes up against that primordial contradiction and learns both to sin and to suffer. The Aryan nations assign to crime the male, the Semites to sin the female gender; and it is quite consistent with these notions that the original act of *hubris* should be attributed to a man, original sin to a woman. For the rest, perhaps not too much should be made of this distinction, cf. the chorus of wizards in Goethe's *Faust*:

> 'Tis no mystery to intuit:
> Far ahead swift woman scurries,
> But no matter how she hurries,
> Man in one bold leap will do it.

Once we have comprehended the substance of the Prometheus myth—the imperative necessity of *hubris* for the titanic individual—we must realize the non-Apollonian character of this pessimistic idea. It is Apollo who tranquilizes the individual by drawing boundary lines, and who, by enjoining again and again the practice of self-knowledge, reminds him of the holy, universal norms. But lest the Apollonian tendency freeze all form into Egyptian rigidity, and in attempting to prescribe its orbit to each particular wave inhibit the movement of the lake, the Dionysiac flood tide periodically destroys all the little circles in which the Apollonian will would confine Hellenism. The swiftly rising Dionysiac tide then shoulders all the small individual wave crests, even as Prometheus' brother, the Titan Atlas, shouldered the world. This titanic urge to be the Atlas of all individuals, to bear them on broad shoulders ever farther and higher, is the common bond between the Promethean and the Dionysiac forces. In this respect the Aeschylean Prometheus appears as a Dionysiac mask, while in his deep hunger for justice Aeschylus reveals his paternal descent from Apollo, god of individuation and just boundaries. We may express the Janus face, at once Dionysiac and Apollonian, of the Aeschylean Prometheus in the following formula: "Whatever exists is both just and unjust, and equally justified in both." What a world!

X

It is an unimpeachable tradition that in its earliest form Greek tragedy records only the sufferings of Dionysos, and that he was the only actor. But it may be claimed with equal justice that, up to Euripides, Dionysos *remains* the sole dramatic protagonist and that all the famous characters of the Greek stage, Prometheus, Oedipus, etc., are only masks of that original hero. The fact that a god hides behind all these masks accounts for the much-admired "ideal" character of those celebrated figures. Someone, I can't recall who, has claimed that all individuals, as individuals, are comic, and therefore untragic; which seems to suggest that the Greeks did not tolerate individuals at all on the tragic stage. And in fact they must have felt this way. The Platonic distinction between the idea and the eidolon is deeply rooted in the Greek temperament. If we wished to use Plato's terminology we might speak of the tragic characters of the Greek stage somewhat as follows: the one true Dionysos appears in a multiplicity of characters, in the mask of warrior hero, and enmeshed in the web of individual will. The god ascends the stage in the likeness of a striving and suffering individual. That he can *appear* at all with this clarity and precision is due to dream interpreter Apollo, who projects before the chorus its Dionysiac condition in this analogical figure. Yet in truth that hero is the suffering Dionysos of the mysteries. He of whom the wonderful myth relates that as a child he was dismembered by Titans now experiences in his own person the pains of individuation, and in this condition is worshiped as Zagreus. We have here an indication that dismemberment—the truly Dionysiac suffering—was like a separation into air, water, earth, and fire, and that individuation should be regarded as the source of all suffering, and rejected. The smile of this Dionysos has given birth to the Olympian gods, his tears have given birth to men. In his existence as dismembered god, Dionysos shows the double nature of a cruel, savage daemon and a mild, gentle ruler.

Every hope of the Eleusinian initiates pointed to a rebirth of Dionysos, which we can now interpret as meaning the end of individuation; the thundering paean of the adepts addressed itself to the coming of the third Dionysos. This hope alone sheds a beam of joy on a ravaged and fragmented world—as is shown by the myth of sorrowing Demeter, who rejoiced only when she was told that she might once again bear Dionysos. In these notions we already find all the components of a profound and mystic philosophy and, by the same token, of the mystery doctrine of tragedy; a recognition that whatever exists is of a piece, and that individuation is the root of all evil; a conception of art as the sanguine hope that the spell of individuation may yet be broken, as an augury of eventual reintegration.

I have said earlier that the Homeric epic was the poetic expression of Olympian culture, its victory song over the terrors of the battle with the Titans. Now, under the overmastering influence of tragic poetry, the Homeric myths were once more transformed and by this metempsychosis proved that in the interim Olympian culture too had been superseded by an even deeper philosophy. The contumacious Titan, Prometheus, now announced to his Olympian tormentor that unless the latter promptly joined forces with him, his reign would be in supreme danger. In the work of Aeschylus we recognize the alliance of the Titan with a frightened Zeus in terror of his end. Thus we find the earlier age of Titans brought back from Tartarus and restored to the light of day. A philosophy of wild, naked nature looks with the bold countenance of truth upon the flitting myths of the Homeric world: they pale and tremble before the lightning eye of this goddess, until the mighty fist of the Dionysiac artist forces them into the service of a new divinity. The Dionysiac truth appropriates the entire realm of myth as symbolic language for its own insights, which it expresses partly in the public rite of tragedy and partly in the secret celebrations of dramatic mysteries, but always under the old mythic veil. What was the power that rescued Prometheus from his vultures and transformed myth into a vehicle of Dionysiac wisdom? It was the Heraclean power of music, which reached its highest form in tragedy and endowed myth with a new and profound significance. Such, as we have said earlier, is the mighty prerogative of music. For it is the lot of every myth to creep gradually into the narrows of supposititious historical fact and to be treated by some later time as a unique event of history. And the Greeks at that time were already well on their way to reinterpreting their childhood dream, cleverly and arbitrarily, into pragmatic childhood history. It is the sure sign of the death of a religion when its mythic presuppositions become systematized, under the severe, rational eyes of an orthodox dogmatism, into a ready sum of historical events, and when people begin timidly defending the veracity of myth but at the same time resist its natural continuance—when the feeling for myth withers and its place is taken by a religion claiming historical foundations. This decaying myth was now seized by the newborn genius of Dionysiac music, in whose hands it flowered once more, with new colors and a fragrance that aroused a wistful longing for a metaphysical world. After this last florescence myth declined, its leaves withered, and before long all the ironic Lucians of antiquity caught at the faded blossoms whirled away by the wind. It was through tragedy that myth achieved its profoundest content, its most expressive form; it arose once again like a wounded warrior, its eyes alight with unspent power and the calm wisdom of the dying.

What were you thinking of, overweening Euripides, when you hoped to press myth, then in its last agony, into your service? It died under your violent hands; but you could easily put in its place an imitation that, like Heracles' monkey, would trick itself out in the master's robes. And even as myth, music too died under your hands; though you plundered greedily all the gardens of music, you could achieve no more than a counterfeit. And because you had deserted Dionysos, you were in turn deserted by Apollo. Though you hunted all the passions up from their couch and conjured them into your circle, though you pointed and burnished a sophistic dialectic for the speeches of your heroes, they have only counterfeit passions and speak counterfeit speeches.

XI

Greek tragedy perished in a manner quite different from the older sister arts: it died by suicide, in consequence of an insoluble conflict, while the others died serene and natural deaths at advanced ages. If it is the sign of a happy natural condition to die painlessly, leaving behind a fair progeny, then the decease of those older genres exhibits such a condition; they sank slowly, and their children, fairer than they, stood before their dying eyes, lifting up their heads in eagerness. The death of Greek tragedy, on the other hand, created a tremendous vacuum that was felt far and wide. As the Greek sailors in the time of Tiberius heard from a lonely island the agonizing cry "Great Pan is dead!" so could be heard ringing now through the entire Greek world these painful cries: "Tragedy is dead! And poetry has perished with it! Away with you, puny, spiritless imitators! Away with you to Hades, where you may eat your fill of the crumbs thrown you by your former masters!"

When after all a new genre sprang into being which honored tragedy as its parent, the child was seen with dismay to bear indeed the features of its mother, but of its mother during her long death struggle. The death struggle of tragedy had been fought by Euripides, while the later art is known as the New Attic comedy. Tragedy lived on there in a degenerate form, a monument to its painful and laborious death.

In this context we can understand the passionate fondness of the writers of the new comedy for Euripides. Now the wish of Philemon—who was willing to be hanged for the pleasure of visiting Euripides in Hades, providing he could be sure that the dead man was still in possession of his senses—no longer seems strange to us. If one were to attempt to say briefly and merely by way of suggestion what Menander and Philemon had in common with Euripides, and what they found so exemplary and exciting in him, one might say that Euripides succeeded in transporting the spectator onto the stage. Once we realize out of what substance the Promethean dramatists before Euripides had formed their heroes and how far it had been from their thoughts to bring onto the stage a true replica of actuality, we shall see clearly how utterly different were Euripides' intentions. Through him the common man found his way from the auditorium onto the stage. That mirror, which previously had shown only the great and bold features, now took on the kind of accuracy that reflects also the paltry traits of nature. Odysseus, the typical Greek of older art, declined under the hands of the new poets to the character of Graeculus, who henceforth held the center of the stage as the good-humored, cunning slave. The merit which Euripides, in Aristophanes' *Frogs,* attributes to himself, of having by his nostrum rid tragic art of its pompous *embonpoint,* is apparent in every one of his tragic heroes. Now every spectator could behold his exact counterpart on the Euripidean stage and was delighted to find him so eloquent. But that was not the only pleasure. People themselves learned to *speak* from Euripides—don't we hear him boast, in his contest with Aeschylus, that through him the populace had learned to observe, make transactions and form conclusions according to all the rules of art, with the utmost cleverness? It was through this revolution in public discourse that the new comedy became possible. From now on the stock phrases to represent everyday affairs were ready to hand. While hitherto the character of dramatic speech had been determined by the demigod in tragedy and the drunken satyr in comedy, that bourgeois mediocrity in which Euripides placed all his political hopes now came to the fore. And so the Aristophanic Euripides could pride himself on having portrayed life "as it really is" and shown men how to attack it: if now all members of the populace were able to philosophize, plead their cases in court and make their business deals with incredible shrewdness, the merit was really his, the result of that wisdom he had inculcated in them.

The new comedy could now address itself to a prepared, enlightened crowd, for whom Euripides had served as choirmaster—only in this case it was the chorus of spectators who had to be trained. As soon as this chorus had acquired a competence in the Euripidean key, the new comedy—that chesslike species of play—with its constant triumphs of cleverness and cunning, arose. Meanwhile choirmaster Euripides was the object of fulsome praise; in fact, people would have killed themselves in order to learn more from him had they not known that the tragic poets were quite as dead as tragedy itself. With tragedy the Greeks had given up the belief in immortality: not only the belief in an ideal past, but also the belief in an ideal future. The words of the famous epitaph "Inconstant and frivolous in old age" apply equally well to the last phase of Hellenism. Its supreme deities are wit, whim, caprice, the pleasure of the moment. The fifth estate, that of the slaves, comes into its own, at least in point of attitude, and if it is possible at all now to speak of Greek serenity, then it must refer to the serenity of the slave, who has no difficult responsibilities, no high aims, and to whom nothing, past or future, is of greater value than the present. It was this semblance of Greek serenity that so outraged the profound and powerful minds of the first four centuries after Christ. This womanish escape from all seriousness and awe, this smug embracing of easy pleasure, seemed to them not only contemptible but the truly anti-Christian frame of mind. It was they who handed on to later generations a picture of Greek antiquity painted entirely in the pale rose hues of serenity—as though there had never been a sixth century with its birth of tragedy, its Mysteries, its Pythagoras and Heracleitus, indeed as though the art works of the great period did not exist at all. And yet none of the latter could, of course, have sprung from the soil of such a trivial ignoble cheer, pointing as they do to an entirely different philosophy as their *raison d'être*.

When I said earlier that Euripides had brought the spectator on the stage in order to enable him to judge the play, I may have created the impression that the older drama had all along stood in a false relation to the spectator; and one might then be tempted to praise Euripides' radical tendency to establish a proper relationship between art work and audience as an advance upon Sophocles. But, after all, *audience* is but a word, not a constant unchanging value. Why should an author feel obliged to accommodate himself to a power whose strength is merely in numbers? If he considers himself superior in his talent and intentions to every single spectator, why should he show respect for the collective expression of all those mediocre capacities rather than for the few members of the audience who seem relatively the most gifted? The truth of the matter is that no Greek artist ever treated his audience with greater audacity and self-sufficiency than Euripides; who at a time when the multitude lay prostrate before him disavowed in noble defiance and publicly his own tendencies—those very tendencies by which he had previously conquered the masses. Had this genius had the slightest reverence for that band of Bedlamites called the public, he would have been struck down long before the mid-point of his career by the bludgeon blows of his unsuccess. We come to realize now that our statement, "Euripides brought the spectator on the stage"—implying that the spectator would be able henceforth to exercise competent judgment —was merely provisional and that we must look for a sounder explanation of his intentions. It is also generally recognized that Aeschylus and Sophocles enjoyed all through their lives and longer the full benefit of popular favor, and that for this reason it would be absurd to speak in either case of a disproportion between art work and public reception. What was it, then, that drove the highly talented and incessantly creative Euripides from a path bathed in the light of those twin luminaries—his great predecessors—and of popular acclaim as well? What peculiar consideration for the spectator made him defy that very same spectator? How did it happen that his great respect for his audience made him treat that audience with utter disrespect?

Euripides—and this may be the solution of our riddle—considered himself quite superior to the crowd as a whole; not, however, to two of his spectators. He would translate the crowd onto the stage but insist, all the same, on revering the two members as the sole judges of his art; on following all their directions and admonitions, and on instilling in the very hearts of his dramatic characters those emotions, passions and recognitions which had heretofore seconded the stage action, like an invisible chorus, from the serried ranks of the amphitheater. It was in deference to these judges that he gave his new characters a new voice, too, and a new music. Their votes, and no others, determined for him the worth of his efforts. And whenever the public rejected his labors it was their encouragement, their faith in his final triumph, which sustained him.

One of the two spectators I just spoke of was Euripides himself—the thinker Euripides, not the poet. Of him it may be said that the extraordinary richness of his critical gift had helped to produce, as in the case of Lessing, an authentic creative offshoot. Endowed with such talent, such remarkable intellectual lucidity and versatility, Euripides watched the performances of his predecessors' plays and tried to rediscover in them those fine lineaments which age, as happens in the case of old paintings, had darkened and almost obliterated. And now something occurred which cannot surprise those among us who are familiar with the deeper secrets of Aeschylean tragedy. Euripides perceived in every line, in every trait, something quite incommensurable: a certain deceptive clarity and, together with it, a mysterious depth, an infinite background. The clearest figure trailed after it a comet's tail which seemed to point to something uncertain, something that could not be wholly elucidated. A similar twilight seemed to invest the very structure of drama, especially the function of the chorus. Then again, how ambiguous did the solutions of all moral problems seem! how problematical the way in which the myths were treated! how irregular the distribution of fortune and misfortune! There was also much in the language of older tragedy that he took exception to, or to say the least, found puzzling: why all this pomp in the representation of simple relationships? why all those tropes and hyperboles, where the characters themselves were simple and straightforward? Euripides sat in the theater pondering, a troubled spectator. In the end he had to admit to himself that he did not understand his great predecessors. But since he looked upon reason as the fountainhead of all doing and enjoying, he had to find out whether anybody shared these notions of his, or whether he was alone in facing up to such incommensurable features. But the multitude, including some of the best individuals, gave him only a smile of distrust; none of them would tell him why, notwithstanding his misgivings and reservations, the great masters were right nonetheless. In this tormented state of mind, Euripides discovered his second spectator—one who did not understand tragedy and for that reason spurned it. Allied with him he could risk coming out of his isolation to fight that tremendous battle against the works of Aeschylus and Sophocles; not by means of polemics, but as a tragic poet determined to make his notion of tragedy prevail over the traditional notions.

XII

Before giving a name to that other spectator, let us stop a moment and call to mind what we have said earlier of the incommensurable and discrepant elements in Aeschylean tragedy. Let us recollect how strangely we were affected by the chorus and by the tragic hero of a kind of tragedy which refused to conform to either our habits or our tradition—until, that is, we discovered that the discrepancy was closely bound up with the very origin and essence of Greek tragedy, as the expression of two interacting artistic impulses, the Apollonian and the Dionysiac. Euripides' basic intention now becomes as clear as day to us: it is to eliminate from tragedy the primitive and pervasive Dionysiac element, and to rebuild the drama on a foundation of non-Dionysiac art, custom and philosophy.

Euripides himself, towards the end of his life, propounded the question of the value and significance of this tendency to his contemporaries in a myth. Has the Dionysiac spirit any right at all to exist? Should it not, rather, be brutally uprooted from the Hellenic soil? Yes, it should, the poet tells us, if only it were possible, but the god Dionysos is too powerful: even the most intelligent opponent, like Pentheus in the *Bacchae*, is unexpectedly enchanted by him, and in his enchantment runs headlong to destruction. The opinion of the two old men in the play—Cadmus and Tiresias—seems to echo the opinion of the aged poet himself: that the cleverest individual cannot by his reasoning overturn an ancient popular tradition like the worship of Dionysos, and that it is the proper part of diplomacy in the face of miraculous powers to make at least a prudent show of sympathy; that it is even possible that the god may still take exception to such tepid interest and—as happened in the case of Cadmus—turn the diplomat into a dragon. We are told this by a poet who all his life had resisted Dionysos heroically, only to end his career with a glorification of his opponent and with suicide—like a man who throws himself from a tower in order to put an end to the unbearable sensation of vertigo. The *Bacchae* acknowledges the failure of Euripides' dramatic intentions when, in fact, these had already succeeded: Dionysos had already been driven from the tragic stage by a daemonic power speaking through Euripides. For in a certain sense Euripides was but a mask, while the divinity which spoke through him was neither Dionysos nor Apollo but a brand-new daemon called Socrates. Thenceforward the real antagonism was to be between the Dionysiac spirit and the Socratic, and tragedy was to perish in the conflict. Try as he may to comfort us with his recantation, Euripides fails. The marvelous temple lies in ruins; of what avail is the destroyer's lament that it was the most beautiful of all temples? And though, by way of punishment, Euripides has been turned into a dragon by all later critics, who can really regard this as adequate compensation?

Let us now look more closely at the Socratic tendency by means of which Euripides fought and conquered Aeschylean tragedy. What, under the most auspicious conditions, could Euripides have hoped to effect in founding his tragedy on purely un-Dionysiac elements? Once it was no longer begotten by music, in the mysterious Dionysiac twilight, what form could drama conceivably take? Only that of the dramatized epic, an Apollonian form which precluded tragic effect. It is not a question here of the events represented. I submit that it would have been impossible for Goethe, in the fifth act of his projected *Nausicäa,* to render tragic the suicide of that idyllic being: the power of the epic Apollonian spirit is such that it transfigures the most horrible deeds before our eyes by the charm of illusion, and redemption through illusion. The poet who writes dramatized narrative can no more become one with his images than can the epic rhapsodist. He too represents serene, wide-eyed contemplation gazing upon its images. The actor in such dramatized epic remains essentially a rhapsodist; the consecration of dream lies upon all his actions and prevents him from ever becoming in the full sense an *actor.*

But what relationship can be said to obtain between such an ideal Apollonian drama and the plays of Euripides? The same as obtains between the early solemn rhapsodist and that more recent variety described in Plato's *Ion:* "When I say something sad my eyes fill with tears; if, however, what I say is terrible and ghastly, then my hair stands on end and my heart beats loudly." Here there is no longer any trace of epic self-forgetfulness, of the true rhapsodist's cool detachment, who at the highest pitch of action, and especially then, becomes wholly illusion and delight in illusion. Euripides is the actor of the beating heart, with hair standing on end. He lays his dramatic plan as Socratic thinker and carries it out as passionate actor. So it happens that the Euripidean drama is at the same time cool and fiery, able alike to freeze and consume us. It cannot possibly achieve the Apollonian effects of the epic, while on the other hand it has severed all connection with the Dionysiac mode; so that in order to have any impact at all it must seek out novel stimulants which are to be found neither in the Apollonian nor in the Dionysiac realm. Those stimulants are, on the one hand, cold paradoxical ideas put in the place of Apollonian contemplation, and on the other fiery emotions put in the place of Dionysiac transports. These last are splendidly realistic counterfeits, but neither ideas nor affects are infused with the spirit of true art.

Having now recognized that Euripides failed in founding the drama solely on Apollonian elements and that, instead, his anti-Dionysiac tendency led him towards inartistic naturalism, we are ready to deal with the phenomenon of esthetic Socratism. Its supreme law may be stated as follows: "Whatever is to be beautiful must also be sensible" —a parallel to the Socratic notion that knowledge alone makes men virtuous. Armed with this canon, Euripides examined every aspect of drama—diction, character, dramatic structure, choral music—and made them fit his specifications. What in Euripidean, as compared with Sophoclean tragedy, has been so frequently censured as poetic lack and retrogression is actually the straight result of the poet's incisive critical gifts, his audacious personality. The Euripidean prologue may serve to illustrate the efficacy of that rationalistic method. Nothing could be more at odds with our dramaturgic notions than the prologue in the drama of Euripides. To have a character appear at the beginning of the play, tell us who he is, what preceded the action, what has happened so far, even what is about to happen in the course of the play—a modern writer for the theater would reject all this as a wanton and unpardonable dismissal of the element of suspense. Now that everyone knows what is going to happen, who will wait to see it happen? Especially since, in this case, the relation is by no means that of a prophetic dream to a later event. But Euripides reasoned quite otherwise. According to him, the effect of tragedy never resided in epic suspense, in a teasing uncertainty as to what was going to happen next. It resided, rather, in those great scenes of lyrical rhetoric in which the passion and dialectic of the protagonist reached heights of eloquence. Everything portended pathos, not action. Whatever did not portend pathos was seen as objectionable. The greatest obstacle to the spectator's most intimate participation in those scenes would be any missing link in the antecedent action: so long as the spectator had to conjecture what this or that figure represented, from whence arose this or that conflict of inclinations and intentions, he could not fully participate in the doings and sufferings of the protagonists, feel with them and fear with them. The tragedy of Aeschylus and Sophocles had used the subtlest devices to furnish the spectator in the early scenes, and as if by chance, with all the necessary information. They had shown an admirable skill in disguising the necessary structural features and making them seem accidental. All the same, Euripides thought he noticed that during those early scenes the spectators were in a peculiar state of unrest—so concerned with figuring out the antecedents of the story that the beauty and pathos of the exposition were lost on them. For this reason he introduced a prologue even before the exposition, and put it into the mouth of a speaker who would command absolute trust. Very often it was a god who had to guarantee to the public the course of the tragedy and so remove any possible doubt as to the reality of the myth; exactly as Descartes could only demonstrate the reality of the empirical world by appealing to God's veracity, his inability to tell a lie. At the end of his drama Euripides required the same divine truthfulness to act as security, so to speak, for the future of his protagonists. This was the function of the ill-famed *deus ex machina*. Between the preview of the prologue and the preview of the epilogue stretched the dramatic-lyric present, the drama proper.

As a poet, then, Euripides was principally concerned with rendering his conscious perceptions, and it is this which gives him his position of importance in the history of Greek drama. With regard to his poetic procedure, which was both critical and creative, he must often have felt that he was applying to drama the opening words of Anaxagoras' treatise: "In the beginning all things were mixed together; then reason came and introduced order." And even as Anaxagoras, with his concept of reason, seems like the first sober philosopher in a company of drunkards, so Euripides may have appeared to himself as the first rational maker of tragedy. Everything was mixed together in a chaotic stew so long as reason, the sole principle of universal order, remained excluded from the creative act. Being of this opinion, Euripides had necessarily to reject his less rational peers. Euripides would never have endorsed Sophocles' statement about Aeschylus—that this poet was doing the right thing, but unconsciously; instead he would have claimed that since Aeschylus created unconsciously he couldn't help doing the wrong thing. Even the divine Plato speaks of the creative power of the poet for the most part ironically and as being on a level with the gifts of the soothsayer and interpreter of dreams, since according to the traditional conception the poet is unable to write until reason and conscious control have deserted him. Euripides set out, as Plato was to do, to show the world the opposite of the "irrational" poet; his esthetic axiom, "whatever is to be beautiful must be conscious" is strictly parallel to the Socratic "whatever is to be good must be conscious." We can hardly go wrong then in calling Euripides the poet of esthetic Socratism. But Socrates was precisely that *second spectator*, incapable of understanding the older tragedy and therefore scorning it, and it was in his company that Euripides dared to usher in a new era of poetic activity. If the old tragedy was wrecked, esthetic Socratism is to blame, and to the extent that the target of the innovators was the Dionysiac principle of the older art we may call Socrates the god's chief opponent, the new Orpheus who, though destined to be torn to pieces by the maenads of Athenian judgment, succeeded in putting the overmastering god to flight. The latter, as before, when he fled from Lycurgus, king of the Edoni, took refuge in the depths of the sea; that is to say, in the flood of a mystery cult that was soon to encompass the world.

XIII

The fact that the aims of Socrates and Euripides were closely allied did not escape the attention of their contemporaries. We have an eloquent illustration of this in the rumor, current at the time in Athens, that Socrates was helping Euripides with his writing. The two names were bracketed by the partisans of the "good old days" whenever it was a question of castigating the upstart demagogues of the present. It was they who were blamed for the disappearance of the Marathonian soundness of body and mind in favor of a dubious enlightenment tending toward a progressive atrophy of the traditional virtues. In the comedy of Aristophanes both men are treated in this vein—half-indignant, half-contemptuous—to the dismay of the rising generation, who, while they were willing enough to sacrifice Euripides, could not forgive the picture of

Socrates as the arch-Sophist. Their only recourse was to pillory Aristophanes in his turn as a dissolute, lying Alcibiades of poetry. I won't pause here to defend the profound instincts of Aristophanes against such attacks but shall proceed to demonstrate the close affinity between Socrates and Euripides, as their contemporaries saw them. It is certainly significant in this connection that Socrates, being a sworn enemy of the tragic art, is said never to have attended the theater except when a new play of Euripides was mounted. The most famous instance of the conjunction of the two names, however, is found in the Delphic oracle which pronounced Socrates the wisest of men yet allowed that Euripides merited the second place. The third place went to Sophocles, who had boasted that, in contrast to Aeschylus, he not only *did* the right thing but knew *why* he did it. Evidently it was the *transparency* of their knowledge that earned for these three men the reputation of true wisdom in their day.

It was Socrates who expressed most clearly this radically new prestige of knowledge and conscious intelligence when he claimed to be the only one who acknowledged to himself that he knew nothing. He roamed all over Athens, visiting the most distinguished statesmen, orators, poets and artists, and found everywhere merely the presumption of knowledge. He was amazed to discover that all these celebrities lacked true and certain knowledge of their callings and pursued those callings by sheer instinct. The expression "sheer instinct" seems to focus perfectly the Socratic attitude. From this point of view Socrates was forced to condemn both the prevailing art and the prevailing ethics. Wherever his penetrating gaze fell he saw nothing but lack of understanding, fictions rampant, and so was led to deduce a state of affairs wholly discreditable and perverse. Socrates believed it was his mission to correct the situation: a solitary man, arrogantly superior and herald of a radically dissimilar culture, art, and ethics, he stepped into a world whose least hem we should have counted it an honor to have touched. This is the reason why the figure of Socrates disturbs us so profoundly whenever we approach it, and why we are tempted again and again to plumb the meaning and intentions of the most problematical character among the ancients. Who was this man who dared, singlehanded, to challenge the entire world of Hellenism—embodied in Homer, Pindar, and Aeschylus, in Phidias, Pericles, Pythia, and Dionysos—which commands our highest reverence? Who was this daemon daring to pour out the magic philter in the dust? this demigod to whom the noblest spirits of mankind must call out:

> *Alas!*
> *With ruthless hand*
> *You have destroyed*
> *This fair edifice:*
> *It falls and decays!*

We are offered a key to the mind of Socrates in that remarkable phenomenon known as his *daimonion*. In certain critical situations, when even his massive intellect faltered, he was able to regain his balance through the agency of a divine voice, which he heard only at such moments. The voice always spoke to *dissuade*. The instinctual wisdom of this anomalous character manifests itself from time to time as a purely inhibitory agent, ready to defy his rational judgment. Whereas in all truly productive men instinct is the strong, affirmative force and reason the dissuader and critic, in the case of Socrates the roles are reversed: instinct is the critic, consciousness the creator. Truly a monstrosity! Because of this lack of every mystical talent Socrates emerges as the perfect pattern of the *non-mystic*, in whom the logical side has become, through superfetation, as overdeveloped as has the instinctual side in the mystic. Yet it was entirely impossible for Socrates' logical impetus to turn against itself. In its unrestrained onrush it exhibited an elemental power such as is commonly found only in men of violent instincts, where we view it with awed surprise. Whoever in reading Plato has experienced the divine directness and sureness of Socrates' whole way of proceeding must have a sense of the gigantic driving wheel of logical Socratism, turning, as it were, *behind* Socrates, which we see through Socrates as through a shadow. That he himself was by no means unaware of this relationship appears from the grave dignity with which he stressed, even at the end and before his judges, his divine mission. It is as impossible to controvert him in this as it is to approve of his corrosive influence upon instinctual life. In this dilemma his accusers, when he was brought before the Athenian forum, could think of one appropriate form of punishment only, namely exile: to turn this wholly unclassifiable, mysterious phenomenon out of the state would have given posterity no cause to charge the Athenians with a disgraceful act. When finally death, not banishment, was pronounced against him, it seems to have been Socrates himself who, with complete lucidity of mind and in the absence of every natural fear of death, insisted on it. He went to his death with the same calm Plato describes when he has him leave the symposium in the early dawn, the last reveler, to begin a new day; while behind him on the benches and on the floor his sleepy companions go on dreaming of Socrates, the true lover. Socrates in his death became the idol of the young Athenian elite. The typical Hellenic youth, Plato, prostrated himself before that image with all the fervent devotion of his enthusiastic mind.

XIV

Let us now imagine Socrates' great Cyclops' eye—that eye which never glowed with the artist's divine frenzy—turned upon tragedy. Bearing in mind that he was unable to look with any pleasure into the Dionysiac abysses, what could Socrates see in that tragic art which to Plato seemed noble and meritorious? Something quite abstruse and irrational, full of causes without effects and effects seemingly without causes, the whole texture so checkered that it must be repugnant to a sober disposition, while it might act as dangerous tinder to a sensitive and impressionable mind. We are told that the only genre of poetry Socrates really appreciated was the Aesopian fable. This he did with the same smiling complaisance with which honest Gellert sings the praise of poetry in his fable of the bee and the hen:

> *I exemplify the use of poetry:*
> *To convey to those who are a bit backward*
> *The truth in a simile.*

The fact is that for Socrates tragic art failed even to "convey the truth," although it did address itself to those who were "a bit backward," which is to say to non-philosophers: a double reason for leaving it alone. Like Plato, he reckoned it among the beguiling arts which represent the agreeable, not the useful, and in consequence exhorted his followers to abstain from such unphilosophical stimu-

lants. His success was such that the young tragic poet
Plato burned all his writings in order to qualify as a student
of Socrates. And while strong native genius might now
and again manage to withstand the Socratic injunction,
the power of the latter was still great enough to force
poetry into entirely new channels.

A good example of this is Plato himself. Although he
did not lag behind the naïve cynicism of his master in the
condemnation of tragedy and of art in general, nevertheless his creative gifts forced him to develop an art form
deeply akin to the existing forms which he had repudi-
ated. The main objection raised by Plato to the older art
(that it was the imitation of an imitation and hence be-
longed to an even lower order of empiric reality) must not,
at all costs, apply to the new genre; and so we see Plato
intent on moving beyond reality and on rendering the idea
which underlies it. By a detour Plato the thinker reached
the very spot where Plato the poet had all along been at
home, and from which Sophocles, and with him the whole
poetic tradition of the past, protested such a charge. Tragedy had assimilated to itself all the older poetic genres. In
a somewhat eccentric sense the same thing can be claimed
for the Platonic dialogue, which was a mixture of all the
available styles and forms and hovered between narrative,
lyric, drama, between prose and poetry, once again breaking through the old law of stylistic unity. The Cynic philosophers went even farther in that direction, seeking, by
their utterly promiscuous style and constant alternation
between verse and prose, to project their image of the
"raving Socrates" in literature, as they sought to enact it
in life. The Platonic dialogue was the lifeboat in which
the shipwrecked older poetry saved itself, together with
its numerous offspring. Crowded together in a narrow

space, and timidly obeying their helmsman Socrates, they moved forward into a new era which never tired of looking at this fantastic spectacle. Plato has furnished for all posterity the pattern of a new art form, the novel, viewed as the Aesopian fable raised to its highest power; a form in which poetry played the same subordinate role with regard to dialectic philosophy as that same philosophy was to play for many centuries with regard to theology. This, then, was the new status of poetry, and it was Plato who, under the pressure of daemonic Socrates, had brought it about.

It is at this point that philosophical ideas begin to entwine themselves about art, forcing the latter to cling closely to the trunk of dialectic. The Apollonian tendency now appears disguised as logical schematism, just as we found in the case of Euripides a corresponding translation of the Dionysiac affect into a naturalistic one. Socrates, the dialectical hero of the Platonic drama, shows a close affinity to the Euripidean hero, who is compelled to justify his actions by proof and counterproof, and for that reason is often in danger of forfeiting our tragic compassion. For who among us can close his eyes to the optimistic element in the nature of dialectics, which sees a triumph in every syllogism and can breathe only in an atmosphere of cool, conscious clarity? Once that optimistic element had entered tragedy, it overgrew its Dionysiac regions and brought about their annihilation and, finally, the leap into genteel domestic drama. Consider the consequences of the Socratic maxims: "Virtue is knowledge; all sins arise from ignorance; only the virtuous are happy"—these three basic formulations of optimism spell the death of tragedy. The virtuous hero must henceforth be a dialectician; virtue and knowledge, belief and ethics, be necessarily and demonstrably connected; Aeschylus' transcendental concept of justice be reduced to the brash and shallow principle of poetic justice with its regular *deus ex machina.*

What is the view taken of the chorus in this new Socratic-optimistic stage world, and of the entire musical and Dionysiac foundation of tragedy? They are seen as accidental features, as reminders of the origin of tragedy, which can well be dispensed with—while we have in fact come to understand that the chorus is the cause of tragedy and the tragic spirit. Already in Sophocles we find some embarrassment with regard to the chorus, which suggests that the Dionysiac floor of tragedy is beginning to give way. Sophocles no longer dares to give the chorus the major role in the tragedy but treats it as almost on the same footing as the actors, as though it had been raised from the *orchestra* onto the *scene.* By so doing he necessarily destroyed its meaning, despite Aristotle's endorsement of this conception of the chorus. This shift in attitude, which Sophocles displayed not only in practice but also, we are told, in theory, was the first step toward the total disintegration of the chorus: a process whose rapid phases we can follow in Euripides, Agathon, and the New Comedy. Optimistic dialectics took up the whip of its syllogisms and drove music out of tragedy. It entirely destroyed the meaning of tragedy—which can be interpreted only as a concrete manifestation of Dionysiac conditions, music made visible, an ecstatic dream world.

Since we have discovered an anti-Dionysiac tendency antedating Socrates, its most brilliant exponent, we must now ask, "Toward what does a figure like Socrates point?" Faced with the evidence of the Platonic dialogues, we are certainly not entitled to see in Socrates merely an agent of disintegration. While it is clear that the immediate result of the Socratic strategy was the destruction of Dionysiac drama, we are forced, nevertheless, by the profundity of the Socratic experience to ask ourselves whether, in fact, art and Socratism are diametrically opposed to one another, whether there is really anything inherently impossible in the idea of a Socratic artist?

It appears that this despotic logician had from time to time a sense of void, loss, unfulfilled duty with regard to art. In prison he told his friends how, on several occasions, a voice had spoken to him in a dream, saying "Practice music, Socrates!" Almost to the end he remained confident that his philosophy represented the highest art of the muses, and would not fully believe that a divinity meant to remind him of "common, popular music." Yet in order to unburden his conscience he finally agreed, in prison, to undertake that music which hitherto he had held in low esteem. In this frame of mind he composed a poem on Apollo and rendered several Aesopian fables in verse. What prompted him to these exercises was something very similar to that warning voice of his daimonion: an Apollonian perception that, like a barbarian king, he had failed to comprehend the nature of a divine effigy, and was in danger of offending his own god through ignorance. These words heard by Socrates in his dream are the only indication that he ever experienced any uneasiness about the limits of his logical universe. He may have asked himself: "Have I been too ready to view what was unintelligible to me as being devoid of meaning? Perhaps there is a realm of wisdom, after all, from which the logician is excluded? Perhaps art must be seen as the necessary complement of rational discourse?"

XV

Keeping in mind these suggestive questions, we must allow that the influence of Socrates (like a shadow cast by the evening sun, ever lengthening into the future) has prompted generation after generation to reconsider the foundations of its art—art taken in its deepest and broadest sense—and as that influence is eternal it also guarantees the eternity of artistic endeavor. But before people were able to realize that all art is intimately dependent on the Greeks from Homer to Socrates, they had necessarily toward the Greeks the same attitude that the Athenians had toward Socrates. Practically every era of Western civilization has at one time or another tried to liberate itself from the Greeks, in deep dissatisfaction because whatever they themselves achieved, seemingly quite original and sincerely admired, lost color and life when held against the Greek model and shrank to a botched copy, a caricature. Time and again a hearty anger has been felt against that presumptuous little nation which had the nerve to brand, for all time, whatever was not created on its own soil as "barbaric." Who are these people, whose historical splendor was ephemeral, their institutions ridiculously narrow, their mores dubious and sometimes objectionable, who yet pretend to the special place among the nations which genius claims among the crowd? None of the later detractors was fortunate enough to find the cup of hemlock with which such a being could be disposed of once and for all: all the poisons of envy, slander, and rage have proved insufficient to destroy that complacent magnificence. And so people have continued to be both ashamed and fearful of the Greeks—though now and again someone has come along who has acknowledged the full truth: that the Greeks are the chariot drivers of every subsequent culture, but that, almost always, chariot and horses are of too poor a quality for the drivers, who then make sport of driving the chariot into the abyss—which they themselves clear with the bold leap of Achilles.

In order to see Socrates as one of these charioteers, it is necessary only to view him as the prototype of an entirely new mode of existence. He is the great exemplar of that *theoretical man* whose significance and aims we must now attempt to understand. Like the artist, theoretical man takes infinite pleasure in all that exists and is thus saved from the practical ethics of pessimism, with its lynx eyes that shine only in the dark. But while the artist, having unveiled the truth garment by garment, remains with his gaze fixed on what is still hidden, theoretical man takes delight in the cast garments and finds his highest satisfaction in the unveiling process itself, which proves to him his own power. Science could not have developed as it has done if its sole concern had been that one naked goddess. For then the adepts of science would have felt like people trying to dig a hole through the earth, each of whom soon realizes that though he toil in lifelong labor he will excavate only an infinitesimal fraction of the great distance and that even this fraction will be covered over before his eyes by another's efforts, so that a third man would do well to find a new spot for his tunneling. Moreover, once it has been proved beyond question that the Antipodes can never be reached by such a direct method, what person in his right mind would want to go on digging—unless it were for the accidental benefit of striking some precious metal or hitting upon a law of nature? For this reason

Lessing, most honest of theoretical men, dared to say that the search for truth was more important to him than truth itself and thereby revealed the innermost secret of inquiry, to the surprise and annoyance of his fellows. Yet, sure enough, alongside sporadic perceptions such as this one of Lessing's, which represented an act of honesty as well as high-spirited defiance, we find a type of deep-seated illusion, first manifested in Socrates: the illusion that thought, guided by the thread of causation, might plumb the farthest abysses of being and even *correct* it. This grand metaphysical illusion has become integral to the scientific endeavor and again and again leads science to those far limits of its inquiry where it becomes art—*which, in this mechanism, is what is really intended.*

If we examine Socrates in the light of this idea, he strikes us as the first who was able not only to live under the guidance of that instinctive scientific certainty but to die by it, which is much more difficult. For this reason the image of the dying Socrates—mortal man freed by knowledge and argument from the fear of death—is the emblem which, hanging above the portal of every science, reminds the adept that his mission is to make existence appear intelligible and thereby justified. If arguments prove insufficient, the element of myth may be used to strengthen them—that myth which I have described as the necessary consequence, and ultimate intention, of all science.

Once we have fully realized how, after Socrates, the mystagogue of science, one school of philosophers after another came upon the scene and departed; how generation after generation of inquirers, spurred by an insatiable thirst for knowledge, explored every aspect of the universe; and how by that ecumenical concern a common net of knowledge was spread over the whole globe, affording glimpses into the workings of an entire solar system—once we have realized all this, and the monumental pyramid of present-day knowledge, we cannot help viewing Socrates as the vortex and turning point of Western civilization. For if we imagine that immense store of energy used, not for the purposes of knowledge, but for the practical, egotistical ends of individuals and nations, we may readily see the consequence: universal wars of extermination and constant migrations of peoples would have weakened man's instinctive zest for life to such an extent that, suicide having become a matter of course, duty might have commanded the son to kill his parents, the friend his friend, as among the Fiji islanders. We know that such wholesale slaughter prevails wherever art in some form or other— especially as religion or science—has not served as antidote to barbarism.

As against this practical pessimism, Socrates represents the archetype of the theoretical optimist, who, strong in the belief that nature can be fathomed, considers knowledge to be the true panacea and error to be radical evil. To Socratic man the one noble and truly human occupation was that of laying bare the workings of nature, of separating true knowledge from illusion and error. So it happened that ever since Socrates the mechanism of concepts, judgments, and syllogisms has come to be regarded as the highest exercise of man's powers, nature's most admirable gift. Socrates and his successors, down to our own day, have considered all moral and sentimental accomplishments— noble deeds, compassion, self-sacrifice, heroism, even that spiritual calm, so difficult of attainment, which the Apollonian Greek called *sophrosyne*—to be ultimately derived from the dialectic of knowledge, and therefore teachable.

Whoever has tasted the delight of a Socratic perception, experienced how it moves to encompass the whole world of phenomena in ever widening circles, knows no sharper incentive to life than his desire to complete the conquest, to weave the net absolutely tight. To such a person the Platonic Socrates appears as the teacher of an entirely new form of "Greek serenity" and affirmation. This positive attitude toward existence must release itself in actions for the most part pedagogic, exercised upon noble youths, to the end of producing genius. But science, spurred on by its energetic notions, approaches irresistibly those outer limits where the optimism implicit in logic must collapse. For the periphery of science has an infinite number of points. Every noble and gifted man has, before reaching the mid-point of his career, come up against some point of the periphery that defied his understanding, quite apart from the fact that we have no way of knowing how the area of the circle is ever to be fully charted. When the inquirer, having pushed to the circumference, realizes how logic in that place curls about itself and bites its own tail, he is struck with a new kind of perception: a tragic perception, which requires, to make it tolerable, the remedy of art.

If we look about us today, with eyes refreshed and fortified by the spectacle of the Greeks, we shall see how the insatiable zest for knowledge, prefigured in Socrates, has been transformed into tragic resignation and the need for art; while, to be sure, on a lower level that same zest appears as hostile to all art and especially to the truly tragic, Dionysiac art, as I have tried to show paradigmatically in the subversion of Aeschylean art by Socratism.

At this point we find ourselves, not without trepidation, knocking at the gates of present and future. Will this dialectic inversion lead to ever new configurations of genius, above all to that of Socrates as the practitioner of music? Will the all-encompassing net of art (whether under the name of religion or science) be woven ever more tightly and delicately? Or will it be torn to shreds by the restless and barbaric activities of our present day? Deeply concerned, yet not unhopeful, we stand aside for a little while as spectators privileged to witness these tremendous struggles and transitions. Alas, it is the spell inherent in such battles that he who watches them must also fight them.

XVI

We have tried to illustrate by this historical example how tragedy, being a product of the spirit of music, must surely perish by the destruction of that spirit. In order to moderate the strangeness of such an assertion and at the same time to demonstrate how we arrived at it, we must now frankly confront certain analogues of our own day. We must step resolutely into the thick of those struggles which are being waged right now between the insatiable thirst for knowledge and man's tragic dependency on art. I will not speak in this connection of those lesser destructive instincts which have at all times opposed art, and especially tragedy, and which in our own day seem to triumph to such an extent that of all the theatrical arts only the farce and the ballet can be said to thrive, with a luxuriance which not all find pleasing. I shall deal here only with the distinguished enemies of the tragic view, that is to say with the exponents of science, all dyed-in-the-wool optimists like their archetype, Socrates. And presently I shall name those forces which seem to promise a rebirth of tragedy and who knows what other fair hopes for the German genius.

Before rushing headlong into the fight let us put on the armor of such perceptions as we have already won. In opposition to all who would derive the arts from a single vital principle, I wish to keep before me those two artistic deities of the Greeks, Apollo and Dionysos. They represent to me, most vividly and concretely, two radically dissimilar realms of art. Apollo embodies the transcendent genius of the *principium individuationis*; through him alone is it possible to achieve redemption in illusion. The mystical jubilation of Dionysos, on the other hand, breaks the spell of individuation and opens a path to the maternal womb of being. Among the great thinkers there is only one who has fully realized the immense discrepancy between the plastic Apollonian art and the Dionysiac art of music. Independently of Greek religious symbols, Schopenhauer assigned to music a totally different character and origin from all the other arts, because it does not, like all the others, represent appearance, but the will directly. It is the metaphysical complement to everything that is physical in the world; the thing-in-itself where all else is appearance (*The World as Will and Idea*, I). Richard Wagner set his seal of approval on this key notion of all esthetics when he wrote in his book on Beethoven that music obeys esthetic principles quite unlike those governing the visual arts and that the category of beauty is altogether inapplicable to it—although a wrongheaded esthetic based on a misguided and decadent art has attempted to make music answer to criteria of beauty proper only to the plastic arts, expecting it to generate *pleasure in beautiful forms*. Once I had become aware of this antinomy I felt strongly moved to explore the nature of Greek tragedy, the profoundest manifestation of Hellenic genius. For the first time I seemed to possess the key enabling me to inspect the problem of tragedy in terms that were no longer derived from conventional esthetics. I was given such a strange and unfamiliar glimpse into the essence of Hellenism that it seemed to me that our classical philology, for all its air of triumphant achievement, had only dealt with phantasmagorias and externals.

We might approach this fundamental problem by posing the following question: what esthetic effect is produced when the Apollonian and Dionysiac forces of art, usually separate, are made to work alongside each other? Or, to put it more succinctly, in what relation does music stand to image and concept? Schopenhauer, whose clarity and perspicuity on that point Wagner praises, has, in *The World as Will and Idea, I,* the following passage, which I shall quote entire: "According to all this, we may regard the phenomenal world, or nature, and music as two different expressions of the same thing, which is therefore itself the only medium of the analogy between these two expressions, so that a knowledge of this medium is required in order to understand that analogy. Music, therefore, if regarded as an expression of the world, is in the highest degree a universal language, which is related indeed to the universality of concepts, much as these are related to the particular things. Its universality, however, is by no means the empty universality of abstraction, but is of quite a different kind, and is united with thorough and distinct definiteness. In this respect it resembles geometrical figures and numbers, which are the universal forms of all possible objects of experience and applicable to them all *a priori*, and yet are not abstract but perceptible and thoroughly determinate. All possible efforts, excitements and manifestations of will, all that goes on in the heart of man and that reason includes in the wide, negative concept of feeling, may be expressed by the infinite number of possible melodies, but always in the universality of mere form, without the material; always according to the thing-in-itself, not the phenomenon—of which melodies reproduce the very soul and essence as it were, without the body. This deep relation which music bears to the true nature of all things also explains the fact that suitable music played to any event or surrounding seems to disclose to us its most secret meaning and appears as the most accurate and distinct commentary upon it; as also the fact that whoever gives himself up entirely to the impression of a symphony seems to see all the possible events of life and the world take place in himself. Nevertheless, upon reflection he can find no likeness between the music and the things that passed before his mind. For, as we have said, music is distinguished from all the other arts by the fact that it is not a copy of the phenomenon, or, more accurately, the adequate objectivity of the will, but is the direct copy of the will itself, and therefore represents the metaphysical of everything physical in the world, and the thing-in-itself of every phenomenon. We might, therefore, just as well call the world embodied music as embodied will: and this is the reason why music makes every picture, and indeed every scene of real life and of the world, at once appear with higher significance; all the more so, to be sure, in proportion as its melody is analogous to the inner spirit of the given phenomenon. It rests upon this that we are able to set a poem to music as a song, or a perceptible representation as a pantomime, or both as an opera. Such particular pictures of human life, set to the universal language of music, are never bound to it or correspond to it with stringent necessity, but stand to it only in the relation of an example chosen at will to a general concept. In the determinateness of the real they represent that which music expresses in the universality of mere form. For melodies are to a certain extent, like general concepts, an abstraction from the actual. This actual world, then, the world of particular things, affords the object of perception, the special and the individual, the particular case, both to the universality of concepts and to the universality of the melodies. But these two universalities are in a certain respect opposed to each other; for the concepts contain only the forms, which are first of all abstracted from perception—the separated outward shell of things, as it were—and hence they are, in the strictest sense of the term, *abstracta*; music, on the other hand, gives the inmost kernel which precedes all forms, or the heart of things. This relation may be very well expressed in the language of the schoolmen by saying: the concepts are the *universalia post rem,* but music gives the *universalia ante rem* and the real world the *universalia in re.* That a relation is generally possible between a composition and a perceptible representation rests, as we have said, upon the fact that both are simply different expressions of the same inner being of the world. When now, in the particular case, such a relation is actually given—that is to say, when the composer has been able to express in the universal language of music the emotions of will which constitute the heart of an event—then the melody of the song, the music of the opera, is expressive. But the analogy discovered by the composer between the two must have proceeded from the direct knowledge of the nature of the world unknown to his reason and must not be an imitation produced with conscious intention by means of conceptions; otherwise the music does not express the inner nature of the will itself, but merely gives an inadequate imitation of its phenomenon: all specially imitative music does this."

In accordance with Schopenhauer's doctrine, we interpret music as the immediate language of the will, and our imaginations are stimulated to embody that immaterial world, which speaks to us with lively motion and yet remains invisible. Image and concept, on the other hand, gain a heightened significance under the influence of truly appropriate music. Dionysiac art, then, affects the Apollonian talent in a twofold manner: first, music incites us to a symbolic intuition of the Dionysiac universality; second, it endows that symbolic image with supreme significance. From these facts, perfectly plausible once we have pondered them well, we deduce that music is capable of giving birth to myth, the most significant of similitudes; and above all, to the tragic myth, which is a parable of Dionysiac knowledge. When I spoke earlier of the lyric poet I demonstrated how, through him, music strives to account for its own essence in Apollonian images. Once we grant that music raised to its highest power must similarly try to find an adequate embodiment, it stands to reason that it will also succeed in discovering a symbolic expression for its proper Dionysiac wisdom. And where should we look for that expression if not in tragedy and the tragic spirit?

It is vain to try to deduce the tragic spirit from the commonly accepted categories of art: illusion and beauty. Music alone allows us to understand the delight felt at the annihilation of the individual. Each single instance of such annihilation will clarify for us the abiding phenomenon of Dionysiac art, which expresses the omnipotent will behind individuation, eternal life continuing beyond all appearance and in spite of destruction. The metaphysical delight in tragedy is a translation of instinctive Dionysiac wisdom into images. The hero, the highest manifestation of the will, is destroyed, and we assent, since he too is merely a phenomenon, and the eternal life of the will remains unaffected. Tragedy cries, "We believe that life is eternal!" and music is the direct expression of that life. The aims of plastic art are very different: here Apollo overcomes individual suffering by the glorious apotheosis of what is eternal in appearance: here beauty vanquishes the suffering that inheres in all existence, and pain is, in a certain sense, glossed away from nature's countenance. That same nature addresses us through Dionysiac art and its tragic symbolism, in a voice that rings authentic: "Be like me, the Original Mother, who, constantly creating, finds satisfaction in the turbulent flux of appearances!"

XVII

Dionysiac art, too, wishes to convince us of the eternal delight of existence, but it insists that we look for this delight not in the phenomena but behind them. It makes us realize that everything that is generated must be prepared to face its painful dissolution. It forces us to gaze into the horror of individual existence, yet without being turned to stone by the vision: a metaphysical solace momentarily lifts us above the whirl of shifting phenomena. For a brief moment we become, ourselves, the primal Being, and we experience its insatiable hunger for existence. Now we see the struggle, the pain, the destruction of appearances, as necessary, because of the constant proliferation of forms pushing into life, because of the extravagant fecundity of the world will. We feel the furious prodding of this travail in the very moment in which we become one with the immense lust for life and are made aware of the eternity and indestructibility of that lust. Pity and terror notwithstanding, we realize our great good fortune in having life—not as individuals, but as part of the life force with whose procreative lust we have become one.

Our study of the genesis of Greek tragedy has shown us clearly how that tragic art arose out of music, and we believe that our interpretation has for the first time done justice to the original and astounding meaning of the chorus. Yet we must admit that the significance of the tragic myth was never clearly conceptualized by the Greek poets, let alone philosophers. Their heroes seem to us always more superficial in their speeches than in their actions: the myth, we might say, never finds an adequate objective correlative in the spoken word. The structure of the scenes and the concrete images convey a deeper wisdom than the poet was able to put into words and concepts. (The same may be claimed for Shakespeare, whose Hamlet speaks more superficially than he acts, so that the interpretation of *Hamlet* given earlier had to be based on a deeper investigation of the whole texture of the play.) As for Greek tragedy, which we experience only through the printed word, I have already indicated that the incongruence between myth and word may lead us to think it more trivial than it actually is and to presume for it a more superficial effect than, according to the ancients, it must have had. It is so easy to forget that what the poet *qua* poet was unable to achieve, namely the supreme spiritualization of myth, might be achieved by him at any moment in his character of musician. Unfortunately, we must reconstruct the superlative effect of tragic music by scholarly means, if we are to experience a measure of that incomparable solace which true tragedy must have afforded. Actually, though, we would have to be Greeks ourselves in order to appreciate the full impact of such music, for—compared with the body of later music with which we are familiar, which seems so infinitely richer—extant Greek music is like the first trial songs of youthful musical genius. As the Egyptian priests have it, the Greeks are eternal children, and children they are in their tragic art too, not knowing what a sublime plaything has grown under their hands and will presently be shattered.

The struggle of the spirit of music to become manifest in image and myth—a struggle that grew in intensity from the beginnings of lyric poetry to the flowering of Attic tragedy—came to a sudden halt and disappeared, as it were, from the Hellenic scene. Yet the Dionysiac world view born of this struggle managed to survive in the Mysteries, and even in its strangest metamorphoses and debasements did not cease to attract thoughtful minds. Who knows whether that conception will not once again rise as art from its mystical depths?

What concerns us here is the question whether those powers to whose influence Greek tragedy succumbed will maintain their ascendancy permanently, thereby blocking for good the renascence of tragedy and the tragic world view. The fact that the dialectical drive toward knowledge and scientific optimism has succeeded in turning tragedy from its course suggests that there may be an eternal conflict between the theoretical and the tragic world view, in which case tragedy could be reborn only when science had at last been pushed to its limits and, faced with those limits, been forced to renounce its claim to universal validity. For the new hypothetical tragedy the music-practicing Socrates might be a fitting symbol.

If we remember the immediate consequences of the restless and inquisitive spirit of science, it can come as no surprise to us that it destroyed myth and, by the same token, displaced poetry from its native soil and rendered it homeless. If we are right in crediting music with the power to revive myth, then we must look for science in those places where it actively opposes the mythopoeic power of music. It did so in the later Attic dithyramb, whose music no longer expressed the innermost being, or will itself, but only reproduced the phenomenon in a mediate, conceptualized form. Truly musical minds turned away from that degenerate kind of music with the same distaste they felt for the anti-artistic tendencies of Socrates. Aristophanes' sure instinct was doubtless right when he lumped together Socrates, the Euripidean drama, and the music of the new dithyrambic poets, castigating them indifferently as symptoms of a degenerate culture. In the new dithyramb, music is degraded to the imitative portrayal of phenomena, such as battles or storms at sea, and thereby robbed of all its mythopoeic power. For we are not in a condition to yield ourselves to the mythic force when music simply tries to beguile us with external analogies between some natural event and certain rhythmical and acoustical combinations, when our reason is called upon to satisfy itself in the recognition of such analogies. Truly Dionysiac music offers us a universal mirror of the world will: every particular incident refracted in that mirror is enlarged into the image of a permanent truth. Conversely, the tone pictures of the new dithyramb strip every such concrete incident at once of its mythic implications. Music here has become a paltry replica of the phenomenon and for that very reason infinitely poorer than the phenomenon itself. And the poverty of the replica further reduces the phenomenon to our consciousness. A battle, thus imitated, becomes a mere sequence of marches, trumpet calls and the like, and our imagination is stopped at the level of such superficialities. Tone painting, then, is in every respect at the opposite pole from the mythopoeic power of true music: it further reduces the phenomenon, while Dionysiac music makes every single phenomenon comprehensive and significant. The anti-Dionysiac spirit won a mighty victory when it estranged music from itself and made it a slave to appearances. Euripides, who, albeit in a higher sense, must be called an absolutely unmusical temperament, was for that very reason a passionate partisan of the new dithyramb and used its entire stock-in-trade with a freebooter's prodigality.

We see a different aspect of this anti-Dionysiac, anti-mythic trend in the increased emphasis on character portrayal and psychological subtlety from Sophocles onward. Character must no longer be broadened so as to become a permanent type, but on the contrary must be so finely individualized, by means of shading and nuances and the strict delineation of every trait, that the spectator ceases to be aware of myth at all and comes to focus on the amazing lifelikeness of the characters and the artist's power of imitation. Here, once again, we see the victory of the particular over the general and the pleasure taken in, as it were, anatomical drawing. We breathe the air of a world of theory, in which scientific knowledge is more revered than the artistic reflection of a universal norm. The cult of the characteristic trait develops apace: Sophocles still paints whole characters and lays myth under contribution in order to render them more fully; Euripides concentrates on large single character traits, projected into violent passions; the new Attic comedy gives us masks, each with a single expression: frivolous old men, hoodwinked panders, roguish slaves, in endless repetition. Where is now the mythopoeic spirit? All that remains to music is to excite jaded nerves or call up memory images, as in tone painting. For the former, the text hardly matters any longer. Already in Euripides things get out of control as soon as his characters or his chorus begin to sing, and heaven only knows what his impudent followers may have been guilty of.

Yet the modish anti-Dionysiac spirit shows itself most clearly in the denouements of the new plays. In the older tragedy one could feel at the end the metaphysical solace, without which it is impossible to imagine our taking pleasure in tragedy. Most purely, perhaps, in *Oedipus at Colonus* we hear those harmonious sounds of reconciliation from another world. But, once the genius of music has departed from tragedy, tragedy is dead, for what, henceforth, is to furnish that metaphysical solace? The new dramatists tried to resolve the tragic dissonance in terrestrial terms: after having been sufficiently buffeted by fate, the hero was compensated in the end by a distinguished marriage and divine honors. He thus resembled a gladiator, who might perchance be set free after he had taken his beating and was covered with wounds. The place of metaphysical solace was now taken by the *deus ex machina*. I do not mean to assert that the tragic spirit was everywhere quite eradicated by the anti-Dionysiac onset; but we do know that it was forced to flee from the realm of art and take refuge in the limbo of aberrant secret rites. Meanwhile, there raged over the entire surface of the Hellenic world the pestilence of that counterfeit "Greek serenity" of which I spoke earlier: a senescent and unproductive affirmation of this life, in utter contrast to the marvelous naïveté of the older Greeks—flower of an Apollonian culture blossoming over a somber abyss, in token of the victory of the Greek will over suffering, and of the wisdom of suffering. The other variety of Greek cheerfulness—the Alexandrian—shows at its best in the man of theory; it exhibits the same characteristics that I have just derived from the general anti-Dionysiac ascendant. It opposes Dionysiac wisdom and art; tries to dissolve the power of myth; puts in place of a metaphysical comfort a terrestrial consonance and a special *deus ex machina*—the god of engines and crucibles: forces of nature put in the service of a higher form of egotism. It believes that the world can be corrected through knowledge and that life should be guided by science; that it is actually in a position to confine man within the narrow circle of soluble tasks, where he can say cheerfully to life: "I want you. You are worth knowing."

XVIII

In age after age the same phenomenon recurs. Over and over the avid will finds means to maintain and perpetuate its creatures in life by spreading over existence the blandishments of illusion. One man is enthralled by the Socratic zest for knowledge and is persuaded that he can staunch the eternal wound of being with its help. Another is beguiled by the veil of art which flutters, tantalizing, before his eyes. Yet another is buoyed up by the metaphysical solace that life flows on, indestructible, beneath the whirlpool of appearances. Not to mention even commoner and more powerful illusions which the will holds in readiness at any moment. The three kinds of illusion I have named answer only to noble natures, who resent the burden of existence more deeply than the rest and who therefore require special beguilements to make them forget this burden. What we call culture is entirely composed of such beguilements. Depending on the proportions of the mixture, we have a culture that is principally Socratic, or artistic, or tragic; or, if historical exemplifications are permitted here, there is either an Alexandrian or a Hellenic or a Brahmanic culture.

Our whole modern world is caught in the net of Alexandrian culture and recognizes as its ideal the man of theory, equipped with the highest cognitive powers, working in the service of science, and whose archetype and progenitor is Socrates. All our pedagogic devices are oriented toward this ideal. Any type of existence that deviates from this model has a hard struggle and lives, at best, on sufferance. It is a rather frightening thought that for centuries the only form of educated man to be found was the scholar. Even our literary arts have been forced to develop out of learned imitations, and the important role rhyme plays in our poetry still betokens the derivation of our poetic forms from artificial experiments with a language not vernacular but properly learned. To any true Greek, that product of modern culture, *Faust*, would have seemed quite unintelligible, though we ourselves understand it well enough. We have only to place Faust, who storms unsatisfied through all the provinces of knowledge and is driven to make a bargain with the powers of darkness, beside Socrates in order to realize that modern man has begun to be aware of the limits of Socratic curiosity and to long, in the wide, waste ocean of knowledge, for a shore. Goethe once said to Eckermann, referring to Napoleon: "Yes indeed, my friend, there is also a productivity of actions." This *aperçu* suggests that for us moderns the man of action is something amazing and incredible, so that the wisdom of a Goethe was needed to find such a strange mode of existence comprehensible, even excusable.

We should acknowledge, then, that Socratic culture is rooted in an optimism which believes itself omnipotent. Nor should we be surprised when we see the fruits of such optimism fully matured, when a society that has been leavened through and through by such convictions begins to quake with extravagant bloatings and appetites, when the belief in general happiness and in the possibility of universal book knowledge becomes by degrees a peremptory demand for such an Alexandrian utopia and the advent of a Euripidean *deus ex machina*. One thing should be remembered: Alexandrian culture requires a slave class for its continued existence, but in its optimism it denies the necessity for such a class; therefore it courts disaster once the effect of its nice slogans concerning the dignity of man and the dignity of labor have worn thin. Nothing can be more terrible than a barbaric slave class that has learned to view its existence as an injustice and prepares to avenge not only its own wrongs but those of all past generations. Under such conditions, who would dare appeal confidently to our weary and etiolated religions, which have long since become "Brahmin" religions? Myth, the prerequisite of all religion, has been paralyzed everywhere, and theology has been invaded by that optimistic spirit which I have just stigmatized as the baneful virus of our society.

The blight which threatens theoretical culture has only begun to frighten modern man, and he is groping uneasily for remedies out of the storehouse of his experience, without having any real conviction that these remedies will prevail against disaster. In the meantime, there have arisen certain men of genius who, with admirable circumspection and consequence, have used the arsenal of science to demonstrate the limitations of science and of the cognitive faculty itself. They have authoritatively rejected science's claim to universal validity and to the attainment of universal goals and exploded for the first time the belief that man may plumb the universe by means of the law of causation. The extraordinary courage and wisdom of Kant and Schopenhauer have won the most difficult victory, that over the optimistic foundations of logic, which form the underpinnings of our culture. Whereas the current optimism had treated the universe as knowable, in the presumption of eternal truths, and space, time, and causality as absolute and universally valid laws, Kant showed how these supposed laws serve only to raise appearance—the work of Maya—to the status of true reality, thereby rendering impossible a genuine understanding of that reality: in the words of Schopenhauer, binding the dreamer even faster in sleep. This perception has initiated a culture which I dare describe as tragic. Its most important characteristic is that wisdom is put in the place of science as the highest goal. This wisdom, unmoved by the pleasant distractions of the sciences, fixes its gaze on the total constellation of the universe and tries to comprehend sympathetically the suffering of that universe as its own. Let us imagine a rising generation with undaunted eyes, with a heroic drive towards the unexplored; let us imagine the bold step of these St. Georges, their reckless pride as they turn their backs on all the valetudinarian doctrines of optimism, preparing to "dwell resolutely in the fullness of being": would it not be necessary for the tragic individual of such a culture, readied by his discipline for every contingency, every terror, to want a novel art of metaphysical solace as his Helena and to exclaim as Faust did:

> *And shall not I, by mightiest desire,*
> *In living shape that precious form acquire?*

Now that Socratic culture has been shaken from two sides and has begun to doubt its own infallibility (first, from fear of its own consequences, which it is just coming to realize, and second, because it is no longer as confident of the solidity of its foundation as it formerly was) it is sad to see how it runs eagerly to embrace one new shape after another, only to let go of it in horror, as Mephistopheles did the seductive lamias. The man of theory, having begun to dread the consequences of his views, no longer dares commit himself freely to the icy flood of existence but runs nervously up and down the bank. He no longer wants to have anything entire with all the natural cruelty of things: to such an extent has the habit of optimism softened him. At the same time, he believes that a culture built on scientific principles must perish once it admits illogic, that is to say, refuses to face its consequences. Our art is a clear example of this universal misery: in vain do we imitate all the great creative periods and masters; in vain do we surround modern man with all of world literature and expect him to name its periods and styles as Adam did the beasts. He remains eternally hungry, the critic without strength or joy, the Alexandrian man who is at bottom a librarian and scholiast, blinding himself miserably over dusty books and typographical errors.

XIX

The best way to characterize the core of Socratic culture is to call it the culture of the opera. It is in this area that Socratism has given an open account of its intentions—a rather surprising one when we compare the evolution of the opera with the abiding Apollonian and Dionysiac truths. First I want to remind the reader of the genesis of the *stilo rappresentativo* and of recitative. How did it happen that this operatic music, so wholly external and incapable of reverence, was enthusiastically greeted by an epoch which, not so very long ago, had produced the inexpressibly noble and sacred music of Palestrina? Can anyone hold the luxury and frivolity of the Florentine court and the vanity of its dramatic singers responsible for the speed and intensity with which the vogue of opera spread? I can explain the passion for a semimusical declamation, at the same period and among the same people who had witnessed the grand architecture of Palestrina's harmonies (in the making of which the whole Christian Middle Ages had conspired), only by reference to an extra-artistic tendency. To the listener who desires to hear the words above the music corresponds the singer who speaks more than he sings, emphasizing the verbal pathos in a kind of half-song. By this emphasis he aids the understanding of the words and gets rid of the remaining half of music. There is a danger that now and again the music will preponderate, spoiling the pathos and clarity of his declamation, while conversely he is always under the temptation to discharge the music of his voice in a virtuoso manner. The pseudopoetic librettist furnishes him ample opportunity for this display in lyrical interjections, repetitions of words and phrases, etc., where the singer may give himself up to the purely musical element without consideration for the text. This constant alternation, so characteristic of the *stilo rappresentativo*, between emotionally charged, only partly sung declamation and wholly musical interjections, this rapid shift of focus between concept and imagination, on the one hand, and the musical response of the listener, on the other, is so completely unnatural, equally opposed to the Dionysiac and the Apollonian spirit, that one must conclude the origin of recitative to have lain outside any artistic instinct. Viewed in these terms, the recitative may be characterized as a mixture of epic and lyric declamation. And yet, since the components are so wholly disparate, the resulting combination is neither harmonious nor constant, but rather a superficial and mosaic-like conglutination, not without precedent in the realm of nature and experience. However, the inventors of recitative took a very different view of it. They, and their age with them, thought they had discovered the secret of ancient music, that secret which alone could account for the amazing feats of an Orpheus or an Amphion or, indeed, for Greek tragedy. They thought that by that novel style they had managed to resuscitate ancient Greek music in all its power; and, given the popular conception of the Homeric world as the primordial world, it was possible to embrace the illusion that one had at last returned to the paradisaical beginnings of mankind, in which music must have had that supreme purity, power, and innocence of which the pastoral poets wrote so movingly. Here we have touched the nerve center of opera, that genuinely modern genre. In it, art satisfies a strong need, but one that can hardly be called esthetic: a hankering for the idyll, a belief in the primordial existence of pure, artistically sensitive man. Recitative stood for the rediscovered language of that archetypal man, opera for the rediscovered country of that idyllic and heroically pure species, who in all their actions followed a natural artistic bent—who, no matter what they had to say, sang at least part of it, and who when their emotions were ever so little aroused burst into full song. It is irrelevant to our inquiry that the humanists of the time used the new image of the paradisaical artist to combat the old ecclesiastical notion of man as totally corrupt and damned; that opera thus represented the opposition dogma of man as essentially good, and furnished an antidote to that pessimism which, given the terrible instability of the epoch, naturally enlisted its strongest and most thoughtful minds. What matters here is our recognition that the peculiar attraction and thus the success of this new art form must be attributed to its satisfaction of a wholly unesthetic need: it was optimistic; it glorified man in himself; it conceived of man as originally good and full of talent. This principle of opera has by degrees become a menacing and rather appalling claim, against which we who are faced with present-day socialist movements cannot stop our ears. The "noble savage" demands his rights: what a paradisaical prospect!

There is still a further point in support of my contention that opera is built on the same principles as our Alexandrian culture. Opera is the product of the man of theory, the critical layman, not the artist. This constitutes one of the most disturbing facts in the entire history of art. Since the demand, coming from essentially unmusical people, was for a clear understanding of the words, a renascence of music could come about only through the discovery of a type of music in which the words lorded it over the counterpoint as a master over his servant. For were not the words nobler than the accompanying harmonic system, as the soul is nobler than the body? It was with precisely that unmusical clumsiness that the combinations of music, image, and word were treated in the beginnings of opera, and in this spirit the first experiments in the new genre were carried out, even in the noble lay circles of Florence, by the poets and singers patronized by those circles. Inartistic man produces his own brand of art, precisely by virtue of his artistic impotence. Having not the faintest conception of the Dionysiac profundity of music, he transforms musical enjoyment into a rationalistic rhetoric of passion in the *stilo rappresentativo*, into a voluptuous indulgence of vocal virtuoso feats; lacking imagination, he must employ engineers and stage designers; being incapable of understanding the true nature of the artist, he invents an "artistic primitive" to suit his taste, i.e. a man who, when his passions are aroused, breaks into song and recites verses. He projects himself into a time when passion sufficed to produce songs and poems—as though mere emotion had ever been able to create art. There lies at the root of opera a fallacious conception of the artistic process, the idyllic belief that every sensitive man is at bottom an artist. In keeping with this belief, opera is the expression of dilettantism in art, dictating its rules with the cheerful optimism of the theorist.

If we were to combine the two tendencies conspiring at the creation of opera into one, we might speak of an idyllic tendency of opera. Here it would be well to refer back to Schiller's account. Nature and ideal, according to Schiller, are objects of grief when the former is felt to be lost, the latter to be beyond reach. But both may become objects of joy when they are represented as actual. Then the first will produce the elegy, in its strict sense, and the second the idyll, in its widest sense. I would like to point out at once the common feature of these two conceptions in the origin of opera: here the ideal is never viewed as unattained nor nature as lost. Rather, a primitive period in the history of man is imagined, in which he lay at the heart of nature and in this state of nature attained immediately the ideal of humanity through Edenic nobility and artistry. From this supposedly perfect primitive we are all said to derive; indeed, we are still his faithful replicas. All we need do in order to recognize ourselves in that primitive is to jettison some of our later achievements, such as our superfluous learning and excess culture. The educated man of the Renaissance used the operatic imitation of Greek tragedy to lead him back to that concord of nature and ideal, to an idyllic reality. He used ancient tragedy the way Dante used Virgil, to lead him to the gates of Paradise, but from there on he went ahead on his own, moving from an imitation of the highest Greek art form to a "restitution of all things," to a re-creation of man's original art world. What confidence and bonhomie these bold enterprises betokened, arising as they did in the very heart of theoretical culture! The only explanation lies in the comforting belief of the day that "essential man" is the perennially virtuous operatic hero, the endlessly piping or singing shepherd, who, if he should ever by chance lose himself for a spell, would inevitably recover himself intact; in the optimism that rises like a perfumed, seductive cloud from the depths of Socratic contemplation.

Opera, then, does not wear the countenance of eternal grief but rather that of joy in an eternal reunion. It expresses the complacent delight in an idyllic reality, or such, at least, as can be viewed as real at any moment. Perhaps people will one day come to *realize* that this supposititious reality is at bottom no more than a fantastic and foolish trifling, which should make anyone who pits against it the immense seriousness of genuine nature and of the true origins of man exclaim in disgust: "Away with that phantom!" And yet it would be self-delusion to think that, trivial as it is, opera can be driven off with a shout, like an apparition. Whoever wants to destroy opera must gird himself for battle with that Alexandrian cheerfulness that has furnished opera its favorite conceptions and whose natural artistic expression it is. As for art proper, what possible benefit can it derive from a form whose origins lie altogether outside the esthetic realm, a form which from a semi-moral sphere has trespassed on the domain of art and can only at rare moments deceive us as to its hybrid origin? What sap nourishes this operatic growth if not that of true art? Are we not right in supposing that its idyllic seductions and Alexandrian blandishments may sophisticate the highest, the truly serious task of art (to deliver the eye from the horror of night, to redeem us by virtue of the healing balm of illusion, from the spastic motions of the will) into an empty and frivolous amusement? What becomes of the enduring Apollonian and Dionysiac truths in such a mixture of styles as we find in the *stilo rappresentativo*; where music acts the part of the servant, the text that of the master; where music is likened to the body, the text to the soul; where the ultimate goal is at best a periphrastic tone painting, similar to that found in the new Attic dithyramb; where music has abrogated its true dignity as the Dionysiac mirror of the universe and seems content to be the slave of appearance, to imitate the play of phenomenal forms, and to stimulate an artificial delight by dallying with lines and proportions? To a careful observer this pernicious influence of opera on music recapitulates the general development of modern music. The optimism that presided at the birth of opera and of the society represented by opera has succeeded with frightening rapidity in divesting music of its grand Dionysiac meanings and stamping it with the trivial character of a *divertissement*, a transformation only equaled in scope by that of Aeschylean man into jovial Alexandrian man.

If we have been justified in suggesting a connection between the disappearance of the Dionysiac spirit and the spectacular, yet hitherto unexplained, degeneration of the Greek species, with what high hopes must we greet the auspicious signs of the opposite development in our own era, namely the gradual reawakening of the Dionysiac spirit! The divine power of Heracles cannot languish forever in the service of Omphale. Out of the Dionysiac recesses of the German soul has sprung a power which has nothing in common with the presuppositions of Socratic culture and which that culture can neither explain nor justify. Quite the contrary, the culture sees it as something to be dreaded and abhorred, something infinitely potent and hostile. I refer to German music, in its mighty course from Bach to Beethoven, and from Beethoven to Wagner. How can the petty intellectualism of our day deal with this monster that has risen out of the infinite deeps? There is no formula to be found, in either the reservoir of operatic filigree and arabesque or the abacus of the fugue and contrapuntal dialectics, that will subdue this monster, make it stand and deliver. What a spectacle to see our estheticians beating the air with the butterfly nets of their pedantic slogans, in vain pursuit of that marvelously volatile musical genius, their movements sadly belying their standards of "eternal" beauty and grandeur! Look at these patrons of music for a moment at close range, as they repeat indefatigably: "Beauty! Beauty!" and judge for yourselves whether they really look like the beautiful darlings of nature, or whether it would not be more correct to say that they have assumed a disguise for their own coarseness, an esthetic pretext for their barren and jejune sensibilities—take the case of Otto Jahn. But liars and prevaricators ought to watch their step in the area of German music. For amidst our degenerate culture music is the only pure and purifying flame, towards which and away from which all things move in a Heracleitean double motion. All that is now called culture, education, civilization will one day have to appear before the incorruptible judge, Dionysos.

Let us now recall how the new German philosophy was nourished from the same sources, how Kant and Schopenhauer succeeded in destroying the complacent acquiescence of intellectual Socratism, how by their labors an infinitely more profound and serious consideration of questions of ethics and art was made possible—a conceptualized form, in fact, of Dionysiac wisdom. To what does this miraculous union between German philosophy and music point if not to a new mode of existence, whose precise nature we can divine only with the aid of Greek analogies? For us, who stand on the watershed between two different modes of existence, the Greek example is still of inestimable value, since it embodies the violent transition to a classical, rationalistic form of suasion; only, we are living through the great phases of Hellenism in reverse order and seem at this very moment to be moving backward from the Alexandrian age into an age of tragedy. And we can't help feeling that the dawn of a new tragic age is for the German spirit only a return to itself, a blessed recovery of its true identity. For an unconscionably long time powerful forces from the outside have compelled the German spirit, which had vegetated in barbaric formlessness, to subserve their forms. But at long last the German spirit may stand before the other nations, free of the leading strings of Romance culture—provided that it continues to be able to learn from that nation from whom to learn at all is a high and rare thing, the Greeks. And was there ever a time when we needed these supreme teachers more urgently than now, as we witness the rebirth of tragedy and are in danger of not knowing either whence it comes or whither it goes?

XX

Someday an incorruptible judge may determine at what period in its history the German spirit has striven most energetically to learn the lessons of the Greeks. If we assume, as we may with some degree of confidence, that the palm goes to Goethe, Schiller and Winckelmann, we must add, with some degree of dismay, that since their time the German effort to assimilate the Greeks has grown progressively weaker. Should this make us despair altogether of the German spirit, or should we not rather propose that even these heroic fighters failed in some crucial points to penetrate the secret of Hellenism and establish a permanent bond between German and Greek culture? An unconscious recognition of this failure may have caused even some of the most thoughtful minds to doubt whether it were possible to outdistance such predecessors along the paths they had marked out and, indeed, whether these paths led to the desired goal. This is why our notions concerning the value of the Greeks for our civilization have deteriorated so alarmingly since our classical era. There are patronizing and condescending views to be heard in most quarters where the question is mooted, but on the other hand one also hears a great deal of ineffectual fine talk about "Greek harmony," "Greek beauty," and "Greek serenity." Most of all in academic circles, whose particular glory it would be to drink deeply from the sources of Hellenism, one has learned betimes to come to easy and comfortable terms with the Greeks, often to the point of abandoning the Hellenic ideal and perverting the true meaning of classical studies altogether. Those university teachers who have not exhausted their energies in the emendation of classical texts or the microscopic inspection of linguistic phenomena will assimilate Greek antiquity by "historical" methods, along with other antiquities, with the conscious superiority of up-to-date scholarship. It can be said truly that the effective power of our academies to educate has never been less than at present; that the journalist, that papery ephemerid, has got the better of the university teacher all along the line, so that the latter's only recourse is to undergo a familiar metamorphosis and—if we may adopt the journalist's jargon—to flutter about with the "easy elegance" of an educated butterfly. How painfully embarrassed our educated classes of today must be in face of the reawakening of the Dionysiac spirit and the rebirth of tragedy, a phenomenon that can be gauged only by analogy to that Greek genius which they have never understood! At no other period in history have the so-called intelligentsia and the artist faced each other with such hostile incomprehension. It is easily understood why such a feeble culture hates a strong art: it is afraid of being destroyed by it. May it not be that this tapering of our culture to such a fine, delicate point spells the end of an entire cultural epoch, the Socratic-Alexandrian? If such heroes as Schiller and Goethe did not succeed in forcing the enchanted gate that leads to the magic mountain of Hellenism, if their most valiant efforts brought them no nearer than the nostalgic look which Goethe's Iphigenia cast from barbaric Taurus toward her homeland across the sea—what can the feeble successors of such heroes hope for, unless the gate should spring open of its own accord in some hitherto unexplored place, to the mystical strains of resurgent tragic music?

No one shall wither our faith in the imminent rebirth of Greek antiquity, for here alone do we see a hope for the rejuvenation and purification of the German spirit through the fire-magic of music. What else, in the desolate waste of present-day culture, holds any promise of a sound, healthy future? In vain we look for a single powerfully branching root, a spot of earth that is fruitful: we see only dust, sand, dullness, and languor. In such hopeless isolation no better symbol comes to mind than that of "The Knight, Death, and the Devil" of Dürer, the steely-eyed armored knight who pursues his dreadful path, undismayed by his ghastly companions and yet without hope, alone with horse and dog. Such a knight was our Schopenhauer, devoid of hope yet persisting in the search for truth. There has been no other like him.

But what amazing change is wrought in that gloomy desert of our culture by the wand of Dionysos! All that is half-alive, rotten, broken and stunted the whirlwind wraps in a red cloud of dust and carries off like a vulture. Our distracted eyes look for all that has vanished and are confused, for what they see has risen from beneath the earth into the golden light, so full and green, so richly alive. In the midst of all this life, joy, and sorrow, tragedy sits in noble ecstasy, listening to a sad, distant song which tells of the mothers of being, whose names are Wish, Will, Woe.

Indeed, my friends, believe with me in this Dionysiac life and in the rebirth of tragedy! Socratic man has run his course; crown your heads with ivy, seize the thyrsus, and do not be surprised if tiger and panther lie down and caress your feet! Dare to lead the life of tragic man, and you will be redeemed. It has fallen to your lot to lead the Dionysiac procession out of India into Greece. Gird yourselves for a severe conflict, but have faith in the thaumaturgy of your god!

XXI

To return from these exhortations to a more sober mood, I wish to repeat that only the Greeks can teach us what such a sudden, miraculous birth of tragedy means to the heart and soul of a nation. The nation of the tragic mysteries fought the war with Persia, and a people who had conducted such a campaign had need of the restorative of tragedy. Who would have expected such strong, steady political feeling, such natural patriotism, such direct joy in combat, of a nation which had undergone the most violent Dionysiac spasms for several generations? We know now that whenever a group has been deeply touched by Dionysiac emotions, the release from the bonds of individuation results in indifference, or even hostility, towards political instinct. On the other hand, Apollo, the founder of states, is also the genius of the *principium individua-*

tionis, and neither commonwealth nor patriotism can subsist without an affirmation of individuality. The only path from orgiastic rites, for a nation, leads to Buddhism, which, given its desire for Nirvana, requires those rare moments of paroxysm that lift man beyond the confines of space, time, and individuation. These paroxysms, in turn, require a philosophy which teaches how the drab intermediate phases can be triumphed over with the aid of the imagination. A nation, on the other hand, in which the political instincts hold absolute sway, necessarily moves toward extreme secularization, of which the most impressive but also most frightening expression is the Roman Empire.

Placed between India and Rome, and tempted to choose one solution or the other, the Greeks managed a classically pure third mode of existence. They could not maintain it for long themselves, but for that very reason it endures for all time. Though the favorites of the gods die young, they also live eternally in the company of the gods. Of what is noblest on earth we cannot reasonably expect that it have the durable toughness of leather: the toughness, for instance, of the Roman national instinct is probably not one of the necessary predicates of perfection. Let us then ask what medicine it was that gave the Greeks in their greatest period—granted the extraordinary force of both their Dionysiac and political instincts—the ability not to exhaust themselves either in ecstatic brooding or a restless bid for universal power and glory but rather to attain that marvelous combination possessed by a noble wine, which at once heats the blood and induces meditation. In order to answer this question we must think of tragedy, whose stimulating and purifying power affected the whole populace and whose supreme value we shall not realize until we see it, as the Greeks did, as the embodiment of all prophylactic powers, reconciling the strongest and most precarious qualities of a nation.

Tragedy absorbs the highest orgiastic music and in so doing consummates music. But then it puts beside it the tragic myth and the tragic hero. Like a mighty titan, the tragic hero shoulders the whole Dionysiac world and removes the burden from us. At the same time, tragic myth, through the figure of the hero, delivers us from our avid thirst for earthly satisfaction and reminds us of another existence and a higher delight. For this delight the hero readies himself, not through his victories but through his undoing. Tragedy interposes a noble parable, *myth,* between the universality of its music and the Dionysiac disposition of the spectator and in so doing creates the illusion that music is but a supreme instrument for bringing to life the plastic world of myth. By virtue of this noble deception it is now able to move its limbs freely in dithyrambic dance and to yield without reserve to an orgiastic abandon, an indulgence which, without this deception, it could not permit itself. Myth shields us from music while at the same time giving music its maximum freedom. In exchange, music endows the tragic myth with a convincing metaphysical significance, which the unsupported word and image could never achieve, and, moreover, assures the spectator of a supreme delight—though the way passes through annihilation and negation, so that he is made to feel that the very womb of things speaks audibly to him.

Since, in this last passage, I have tentatively set forth a difficult notion, which may not be immediately clear to many, I would now invite my friends to consider a particular instance that is within our common experience and which may support my general thesis. I shall not address myself to those who use the scenic representation and the words and emotions of the actors to help them respond to the music. To none of these is music as a mother tongue, and, notwithstanding that help, they never penetrate beyond the vestibule of musical perception. Some, like Gervinus, do not even attain the vestibule by this means. I address myself only to those having immediate kinship with music, who communicate with things almost entirely through unconscious musical relations. To these genuine musicians I direct my question: 'how can anyone experience the third act of *Tristan and Isolde,* apart from either word or image, simply as the movement of a mighty symphony, without exhausting himself in the overstretching of his soul's pinions?' How is it possible for a man who has listened to the very heartbeat of the world-will and felt the unruly lust for life rush into all the veins of the world, now as a thundering torrent and now as a delicately foaming brook—how is it possible for him to remain unshattered? How can he bear, shut in the paltry glass bell of his individuality, to hear the echoes of innumerable cries of weal and woe sounding out of the "vast spaces of cosmic night," and not wish, amidst these pipings of metaphysical pastoral, to flee incontinent to his primordial home? And yet the reception of such a work does not shatter the recipient, the creation of it the creator. What are we to make of this contradiction?

It is at this point that the tragic myth and the tragic hero interpose between our highest musical excitement and the music, giving us a parable of those cosmic facts of which music alone can speak directly. And yet, if we reacted wholly as Dionysiac beings, the parable would fail entirely of effect, and not for a single moment would it distract our attention from the reverberations of the *universalia ante rem.* But now the Apollonian power, bent upon reconstituting the nearly shattered individual, asserts itself, proffering the balm of a delightful illusion. Suddenly we see only Tristan, lying motionless and torpid, and hear him ask, "Why does that familiar strain waken me?" And what before had seemed a hollow sigh echoing from the womb of things now says to us simply, "Waste and empty the sea." And where, before, we had felt ourselves about to expire in a violent paroxysm of feeling, held by a most tenuous bond to this our life, we now see only the hero, mortally wounded yet not dying, and hear his despairing cry: "To long, even in death, and be unable to die for longing!" And where, before, the jubilation of the horn after such an excess of feeling and such consuming pains would have cut us to the quick, as though it had been the crowning pain, now there stands between us and this absolute jubilation the rejoicing Kurwenal, turned toward the ship which brings Isolde. No matter how deeply pity moves us, that pity saves us from the radical "pity of things," even as the parable of myth saves us from the direct intuition of the cosmic idea, as idea and word save us from the undammed pouring forth of the unconscious will. It is through the workings of that marvelous Apollonian illusion that even the realm of sound takes plastic shape before us, as though it were only a question of the destinies of Tristan and Isolde, molded in the finest, most expressive material.

Thus the Apollonian spirit rescues us from the Dionysiac universality and makes us attend, delightedly, to individual forms. It focuses our pity on these forms and so satisfies our instinct for beauty, which longs for great and noble embodiments. It parades the images of life before us and incites us to seize their ideational essence. Through the massive impact of image, concept, ethical doctrine, and sympathy, the Apollonian spirit wrests man from his Dionysiac self-destruction and deceives him as to the universality of the Dionysiac event. It pretends that he sees only the particular image, e.g., Tristan and Isolde, and that the music serves only to make him see it more intensely. What could possibly be immune from the salutary Apollonian charm, if it is able to create in us the illusion that Dionysos may be an aid to Apollo and further enhance his effects? that music is at bottom a vehicle for Apollonian representations? In the pre-established harmony obtaining between the consummate drama and its music, that drama reaches an acme of visual power unobtainable to the drama of words merely. As we watch the rhythmically moving characters of the stage merge with the independently moving lines of melody into a single curving line of motion, we experience the most delicate harmony of sound and visual movement. The relationships of things thus become directly available to the senses, and we realize that in these relationships the essence of a character and of a melodic line are simultaneously made manifest. And as music forces us to see more, and more inwardly than usual, and spreads before us like a delicate tissue the curtain of the scene, our spiritualized vision beholds the world of the stage at once infinitely expanded and illuminated from within. What analogue could the verbal poet possibly furnish—he who tries to bring about that inward expansion of the visible stage world, its inner illumination, by much more indirect and imperfect means, namely word and concept? But, once musical tragedy has appropriated the word, it can at the same time present the birthplace and subsoil of the word and illuminate the genesis of the word from within. And yet it must be emphatically stated that the process I have described is only a marvelous illusion, by whose effects we are delivered from the Dionysiac extravagance and onrush. For, at bottom, music and drama stand in the opposite relation: music is the true idea of the cosmos, drama but a reflection of that idea. The identity between the melodic line and the dramatic character, between relations of harmony and character, obtains in an opposite sense from what we experience when we witness a musical tragedy. However concretely we move, enliven, and illuminate the characters from within, they will always remain mere appearance, from which there is no gateway leading to the true heart of reality. But music addresses us from that center; and though countless appearances were to file past that same music, they would never exhaust its nature but remain external replicas only. Nothing is gained for the understanding of either music or drama by resorting to that popular and utterly false pair of opposites, body and soul. Yet this contrast, crude and unphilosophical as it is, seems to have developed among our estheticians into an article of faith. About the contrast between the phenomenon and the thing-in-itself, on the other hand, they have never learned anything nor, for some obscure reason, wanted to learn.

If our analysis has shown that the Apollonian element in tragedy has utterly triumphed over the Dionysiac quintessence of music, bending the latter to its own purposes —which are to define the drama completely—still an important reservation must be made. At the point that matters most the Apollonian illusion has been broken through and destroyed. This drama which deploys before us, having all its movements and characters illumined from within by the aid of music—as though we witnessed the coming and going of the shuttle as it weaves the tissue—this drama achieves a total effect quite beyond the scope of any Apollonian artifice. In the final effect of tragedy the Dionysiac element triumphs once again: its closing sounds are such as were never heard in the Apollonian realm. The Apollonian illusion reveals its identity as the veil thrown over the Dionysiac meanings for the duration of the play, and yet the illusion is so potent that at its close the Apollonian drama is projected into a sphere where it begins to speak with Dionysiac wisdom, thereby denying itself and its Apollonian concreteness. The difficult relations between the two elements in tragedy may be symbolized by a fraternal union between the two deities: Dionysos speaks the language of Apollo, but Apollo, finally, the language of Dionysos; thereby the highest goal of tragedy and of art in general is reached.

XXII

Let the reader invoke, truly and purely, the effects upon him of genuine musical tragedy by harkening back to his own experience. I believe I have described those effects in such a way that he will now be able to interpret his experiences. He will remember how, watching the myth unfold before him, he felt himself raised to a kind of omniscience, as though his visual power were no longer limited to surfaces but capable of penetrating beyond them; as though he were able to perceive with utter visual clarity the motions of the will, the struggle of motives, the mounting current of passions, all with the aid of music. Yet, though he was conscious of a tremendous intensification of his visual and imaginative instincts, he will nevertheless feel that this long series of Apollonian effects did

not result in that blissful dwelling in will-less contemplation which the sculptor and epic poet—those truly Apollonian artists—induce in him by their productions. He will
not have felt that justification of the individuated world
which is the essence of Apollonian art. He will have beheld the transfigured world of the stage and yet denied
it, seen before him the tragic hero in epic clarity and
beauty and yet rejoiced in his destruction. He will have
responded profoundly to the events presented on the stage
and yet fled willingly into that which passes understanding. He will have considered the actions of the hero
justified and yet felt an even greater exaltation when these
very actions brought about his destruction. He will have
shuddered at the sufferings about to befall the hero and
yet divined in them a higher, overmastering joy. He will
have seen more, and more deeply, than ever and yet wished
for blindness. How are we to account for this strange inner
conflict, this splintering of the Apollonian lance point, if
not by the Dionysiac magic, which, though it seems to
raise the Apollonian motions to their highest pitch, nevertheless manages to enlist this extravagance of Apollonian
power in its own service? To understand tragic myth we
must see it as Dionysiac wisdom made concrete through
Apollonian artifice. In that myth the world of appearance
is pushed to its limits, where it denies itself and seeks to
escape back into the world of primordial reality. There,
with Isolde, it seems to sing its metaphysical swan song:

> *In the sea of pleasure's*
> *Billowing roll,*
> *In the ether waves'*
> *Knelling and toll,*
> *In the world-breath's*
> *Wavering whole—*

To drown in, go down in—
Lost in swoon—greatest boon!

In thus retracing the experiences of the truly responsive listener we gain an understanding of the tragic artist, of how, like a prodigal deity of individuation, he creates his characters—a far cry from mere imitation of nature—and how his mighty Dionysiac desire then engulfs this entire world of phenomena, in order to reveal behind it a sublime esthetic joy in the heart of original Oneness. Our estheticians have nothing to say about this grand return, about the fraternal union in tragedy of the two deities, or about the alternation of Apollonian and Dionysiac excitation in the spectator. But they never tire of telling us about the hero's struggle with destiny, about the triumph of the moral order, and about the purging of the emotions through tragedy. Such doggedness makes me wonder whether these men are at all responsive to esthetic values, whether they do not respond to tragedy merely as moralists. No one, not even Aristotle, has analyzed the effect of tragedy in terms of its esthetic conditions and the esthetic activity of the audience. At one moment we are told of the release of pity and terror through the serious events of the action, at another we are asked to be elevated by the victory of noble principles and the hero's sacrifice to a sublime moral norm. I am sure that the effect of tragedy for many people resides in precisely this, but I am equally sure that these people, and those who interpret to them, have not the slightest inkling of tragedy as a supreme form of art. Aristotle's *catharsis,* that pathological release of which philologists are unsure whether to place it among medical or moral phenomena, reminds me of a curious perception of Goethe's. "Without a lively pathological in-

terest," Goethe writes, "I have never been able to manage
a tragic situation, and for that reason I have rather avoided
them than sought them out. Can it have been one of the
virtues of the ancients that, for them, the highest pathos
was but a form of esthetic play, while for us there is need
of verisimilitude in the production of such a work?" We
may now answer this profound question in the affirmative,
having seen, to our amazement, how in the case of musical
tragedy the highest pathos was, indeed, but a sublime
esthetic play. Only in these terms can the radical tragic
phenomenon be described with some degree of success.
Whoever, after this, goes on talking about those vicarious
pathological and moral effects may as well despair altogether of his esthetic sensibility. To such persons we rec-
ommend, as a harmless substitute, the study of Shakespeare
after the manner of Gervinus and the diligent tracing of
"poetic justice."

Together with tragedy, the esthetic spectator has been
reborn, whose place in our theaters had heretofore been
taken by an odd *quid pro quo* of partly moral and partly
learned pretensions, the "critic." In the sphere where the
latter had his being everything was artificial and only
painted with a semblance of life. The actor was really at
a loss what to do with such a captious and pretentious
spectator and kept looking nervously, together with the
playwright or operatic composer, for the last vestiges of
life in that aridity. Our audiences have hitherto consisted
of precisely this type of critic: schoolboy and student, even
the most naïve female spectator, were unconsciously pre-
conditioned for such response by education and journal-
ism. Faced with such an audience, our better artists concentrated their effort on arousing moral and religious
responses, and the moral norm was vicariously invoked

where by rights a powerful esthetic magic should have transported the listeners. Or else—more grandly, or at least more excitingly—the dramatist presented some feature of the contemporary scene so clearly that the spectators could forget their critical impotence and give themselves up to the same emotions they would have experienced during a military emergency or before the tribune of parliament or at the judgment of crime or vice. Such a perversion of the true purposes of art necessarily resulted in many cases in a cult of "ends." What happened next was what always happens when art becomes adulterated: a rapid deterioration of those "ends." A good example is the notion of the stage as furthering the moral advancement of the people, a notion that was taken seriously in Schiller's day but which is now looked upon as part of the lumber of an obsolete civilization. As the critic gained ascendancy in theater and concert, the journalist in the schoolroom, and the newspaper in society, art degenerated into the lowest kind of amusement and esthetic criticism into the cement of a social group that was vain, distracted, egotistic, and totally unoriginal, whose complexion is best portrayed in Schopenhauer's parable of the porcupine. Never has there been so much loose talk about art and so little respect for it. But what intercourse is possible with a person who uses Beethoven and Shakespeare as subjects for light conversation? Let everyone answer according to his own taste: his answer will reveal what meaning civilization has for him—providing he attempts to answer at all and does not simply fall silent in amazement.

On the other hand, many nobler and more delicately organized people, though their critical perceptions have been barbarized, may recall the unexpected and to them quite incomprehensible effect of a successful performance of *Lohengrin*. Only the hand which might have supported them and led them through this incomprehensible and incomparable experience has been absent, so that the experience remained a solitary one, like a brief comet that leaves darkness in its wake. Yet for that brief moment these people have sensed what it means to be an esthetically responsive spectator.

XXIII

If one wants to try whether he is such a spectator or whether he belongs, rather, to the community of Socratic men, he may ask himself honestly with what emotion he responds to the *miracle* on the stage; whether he feels that his historical sense, trained to look everywhere for strict psychological causation, has been outraged, whether he admits the miracle as a phenomenon that seems natural to child minds but rather remote from himself, or whether he has some different sort of response. Depending on what answer he makes, he will be able to tell whether he has any understanding at all of myth, which, being a concentrated image of the world, an emblem of appearance, cannot dispense with the miracle. The chances are that almost every one of us, upon close examination, will have to admit that he is able to approach the once-living reality of myth only by means of intellectual constructs. Yet every culture that has lost myth has lost, by the same token, its natural, healthy creativity. Only a horizon ringed about with myths can unify a culture. The forces of imagination and of Apollonian dream are saved only by myth from indiscriminate rambling. The images of myth must be the daemonic guardians, ubiquitous but unnoticed, presiding over the growth of the child's mind and interpreting to the mature man his life and struggles. Nor does the commonwealth know any more potent unwritten law than that mythic foundation which guarantees its union with religion and its basis in mythic conceptions. Over against this, let us consider abstract man stripped of myth, abstract education, abstract mores, abstract law, abstract government; the random vagaries of the artistic imagination unchanneled by any native myth; a culture without any fixed and consecrated place of origin, condemned to exhaust all possibilities and feed miserably and parasitically on every culture under the sun. Here we have our present age, the result of a Socratism bent on the extermination of myth. Man today, stripped of myth, stands famished among all his pasts and must dig frantically for roots, be it among the most remote antiquities. What does our great historical hunger signify, our clutching about us of countless other cultures, our consuming desire for knowledge, if not the loss of myth, of a mythic home, the mythic womb? Let us ask ourselves whether our feverish and frightening agitation is anything but the greedy grasping for food of a hungry man. And who would care to offer further nourishment to a culture which, no matter how much it consumes, remains insatiable and which converts the strongest and most wholesome food into "history" and "criticism"?

If the German spirit were, like that of "civilized" France, indissolubly bound up with its culture, we might well despair of it. That oneness of her people with her culture which for so long constituted France's great virtue and was the cause of her supremacy might make us shudder as we look at her today and indeed congratulate ourselves that our own dubious culture has so far nothing in common with the noble core of our national character. All our hopes center on the fact that underneath the hectic movements of our civilization there dwells a marvelous ancient power, which arouses itself mightily only at certain grand moments and then sinks back to dream again of the future. Out of this subsoil grew the German Reformation, in whose choral music the future strains of German music sounded for the first time. Luther's chorales, so inward, courageous, spiritual, and tender, are like the first Dionysiac cry from the thicket at the approach of spring. They are answered antiphonally by the sacred and exuberant procession of Dionysiac enthusiasts to whom we are indebted for German music, to whom we shall one day be indebted for the rebirth of German myth.

I realize that I must now conduct the sympathetic reader to a mountain peak of lonely contemplation where he will have few companions, and I would call out to him by way of encouragement that we must hold fast to our luminous guides, the Greeks. It is from them that we have borrowed, for the purification of our esthetic notions, the twin divine images, each of whom governs his own realm and whose commerce and mutual enhancement we have been able to guess at through the medium of Greek tragedy. We have seen how Greek tragedy declined through a curious sundering of the two sources that nourished it, a process which went hand in hand with the degeneration of the Greek national character and which should make us consider how inextricably bound up with one another are art and the people, myth and custom, tragedy and the commonwealth. The disappearance of tragedy also spelled the disappearance of myth. Heretofore the Greeks had felt an instinctive need to relate their experience at once to their myth, indeed to understand it only through that connection. In this way even the immediate present appeared to them *sub specie aeternitatis* and in a certain sense as timeless. The commonwealth, as well as art, submerged itself in that timeless stream in order to find respite from the burden and avidity of the immediate moment. It may be claimed that a nation, like an individual, is valuable only insofar as it is able to give to quotidian experience the stamp of the eternal. Only by so doing can it express its profound, if unconscious, conviction of the relativity of time and the metaphysical meaning of life. The opposite happens when a nation begins to view itself historically and to demolish the mythical bulwarks that surround it. The result is usually a definite secularization, a break with the unconscious metaphysic of its earlier mode of existence, with all the accompanying dismal moral consequences. Greek art, and specifically Greek tragedy, were the factors preventing the destruction of myth; they too had to be destroyed if one were to live recklessly, out of touch with the native soil, in a wilderness of thought, custom, and action. Even so, the metaphysical urge endeavored to create for itself a weaker embodiment through the intense Socratism of science, but on that pedestrian plane it led only to a feverish search, dissipating itself by degrees in a pandemonium of myths and superstitions collected at random. In the midst of these the Greek remained unsatisfied, until he finally learned to dissemble, as Graeculus, his fever under Greek jollity and frivolity or else to drug himself in some crass oriental superstition.

We have approximated the same conditions ever since the Alexandrian-Roman revival in the fifteenth century, after the long entr'acte so difficult to describe. Today we experience the same extravagant thirst for knowledge, the same insatiable curiosity, the same drastic secularization, the nomadic wandering, the greedy rush to alien tables, the frivolous apotheosis of the present or the stupefied negation of it, and all *sub specie saeculi*—like symptoms, pointing to a comparable lack in our own culture, which has also destroyed myth. It seems scarcely possible to graft an alien myth onto a native culture without damaging the tree beyond repair in the process. Occasionally the tree proves strong and healthy enough to eliminate the foreign element after a prolonged struggle, but as a rule it must wither or continue in a state of morbid growth. We have a sufficiently high opinion of the pure and vigorous substance of the German spirit to entertain the hope that it will eliminate those elements grafted on it by force and remember its own true nature. It might be thought that the battle should begin with the eradication of all elements of Romance culture. Our victory in the last war might be taken as an encouraging sign, yet it is merely external: the internal challenge must be sought in the desire to prove ourselves worthy of our great predecessors, Luther as well as our best artists and poets. But no one should think that such battles can be fought without one's household gods, one's mythic roots, without a true "recovery" of all things German. And if the German should despond in his endeavor to find his way back to his lost homeland, whose familiar paths he has forgotten, he has only to listen to the call of the Dionysiac bird, which hovers above his head and will show him the way.

XXIV

When speaking of the peculiar effects of musical tragedy we laid stress on that Apollonian illusion which saves us from the direct identification with Dionysiac music and allows us to discharge our musical excitement on an interposed Apollonian medium. At the same time we observed how, by virtue of that discharge, the medium of drama was made visible and understandable from within to a degree that is outside the scope of Apollonian art *per se*. We were led to the conclusion that when Apollonian art is elevated by the spirit of music it reaches its maximum intensity; thus the fraternal union of Apollo and Dionysos may be said to represent the final consummation of both the Apollonian and Dionysiac tendencies.

When it is thus illuminated from within, the Apollonian image no longer resembles the weaker manifestations of Apollonian art. What epic and sculpture are able to do, namely to force the contemplative eye to a tranquil delight in individual forms, is not here aimed at, despite the greater clarity and more profound animation. We regarded the drama and penetrated the tumultuous world of its motives and yet felt as though what was passing before us was merely a symbolic image, whose deepest meaning we almost divined and which we longed to tear away in order to reveal the original image behind it. The intense clarity of the image failed to satisfy us, for it seemed to hide as much as it revealed; and while it seemed to invite us to pierce the veil and examine the mystery behind it, its luminous concreteness nevertheless held the eye entranced and kept it from probing deeper.

No one who has not experienced the need to look and at the same time to go beyond that look will understand how clearly these two processes are associated for the understanding of tragic myth. Yet the truly sensitive spectator will bear me out that of all the strange effects of tragedy this double claim is the most peculiar. If we can project this phenomenon from the spectator onto the tragic artist, we shall understand the genesis of tragic myth. It shares with the Apollonian the strong delight in illusion and contemplation, and yet it denies that delight, finding an even higher satisfaction in the annihilation of concrete semblances. At first blush the tragic myth appears as an epic event having to do with the glorification of the hero and his struggles. Yet how are we to account for the fact that the hero's sufferings, his most painful dilemmas—all the ugly, discordant things which support the wisdom of Silenus—are depicted again and again with such relish, and all this during the Greeks' most prosperous and vigorous period, unless we assume that these representations engender a higher kind of delight?

The genesis of tragedy cannot be explained by saying that things happen, after all, just as tragically in real life. Art is not an imitation of nature but its metaphysical supplement, raised up beside it in order to overcome it. Insofar as tragic myth belongs to art, it fully shares its transcendent intentions. Yet what is transcended by myth when it presents the world of phenomena under the figure of the suffering hero? Certainly not the "reality" of that phenomenal world, for myth tells us on the contrary: "Just look! Look closely! This is your life. This is the hour hand on the clock of your existence." Is this the life that myth shows us in order to transcend it? And if not, how are we to account for the delight we feel in viewing these images? I am speaking of *esthetic* delight, being at the same time fully aware that many of these images yield a moral delight as well, in the form of compassion or ethical triumph. But whoever tries to trace the tragic effect solely to these moral sources, as has been the custom among estheticians for so long, need not think that he is doing art a service. Art must insist on interpretations that are germane to its essence. In examining the peculiar delight arising from tragedy, we must look for it in the esthetic sphere, without trespassing on the areas of pity, terror, or moral grandeur. How can ugliness and disharmony, which are the content of tragic myth, inspire an esthetic delight?

At this point we must take a leap into the metaphysics of art by reiterating our earlier contention that this world can be justified only as an esthetic phenomenon. On this view, tragic myth has convinced us that even the ugly and discordant are merely an esthetic game which the will, in its utter exuberance, plays with itself. In order to understand the difficult phenomenon of Dionysiac art directly, we must now attend to the supreme significance of *musical dissonance*. The delight created by tragic myth has the same origin as the delight dissonance in music creates. That primal Dionysiac delight, experienced even in the presence of pain, is the source common to both music and tragic myth.

Now that we have touched upon the musical relation of dissonance we have perhaps come an important step nearer to the solution of the problem of tragedy. For now we can really grasp the significance of the need to look and yet go beyond that look. The auditory analogue of this experience is musical dissonance, as used by a master, which makes us need to hear and at the same time to go beyond that hearing. This forward propulsion, notwithstanding our supreme delight in a reality perceived in all its features, reminds us that both conditions are aspects of one and the same Dionysiac phenomenon, of that spirit which playfully shatters and rebuilds the teeming world of individuals—much as, in Heracleitus, the plastic power of the universe is compared to a child tossing pebbles or building in a sand pile and then destroying what he has built.

In order to assess the Dionysiac capacities of a people correctly we must advert not only to their music but equally to the tragic myth prevailing among them. Given this close affinity between myth and music, we may suppose that when one degenerates the other is likely to atrophy too. One glance at the development of the German people will convince us of the truth of this proposition. The inartistic and parasitical nature of Socratic optimism has shown itself both in our art, reduced to mere amusement, and in our lives, governed by empty concepts. And yet there have been indications that the German spirit is still alive, and marvelously alive, like a knight who sleeps his enchanted sleep and dreams far underground. From out of these depths a Dionysiac song rises, letting us know that this German knight in his austere enchantment is still dreaming of the age-old Dionysiac myth. Let no one believe that the German spirit has irrevocably lost its Dionysiac home so long as those bird voices can clearly be heard telling of that home. One day the knight will awaken, in all the morning freshness of his long sleep. He will slay dragons, destroy the cunning dwarfs, rouse Brünnhilde, and not even Wotan's spear will be able to bar his way.

You, my friends, who believe in Dionysiac music, also know what tragedy means to us. In tragedy the tragic myth is reborn from the matrix of music. It inspires the most extravagant hopes and promises oblivion of the bitterest pain. But for all of us the most bitter pain has been the long humiliation which German genius has had to suffer in the vassalage of evil dwarfs. You will understand my meaning, as you will also understand the nature of my hopes.

XXV

Music and tragic myth are equally expressive of the Dionysiac talent of a nation and cannot be divorced from one
another. Both have their origin in a realm of art which
lies beyond the Apollonian; both shed their transfiguring
light on a region in whose rapt harmony dissonance and
the horror of existence fade away in enchantment. Confident of their supreme powers, they both toy with the
sting of displeasure, and by their toying they both justify
the existence of even the "worst possible world." Thus
the Dionysiac element, as against the Apollonian, proves
itself to be the eternal and original power of art, since it
calls into being the entire world of phenomena. Yet in the
midst of that world a new transfiguring light is needed to
catch and hold in life the stream of individual forms. If
we could imagine an incarnation of dissonance—and what
is man if not that?—that dissonance, in order to endure life,
would need a marvelous illusion to cover it with a veil of
beauty. This is the proper artistic intention of Apollo, in
whose name are gathered together all those countless illusions of fair semblance which at any moment make life
worth living and whet our appetite for the next moment.

But only so much of the Dionysiac substratum of the
universe may enter an individual consciousness as can be
dealt with by that Apollonian transfiguration; so that these
two prime agencies must develop in strict proportion, con-
formable to the laws of eternal justice. Whenever the Dionysiac forces become too obstreperous, as is the case today, we are safe in assuming that Apollo is close at hand,

though wrapped in a cloud, and that the rich effects of his beauty will be witnessed by a later generation.

The reader may intuit these effects if he has ever, though only in a dream, been carried back to the ancient Hellenic way of life. Walking beneath high Ionic peristyles, looking toward a horizon defined by pure and noble lines, seeing on either hand the glorified reflections of his shape in gleaming marble and all about him men moving solemnly or delicately, with harmonious sounds and rhythmic gestures: would he not then, overwhelmed by this steady stream of beauty, be forced to raise his hands to Apollo and call out: "Blessed Greeks! how great must be your Dionysos, if the Delic god thinks such enchantments necessary to cure you of your dithyrambic madness!" To one so moved, an ancient Athenian with the august countenance of Aeschylus might reply: "But you should add, extraordinary stranger, what suffering must this race have endured in order to achieve such beauty! Now come with me to the tragedy and let us sacrifice in the temple of both gods."

THE GENEALOGY OF MORALS:
AN ATTACK

(1887)

Preface

I

We knowers are unknown to ourselves, and for a good reason: how can we ever hope to find what we have never looked for? There is a sound adage which runs: "Where a man's treasure lies, there lies his heart." Our treasure lies in the beehives of our knowledge. We are perpetually on our way thither, being by nature winged insects and honey gatherers of the mind. The only thing that lies close to our heart is the desire to bring something home to the hive. As for the rest of life—so-called "experience"—who among us is serious enough for that? Or has time enough? When it comes to such matters, our heart is simply not in it— we don't even lend our ear. Rather, as a man divinely abstracted and self-absorbed into whose ears the bell has just drummed the twelve strokes of noon will suddenly awake with a start and ask himself what hour has actually struck, we sometimes rub our ears after the event and ask ourselves, astonished and at a loss, "What have we really experienced?"—or rather, "Who are we, really?" And we recount the twelve tremulous strokes of our experience, our life, our being, but unfortunately count wrong. The sad truth is that we remain necessarily strangers to ourselves, we don't understand our own substance, we *must* mistake ourselves; the axiom, "Each man is farthest from himself," will hold for us to all eternity. Of ourselves we are not "knowers". . . .

11

My ideas about the provenance of our moral prejudices (for that is to be the subject of the present work) found their first brief and tentative formulation in a collection of aphorisms called *Human, All Too Human: A Book for Free Spirits.* I began that book one winter in Sorrento, at a moment when it was given me to pause, as a wanderer might pause, and to look back over the wild and dangerous territory my mind had crossed. It was the winter of 1876–77; the ideas themselves had come to me earlier, however. And it is those same ideas I wish to take up in the present treatise: let us hope that the long interval has done them good, making them stronger and more luminous. At all events, the fact that I still hold them fast today, that through all these years they have continued to intertwine and draw nourishment from each other, encourages me to believe that from the very beginning they were not isolated thoughts, nor random or sporadic ones, but sprang from a common root, from a primary desire for knowledge, legislating from deep down in increasingly precise terms, increasingly precise demands. A philosopher should proceed in no other way. We have no right to isolated thoughts, whether truthful or erroneous. Our thoughts should grow out of our values with the same necessity as the fruit out of the tree. Our yeas and nays, our ifs and buts should all be intimately related and bear testimony to one will, one health, one soil, one sun. Supposing you find these fruits unpalatable? What concern is that of the trees—or of us, the philosophers?

III

Because of a qualm peculiar to me and which I am loath
to admit, since it refers to morals, or rather to anything
that has ever been cried up as ethics—a qualm which, un-
bidden and irresistible, put me so at variance, from my
earliest childhood, with environment, age, precepts, tradition that I feel almost entitled to call it my *a priori*—both
my curiosity and my suspicions were focused betimes on
the provenance of our notions of good and evil. Already
at the age of thirteen I was exercised by the problem of
evil. At an age when one's interests are "divided between
childish games and God" I wrote my first essay on ethics.
My solution of the problem was to give the honor to God,
as is only just, and make him the father of evil. Was this
what my *a priori* demanded of me—that new, immoral, or
at any rate non-moral *a priori*—and that mysterious anti-
Kantian "categorical imperative" to which I have hearkened more and more ever since, and not only hearkened?
Fortunately I learned in good time to divorce the theological prejudice from the moral and no longer to seek the
origin of evil *behind* the world. A certain amount of historical and philological training, together with a native
fastidiousness in matters of psychology, before long transformed this problem into another, to wit, "Under what
conditions did man construct the value judgments *good*
and *evil?*" And what is their intrinsic worth? Have they
thus far benefited or retarded mankind? Do they betoken
misery, curtailment, degeneracy or, on the contrary, power,
fullness of being, energy, courage in the face of life, and
confidence in the future? A great variety of answers sug-

gested themselves. I began to distinguish among periods,
nations, individuals; I narrowed the problem down; the
answers grew into new questions, investigations, supposi-
tions, probabilities, until I had staked off at last my own
domain, a whole hidden, growing and blooming world,
secret gardens as it were, of whose existence no one must
have an inkling. . . . How blessed are we knowers, provided we know how to keep silent long enough!

IV

I was first moved to make public some of my hypotheses
concerning the origin of moral ideas by a well-written and
clever (if somewhat pert) essay, which brought me face
to face with a perverse and upside-down variety of genea-
logical hypothesis—the English variety. It had that attraction for me which ideas at the opposite pole from our own
usually have. The title of the little book was *The Origin of
Moral Perceptions,* its author Dr. Paul Rée, the year of
its publication 1877. I believe I have never read anything
from which I dissented so thoroughly from beginning to
end, and yet I did so entirely without rancor. In the work
mentioned earlier, which I was engaged on at the time,
I made reference to certain passages from Rée's essay, not
by way of controverting them—what have I to do with
controversy?—but rather, as becomes a constructive spirit,
to replace the improbable with the probable, or sometimes,
no doubt, to replace his error with my own. On that occasion I formulated for the first time those hypotheses
which are also the concern of the present work—awkwardly, as I am the last to deny, without freedom or the
style proper to such a subject, and with occasional vacilla-

tions and backslidings. The reader may want to go back
to what I had to say in *Human, All Too Human* about
the double evolution of "good" and "evil"—in the ruling
class and the slave class, respectively; about the origin and
value of the ascetic code of ethics; about the "morality of
custom," that much more ancient type of morality, which
is worlds apart from any system of altruistic valuations,
though Dr. Rée, like the English psychologists of ethics,
considers the latter *the* moral valuation; also to what I said
in *The Wanderer* and *Daybreak* about the origin of justice
as a mutual adjustment between roughly equal powers
(balance being the precondition of all covenants, and
hence of all law); further, to what I said in *The Wanderer*
about the origin of punishment, which cannot possibly be
reduced to motives of intimidation (as Dr. Rée assumes;
those motives being always secondary and only coming
into play under special circumstances).

v

At bottom, I was concerned at that time with something
much more important than either my own or someone else's
hypotheses about the origin of ethics—more precisely, this
origin mattered to me only as one of the means toward
an end. The end was the *value* of ethics, and I had to
fight this issue out almost alone with my great teacher
Schopenhauer, to whom *Human, All Too Human,* with
all its passion and hidden contradictions, addresses itself
as though he were still alive. That book, be it observed,
was likewise an attack. The point at issue was the value
of the non-egotistical instincts, the instincts of compassion,
self-denial, and self-sacrifice, which Schopenhauer above

all others had consistently gilded, glorified, "transcenden-talized" until he came to see them as *absolute* values allowing him to deny life and even himself. Yet it was these very same instincts which aroused my suspicion, and that suspicion deepened as time went on. It was here, precisely, that I sensed the greatest danger for humanity, its sublimest delusion and temptation—leading it whither? into nothingness? Here I sensed the beginning of the end, stagnation, nostalgic fatigue, a will that had turned *against* life. I began to understand that the constantly spreading ethics of pity, which had tainted and debilitated even the philosophers, was the most sinister symptom of our sinister European civilization—a detour to a new Buddhism? to a European species of Buddhism? to nihilism? This preference for and overestimation of pity, among philos-ophers, is an entirely new development in Western civiliza-tion. The philosophers of the past deny, to a man, all value to pity. I need only instance Plato, Spinoza, La Rochefou-cauld, and Kant, four minds as different from each other as possible yet agreeing in this one regard, the low esteem in which they hold pity.

VI

At first sight, this problem of pity and the ethics of pity (I am strongly opposed to our modern sentimentality in these matters) may seem very special, a marginal issue. But whoever sticks with it and learns how to ask questions will have the same experience that I had: a vast new panorama will open up before him; strange and vertiginous possibil-ities will invade him; every variety of suspicion, distrust, fear will come to the surface; his belief in ethics of any kind will begin to be shaken. Finally he will be forced to listen to a new claim. Let us articulate that new claim: we need a critique of all moral values; the intrinsic worth of these values must, first of all, be called in question. To this end we need to know the conditions from which those values have sprung and how they have developed and changed: morality as consequence, symptom, mask, *tartufferie*, sickness, misunderstanding; but, also, morality as cause, remedy, stimulant, inhibition, poison. Hitherto such knowledge has neither been forthcoming nor considered a desideratum. The intrinsic worth of these values was taken for granted as a fact of experience and put beyond question. Nobody, up to now, has doubted that the "good" man represents a higher value than the "evil," in terms of promoting and benefiting mankind generally, even taking the long view. But suppose the exact opposite were true. What if the "good" man represents not merely a retrogression but even a danger, a temptation, a narcotic drug enabling the present to live at the expense of the future? More comfortable, less hazardous, perhaps, but also baser, more petty—so that morality itself would be responsible for man, as a species, failing to reach the peak of magnificence of which he is capable? What if morality should turn out to be the danger of dangers? . . .

VII

Suffice it to say that ever since that vista opened before me I have been on the lookout for learned, bold and industrious comrades in arms—I am still looking. The object is to explore the huge, distant and thoroughly hidden country of morality, morality as it has actually existed and actually been lived, with new questions in mind and with fresh eyes. Is not this tantamount to saying that that country must be discovered anew? If, in this connection, among other possible assistants Dr. Rée came to mind, it was because I had not the slightest doubt that the nature of his investigations would lead him almost automatically to a more promising method. Have I deceived myself in entertaining such hopes? At all events I hoped to orient such a sharp and impartial thinker toward a sound history of ethics and to warn him, before it was too late, against random hypothesizing in the English manner. For it should be obvious that all that matters to a psychologist of morals is what has really existed and is attested by documents, the endless hieroglyphic record, so difficult to decipher, of our moral past. That past was unknown to Dr. Rée, but he had read Darwin. So it happened that in his hypotheses, most amusingly, the Darwinian brute and the ultramodern moral milksop who no longer bites walk hand in hand, the latter wearing an expression of bonhomie and refined indolence, even a shade of pessimism, of fatigue—as though it were really not worth-while to take all these things (the problems of morality) quite so seriously. My point of view is exactly the opposite, that nothing under the sun is more rewarding to take seriously; and part of the reward might be that someday we will be allowed to take it *lightly*. For lightheartedness, or to use my own phrase, a "gay science" is the reward of a long, courageous, painstaking, inward seriousness, which to be sure is not within every man's compass. On the day when we can honestly exclaim "Let's get on with the comedy! These antiquated morals are part of it too!" we shall have given a new turn to the Dionysiac drama of man's destiny, and doubtless the grand old writer of life's comedy will make good use of it.

VIII

Should this treatise seem unintelligible or jarring to some readers, I think the fault need not necessarily be laid at my door. It is plain enough, and it presumes only that the reader will have read my earlier works with some care— for they do, in fact, require careful reading. As regards my *Zarathustra*, I think no one should claim to know it who has not been, by turns, deeply wounded and deeply delighted by what it says. Only such readers will have gained the right to participate in the halcyon element from which it sprang, with all its sunniness, sweep, and assurance. Also, the aphoristic form may present a stumbling block, the difficulty being that this form is no longer taken "hard" enough. An aphorism that has been honestly struck cannot be deciphered simply by reading it off; this is only the beginning of the work of interpretation proper, which requires a whole science of hermeneutics. In the third essay of this book I give an example of what I mean by true interpretation: an aphorism stands at the head of that essay, and the body of the essay forms the commentary. One skill is needed—lost today, unfortunately—for the practice of reading as an art: the skill to ruminate, which cows possess but modern man lacks. This is why my writings will, for some time yet, remain difficult to digest.

Sils-Maria, Upper Engadine
July 1887

First Essay

"GOOD AND EVIL," "GOOD AND BAD"

I

The English psychologists to whom we owe the only attempts that have thus far been made to write a genealogy of morals are no mean posers of riddles, but the riddles they pose are themselves, and being incarnate have one advantage over their books—they are interesting. What are these English psychologists really after? One finds them always, whether intentionally or not, engaged in the same task of pushing into the foreground the nasty part of the psyche, looking for the effective motive forces of human development in the very last place we would wish to have them found, e.g., in the inertia of habit, in forgetfulness, in the blind and fortuitous association of ideas: always in something that is purely passive, automatic, reflexive, molecular, and, moreover, profoundly stupid. What drives these psychologists forever in the same direction? A secret, malicious desire to belittle humanity, which they do not acknowledge even to themselves? A pessimistic distrust, the suspiciousness of the soured idealist? Some petty resentment of Christianity (and Plato) which does not rise above the threshold of consciousness? Or could it be a prurient taste for whatever is embarrassing, painfully paradoxical, dubious and absurd in existence? Or is it, perhaps, a kind of stew—a little meanness, a little bitterness, a bit of anti-Christianity, a touch of prurience and desire for condiments? . . . But, again, people tell me that these men are simply dull old frogs who hop and creep in and around man as in their own element—as though man were a bog. However, I am reluctant to listen to this, in fact I refuse to believe it; and if I may express a wish where I cannot express a conviction, I do wish wholeheartedly that things may be otherwise with these men—that these microscopic examiners of the soul may be really courageous, magnanimous, and proud animals, who know how to contain their emotions and have trained themselves to subordinate all wishful thinking to the truth—any truth, even a homespun, severe, ugly, obnoxious, un-Christian, unmoral truth. For such truths do exist.

11

All honor to the beneficent spirits that may motivate these historians of ethics! One thing is certain, however, they have been quite deserted by the true spirit of history. They all, to a man, think unhistorically, as is the age-old custom among philosophers. The amateurishness of their procedure is made plain from the very beginning, when it is a question of explaining the provenance of the concept and judgment *good*. "Originally," they decree, "altruistic actions were praised and approved by their recipients, that is, by those to whom they were useful. Later on, the origin of that praise having been forgotten, such actions were felt to be good simply because it was the habit to commend them." We notice at once that this first derivation has all the earmarks of the English psychologists' work. Here are the key ideas of utility, forgetfulness, habit, and, finally, error, seen as lying at the root of that value system which civilized man had hitherto regarded with pride as the prerogative of all men. This pride must now be humbled, these values devalued. Have the debunkers succeeded?

Now it is obvious to me, first of all, that their theory looks for the genesis of the concept *good* in the wrong place: the judgment *good* does not originate with those to whom the good has been done. Rather it was the "good" themselves, that is to say the noble, mighty, highly placed, and high-minded who decreed themselves and their actions to be good, i.e., belonging to the highest rank, in contradistinction to all that was base, low-minded and plebeian. It was only this *pathos of distance* that authorized them to create values and name them—what was utility to them? The notion of utility seems singularly inept to account for such a quick jetting forth of supreme value judgments. Here we come face to face with the exact opposite of that lukewarmness which every scheming prudence, every utilitarian calculus presupposes—and not for a time only, for the rare, exceptional hour, but permanently. The origin of the opposites *good* and *bad* is to be found in the pathos of nobility and distance, representing the dominant temper of a higher, ruling class in relation to a lower, dependent one. (The lordly right of bestowing names is such that one would almost be justified in seeing the origin of language itself as an expression of the rulers' power. They say, "This *is* that or that"; they seal off each thing and action with a sound and thereby take symbolic possession of it.) Such an origin would suggest that there is no *a priori* necessity for associating the word *good* with altruistic deeds, as those moral psychologists are fond of claiming. In fact, it is only after aristocratic values have begun to decline that the egotism-altruism dichotomy takes possession of the human conscience; to use my own terms, it is the herd instinct that now asserts itself. Yet it takes quite a while for this instinct to assume such sway that it can reduce all moral valuations to that dichotomy—as is currently happening throughout Europe, where the prejudice equating the terms *moral, altruistic,* and *disinterested* has assumed the obsessive force of an *idée fixe.*

III

Quite apart from the fact that this hypothesis about the origin of the value judgment *good* is historically untenable, its psychology is intrinsically unsound. Altruistic deeds were originally commended for their usefulness, but this original reason has now been forgotten—so the claim goes. How is such a forgetting conceivable? Has there ever been a point in history at which such deeds lost their usefulness? Quite the contrary, this usefulness has been apparent to every age, a thing that has been emphasized over and over again. Therefore, instead of being forgotten, it must have impressed itself on the consciousness with ever increasing clearness. The opposite theory is far more sensible, though this does not necessarily make it any the truer—the theory held by Herbert Spencer, for example, who considers the concept *good* qualitatively the same as the concepts *useful* or *practical;* so that in the judgments *good* and *bad,* humanity is said to have summed up and sanctioned precisely its unforgotten and unforgettable experiences of the *useful practical* and the *harmful impractical.* According to this theory, the *good* is that which all along has proved itself useful and which therefore may lay the highest claim to be considered valuable. As I have said, the derivation of this theory is suspect, but at least the explanation is self-consistent and psychologically tenable within its limits.

IV

The clue to the correct explanation was furnished me by the question "What does the etymology of the terms for good in various languages tell us?" I discovered that all these terms lead us back to the same conceptual transformation. The basic concept is always *noble* in the hierarchical, class sense, and from this has developed, by historical necessity, the concept *good* embracing nobility of mind, spiritual distinction. This development is strictly parallel to that other which eventually converted the notions *common, plebeian, base* into the notion *bad*.[1] Here we have an important clue to the actual genealogy of morals; that it has not been hit upon earlier is due to the retarding influence which democratic prejudice has had upon all investigation of origins. This holds equally true with regard to the seemingly quite objective areas of natural science and physiology, though I cannot enlarge upon the question now. The amount of damage such prejudice is capable of doing in ethics and history, once it becomes inflamed with hatred, is clearly shown by the case of Buckle. Here we see the plebeian bias of the modern mind, which stems from England, erupt once

[1] The most eloquent proof of this is the etymological relationship between the German words *schlecht* (bad) and *schlicht* (simple). For a long time the first term was used interchangeably with the second, without any contemptuous connotation as yet, merely to designate the commoner as opposed to the nobleman. About the time of the Thirty Years' War the meaning changed to the present one.

again on its native soil with all the violence of a muddy volcano and all the vulgar and oversalted eloquence characteristic of volcanoes.

V

As for our own problem, which we may justly call a *quiet* one, addressing itself to a very restricted audience, it is of interest to note that many of the words and roots denominating *good* still, to this day, carry overtones of the meanings according to which the nobility regarded themselves as possessing the highest moral rank. It is true that, most often, they described themselves simply in terms of their superior power (as the rulers, lords, sovereigns) or else in terms of the visible signs of their superiority, as the rich, the possessors (this is the meaning of *arya*, and there are corresponding terms in the Iranian and Slavic languages); but also in terms of a typical character trait, and this is the case that concerns us here. They speak of themselves as "the truthful"; most resolute in doing this were members of the Greek aristocracy, whose mouthpiece is the Megarian poet Theognis. The word they used was *esthlos*, meaning one who *is*, who has true reality, who is true. By a subjective turn the *true* later became the *truthful*. During this phase the word provided the shibboleth of the nobility, describing the aristocrat, as Theognis saw and portrayed him, in distinction from the lying plebeian, until finally, after the decline of the aristocracy, the word came to stand for spiritual nobility, and ripened and sweetened. The words *kakos* and *deilos* (the plebeian, in contrast to the *agathos*) emphasize cowardice and provide a hint as to the direction in which we should look for the etymology of *agathos,* a word allowing of more than one interpretation. The Latin *malus* (beside which I place *melas*) might designate the common man as dark, especially black-haired ("hic niger est"), as the pre-Aryan settler of the Italian soil, notably distinguished from the new blond conqueror race by his color. At any rate, the Gaelic presented me with an exactly analogous case: *fin,* as in the name Fingal, the characteristic term for nobility, eventually the good, noble, pure, originally the fair-haired as opposed to the dark, black-haired native population. The Celts, by the way, were definitely a fair-haired race; and it is a mistake to try to relate the area of dark-haired people found on ethnographic maps of Germany to Celtic bloodlines, as Virchow does. These are the last vestiges of the pre-Aryan population of Germany. (The subject races are seen to prevail once more, throughout almost all of Europe: in color, shortness of skull, perhaps also in intellectual and social instincts. Who knows whether modern democracy, the even more fashionable anarchism, and especially that preference for the *commune,* the most primitive of all social forms, which is now shared by all European socialists—whether all these do not represent a throwback, and whether, even physiologically, the Aryan race of conquerors is not doomed?) The Latin *bonus* I venture to interpret as warrior; providing that I am justified in deriving *bonus* from an older *duonus* (c.f. *bellum* → *duellum* → *duen-lum,* which seems to preserve that *duonus*). *Bonus* would then spell the man of strife, of discord, the warrior: we can now form some idea of what, in ancient Rome, constituted a man's goodness. And might not our German *gut* signify *göttlich,* the man of divine race? And further be identical with the racial term, earlier also a term of rank, *Goth?* My arguments in support of this conjecture do not belong here.

VI

Granting that political supremacy always gives rise to notions of spiritual supremacy, it at first creates no difficulties (though difficulties might arise later) if the ruling caste is also the priestly caste and elects to characterize itself by a term which reminds us of its priestly function. In this context we encounter for the first time concepts of *pure* and *impure* opposing each other as signs of class, and here, too, *good* and *bad* as terms no longer referring to class, develop before long. The reader should be cautioned, however, against taking pure and impure in too large or profound or symbolic a sense: all the ideas of ancient man were understood in a sense much more crude, narrow, superficial and non-symbolic than we are able to imagine today. The pure man was originally one who washed himself, who refused to eat certain foods entailing skin diseases, who did not sleep with the unwashed plebeian women, who held blood in abomination—hardly more than that. At the same time, given the peculiar nature of a priestly aristocracy, it becomes clear why the value opposites would early turn inward and become dangerously exacerbated; and in fact the tension between such opposites has opened abysses between man and man, over which not even an Achilles of free thought would leap without a shudder. There is from the very start something unwholesome about such priestly aristocracies, about their way of life, which is turned away from action and swings between brooding and emotional explosions: a way of life which may be seen as responsible for the morbidity and neurasthenia of priests of all periods. Yet are we not right in maintaining that the cures which they have developed for their morbidities have proved a hundred times more dangerous than the ills themselves? Humanity is still suffering from the after-effects of those priestly cures. Think, for example, of certain forms of diet (abstinence from meat), fasting, sexual continence, escape "into the desert"; think further of the whole anti-sensual metaphysics of the priests, conducive to inertia and false refinement; of the self-hypnosis encouraged by the example of fakirs and Brahmans, where a glass knob and an *idée fixe* take the place of the god. And at last, supervening on all this, comes utter satiety, together with its radical remedy, nothingness—or God, for the desire for a mystical union with God is nothing other than the Buddhist's desire to sink himself in nirvana. Among the priests everything becomes more dangerous, not cures and specifics alone but also arrogance, vindictiveness, acumen, profligacy, love, the desire for power, disease. In all fairness it should be added, however, that only on this soil, the precarious soil of priestly existence, has man been able to develop into an interesting creature; that only here has the human mind grown both profound and evil; and it is in these two respects, after all, that man has proved his superiority over the rest of creation.

VII

By now the reader will have got some notion how readily the priestly system of valuations can branch off from the aristocratic and develop into its opposite. An occasion for such a division is furnished whenever the priest caste and the warrior caste jealously clash with one another and find themselves unable to come to terms. The chivalrous and aristocratic valuations presuppose a strong physique, blooming, even exuberant health, together with all the conditions that guarantee its preservation: combat, adventure, the chase, the dance, war games, etc. The value system of the priestly aristocracy is founded on different presuppositions. So much the worse for them when it becomes a question of war! As we all know, priests are the most evil enemies to have—why should this be so? Because they are the most impotent. It is their impotence which makes their hate so violent and sinister, so cerebral and poisonous. The greatest haters in history—but also the most intelligent haters—have been priests. Beside the brilliance of priestly vengeance all other brilliance fades. Human history would be a dull and stupid thing without the intelligence furnished by its impotents. Let us begin with the most striking example. Whatever else has been done to damage the powerful and great of this earth seems trivial compared with what the Jews have done, that priestly people who succeeded in avenging themselves on their enemies and oppressors by radically inverting all their values, that is, by an act of the most spiritual vengeance. This was a strategy entirely appropriate to a priestly people in whom vindictiveness had gone most deeply underground. It was the Jew who, with frightening consistency, dared to invert the aristocratic value equations good/noble/powerful/beautiful/happy/favored-of-the-gods and maintain, with the furious hatred of the underprivileged and impotent, that "only the poor, the powerless, are good; only the suffering, sick, and ugly, truly blessed. But you noble and mighty ones of the earth will be, to all eternity, the evil, the cruel, the avaricious, the godless, and thus the cursed and damned!" . . . We know who has fallen heir to this Jewish inversion of values. . . . In reference to the grand and unspeakably disastrous initiative which the Jews have launched by this most radical of all declarations of war, I wish to repeat a statement I made in a different context (*Beyond Good and Evil*), to wit, that it was the Jews who started the slave revolt in morals; a revolt with two millennia of history behind it, which we have lost sight of today simply because it has triumphed so completely.

VIII

You find that difficult to understand? You have no eyes for something that took two millennia to prevail? . . . There is nothing strange about this: all long developments are difficult to see in the round. From the tree trunk of Jewish vengeance and hatred—the deepest and sublimest hatred in human history, since it gave birth to ideals and a new set of values—grew a branch that was equally unique: a new love, the deepest and sublimest of loves. From what other trunk could this branch have sprung? But let no one surmise that this love represented a denial of the thirst for vengeance, that it contravened the Jewish hatred. Exactly the opposite is true. Love grew out of hatred as the tree's crown, spreading triumphantly in the purest sunlight, yet having, in its high and sunny realm, the same aims—victory, aggrandizement, temptation—which hatred pursued by digging its roots ever deeper into all that was profound and evil. Jesus of Nazareth, the gospel of love made flesh, the "redeemer," who brought

blessing and victory to the poor, the sick, the sinners—
what was he but temptation in its most sinister and irresistible form, bringing men by a roundabout way to
precisely those Jewish values and renovations of the ideal?
Has not Israel, precisely by the detour of this "redeemer,"
this seeming antagonist and destroyer of Israel, reached the
final goal of its sublime vindictiveness? Was it not a necessary feature of a truly brilliant politics of vengeance, a far-
sighted, subterranean, slowly and carefully planned vengeance, that Israel had to deny its true instrument publicly
and nail him to the cross like a mortal enemy, so that "the
whole world" (meaning all the enemies of Israel) might
naïvely swallow the bait? And could one, by straining
every resource, hit upon a bait more dangerous than this?
What could equal in debilitating narcotic power the
symbol of the "holy cross," the ghastly paradox of a
crucified god, the unspeakably cruel mystery of God's self-
crucifixion for the benefit of mankind? One thing is certain, that in this sign Israel has by now triumphed over
all other, nobler values.

IX

—"But what is all this talk about nobler values? Let us
face facts: the people have triumphed—or the slaves, the
mob, the herd, whatever you wish to call them—and if the
Jews brought it about, then no nation ever had a more
universal mission on this earth. The lords are a thing of
the past, and the ethics of the common man is completely
triumphant. I don't deny that this triumph might be
looked upon as a kind of blood poisoning, since it has
resulted in a mingling of the races, but there can be no

doubt that the intoxication has succeeded. The 'redemption' of the human race (from the lords, that is) is well under way; everything is rapidly becoming Judaized, or Christianized, or mob-ized—the word makes no difference. The progress of this poison throughout the body of mankind cannot be stayed; as for its tempo, it can now afford to slow down, become finer, barely audible—there's all the time in the world. . . . Does the Church any longer have a necessary mission, or even a *raison d'être*? Or could it be done without? *Quaeritur*. It would almost seem that it retards rather than accelerates that progress. In which case we might consider it useful. But one thing is certain, it has gradually become something crude and lumpish, repugnant to a sensitive intelligence, a truly modern taste. Should it not, at least, be asked to refine itself a bit? . . . It alienates more people today than it seduces. . . . Who among us would be a freethinker, were it not for the Church? It is the Church which offends us, not its poison. . . . Apart from the Church we, too, like the poison. . . ." This was a "freethinker's" reaction to my argument—an honest fellow, as he has abundantly proved, and a democrat to boot. He had been listening to me until that moment, and could not stand to hear my silence. For I have a great deal to be silent about in this matter.

x

The slave revolt in morals begins by rancor turning creative and giving birth to values—the rancor of beings who, deprived of the direct outlet of action, compensate by an imaginary vengeance. All truly noble morality grows out of triumphant self-affirmation. Slave ethics, on the other hand, begins by saying *no* to an "outside," an "other," a non-self, and that *no* is its creative act. This reversal of direction of the evaluating look, this invariable looking outward instead of inward, is a fundamental feature of rancor. Slave ethics requires for its inception a sphere different from and hostile to its own. Physiologically speaking, it requires an outside stimulus in order to act at all; all its action is reaction. The opposite is true of aristocratic valuations: such values grow and act spontaneously, seeking out their contraries only in order to affirm themselves even more gratefully and delightedly. Here the negative concepts, *humble, base, bad,* are late, pallid counterparts of the positive, intense and passionate credo, "We noble, good, beautiful, happy ones." Aristocratic valuations may go amiss and do violence to reality, but this happens only with regard to spheres which they do not know well, or from the knowledge of which they austerely guard themselves: the aristocrat will, on occasion, misjudge a sphere which he holds in contempt, the sphere of the common man, the people. On the other hand we should remember that the emotion of contempt, of looking down, provided that it falsifies at all, is as nothing compared with the falsification which suppressed hatred, impotent vindictiveness, effects upon its opponent, though only in effigy. There is in all contempt too much casualness and nonchalance, too much blinking of facts and impatience, and too much inborn gaiety for it ever to make of its object a downright caricature and monster. Hear the almost benevolent nuances the Greek aristocracy, for example, puts into all its terms for the commoner; how emotions of compassion, consideration, indulgence, sugar-coat these words until, in the end, almost all terms referring to the common man survive as expressions for "unhappy," "pitiable" (cf.

deilos, deilaios, poneros, mochtheros, the last two of which
properly characterize the common man as a drudge and
beast of burden); how, on the other hand, the words *bad,
base, unhappy* have continued to strike a similar note for
the Greek ear, with the timbre "unhappy" preponderating.
The "wellborn" really felt that they were also the "happy."
They did not have to construct their happiness factitiously
by looking at their enemies, as all rancorous men are wont
to do, and being fully active, energetic people they were
incapable of divorcing happiness from action. They ac-
counted activity a necessary part of happiness (which explains the origin of the phrase *eu prattein*).

All this stands in utter contrast to what is called happiness among the impotent and oppressed, who are full of
bottled-up aggressions. Their happiness is purely passive
and takes the form of drugged tranquillity, stretching and
yawning, peace, "sabbath," emotional slackness. Whereas
the noble lives before his own conscience with confidence
and frankness (*gennaîos* "nobly bred" emphasizes the
nuance "truthful" and perhaps also "ingenuous"), the
rancorous person is neither truthful nor ingenuous nor
honest and forthright with himself. His soul squints; his
mind loves hide-outs, secret paths, and back doors; everything that is hidden seems to him his own world, his
security, his comfort; he is expert in silence, in long
memory, in waiting, in provisional self-depreciation, and
in self-humiliation. A race of such men will, in the end,
inevitably be cleverer than a race of aristocrats, and it will
honor sharp-wittedness to a much greater degree, i.e., as
an absolutely vital condition for its existence. Among the
noble, mental acuteness always tends slightly to suggest
luxury and overrefinement. The fact is that with them it
is much less important than is the perfect functioning of

the ruling, unconscious instincts or even a certain temerity to follow sudden impulses, court danger, or indulge spurts of violent rage, love, worship, gratitude, or vengeance. When a noble man feels resentment, it is absorbed in his instantaneous reaction and therefore does not poison him. Moreover, in countless cases where we might expect it, it never arises, while with weak and impotent people it occurs without fail. It is a sign of strong, rich temperaments that they cannot for long take seriously their enemies, their misfortunes, their *misdeeds;* for such characters have in them an excess of plastic curative power, and also a power of oblivion. (A good modern example of the latter is Mirabeau, who lacked all memory for insults and meannesses done him, and who was unable to forgive because he had forgotten). Such a man simply shakes off vermin which would get beneath another's skin—and only here, if anywhere on earth, is it possible to speak of "loving one's enemy." The noble person will respect his enemy, and respect is already a bridge to love. . . . Indeed he requires his enemy for himself, as his mark of distinction, nor could he tolerate any other enemy than one in whom he finds nothing to despise and much to esteem. Imagine, on the other hand, the "enemy" as conceived by the rancorous man! For this is his true creative achievement: he has conceived the "evil enemy," the Evil One, as a fundamental idea, and then as a pendant he has conceived a Good One—himself.

XI

The exact opposite is true of the noble-minded, who spontaneously creates the notion *good,* and later derives from it the conception of the *bad*. How ill-matched these two concepts look, placed side by side: the bad of noble origin, and the *evil* that has risen out of the cauldron of unquenched hatred! The first is a by-product, a complementary color, almost an afterthought; the second is the beginning, the original creative act of slave ethics. But neither is the conception of good the same in both cases, as we soon find out when we ask ourselves who it is that is really evil according to the code of rancor. The answer is: precisely the good one of the opposite code, that is the noble, the powerful—only colored, reinterpreted, re-envisaged by the poisonous eye of resentment. And we are the first to admit that anyone who knew these "good" ones only as enemies would find them evil enemies indeed. For these same men who, amongst themselves, are so strictly constrained by custom, worship, ritual, gratitude, and by mutual surveillance and jealousy, who are so resourceful in consideration, tenderness, loyalty, pride and friendship, when once they step outside their circle become little better than uncaged beasts of prey. Once abroad in the wilderness, they revel in the freedom from social constraint and compensate for their long confinement in the quietude of their own community. They revert to the innocence of wild animals: we can imagine them returning from an orgy of murder, arson, rape, and torture, jubilant and at peace with themselves as though they had committed a fraternity prank—convinced, moreover, that the poets for a long time to come will have something to sing about and to praise. Deep within all these noble races there lurks the beast of prey, bent on spoil and conquest. This hidden urge has to be satisfied from time to time, the beast let loose in the wilderness. This goes as well for the Roman, Arabian, German, Japanese nobility as for the

Homeric heroes and the Scandinavian vikings. The noble races have everywhere left in their wake the catchword "barbarian." And even their highest culture shows an awareness of this trait and a certain pride in it (as we see, for example, in Pericles' famous funeral oration, when he tells the Athenians: "Our boldness has gained us access to every land and sea, and erected monuments to itself *for both good and evil*.") This "boldness" of noble races, so headstrong, absurd, incalculable, sudden, improbable (Pericles commends the Athenians especially for their *rathumia*), their utter indifference to safety and comfort, their terrible pleasure in destruction, their taste for cruelty —all these traits are embodied by their victims in the image of the "barbarian," the "evil enemy," the Goth or the Vandal. The profound and icy suspicion which the German arouses as soon as he assumes power (we see it happening again today) harks back to the persistent horror with which Europe for many centuries witnessed the raging of the blond Teutonic beast (although all racial connection between the old Teutonic tribes and ourselves has been lost). I once drew attention to the embarrassment Hesiod must have felt when he tried to embody the cultural epochs of mankind in the gold, silver, and iron ages. He could cope with the contradictions inherent in Homer's world, so marvelous on the one hand, so ghastly and brutal on the other, only by making two ages out of one and presenting them in temporal sequence; first, the age of the heroes and demigods of Troy and Thebes, as that world was still remembered by the noble tribes who traced their ancestry to it; and second, the iron age, which presented the same world as seen by the descendants of those who had been crushed, despoiled, brutalized, sold into slavery. If it were true, as passes current nowadays, that the real meaning of culture resides in its power to domesticate man's savage instincts, then we might be justified in viewing all those rancorous machinations by which the noble tribes, and their ideals, have been laid low as the true instruments of culture. But this would still not amount to saying that the *organizers* themselves represent culture. Rather, the exact opposite would be true, as is vividly shown by the current state of affairs. These carriers of the leveling and retributive instincts, these descendants of every European and extra-European slavedom, and especially of the pre-Aryan populations, represent human retrogression most flagrantly. Such "instruments of culture" are a disgrace to man and might make one suspicious of culture altogether. One might be justified in fearing the wild beast lurking within all noble races and in being on one's guard against it, but who would not a thousand times prefer fear when it is accompanied with admiration to security accompanied by the loathsome sight of perversion, dwarfishness, degeneracy? And is not the latter our predicament today? What accounts for our repugnance to man—for there is no question that he makes us suffer? Certainly not our fear of him, rather the fact that there is no longer anything to be feared from him; that the vermin "man" occupies the entire stage; that, tame, hopelessly mediocre, and savorless, he considers himself the apex of historical evolution; and not entirely without justice, since he is still somewhat removed from the mass of sickly and effete creatures whom Europe is beginning to stink of today.

XII

Here I want to give vent to a sigh and a last hope. Exactly what is it that I, especially, find intolerable; that I am unable to cope with; that asphyxiates me? A bad smell. The smell of failure, of a soul that has gone stale. God knows it is possible to endure all kinds of misery—vile weather, sickness, trouble, isolation. All this can be coped with, if one is born to a life of anonymity and battle. There will always be moments of re-emergence into the light, when one tastes the golden hour of victory and once again stands foursquare, unshakable, ready to face even harder things, like a bowstring drawn taut against new perils. But, you divine patronesses—if there are any such in the realm beyond good and evil—grant me now and again the sight of something perfect, wholly achieved, happy, magnificently triumphant, something still capable of inspiring fear! Of a man who will justify the existence of mankind, for whose sake one may continue to believe in mankind! . . . The leveling and diminution of European man is our greatest danger; because the sight of him makes us despond. . . . We no longer see anything these days that aspires to grow greater; instead, we have a suspicion that things will continue to go downhill, becoming ever thinner, more placid, smarter, cosier, more ordinary, more indifferent, more Chinese, more Christian—without doubt man is getting "better" all the time. . . . This is Europe's true predicament: together with the fear of man we have also lost the love of man, reverence for man, confidence in man, indeed the *will to man*. Now the sight of man makes us despond. What is nihilism today if not that?

But to return to business: our inquiry into the origins of that other notion of goodness, as conceived by the resentful, demands to be completed. There is nothing very odd about lambs disliking birds of prey, but this is no reason for holding it against large birds of prey that they carry off lambs. And when the lambs whisper among themselves, "These birds of prey are evil, and does not this give us a right to say that whatever is the opposite of a bird of prey must be good?" there is nothing intrinsically wrong with such an argument—though the birds of prey will look somewhat quizzically and say, "*We* have nothing against these good lambs; in fact, we love them; nothing tastes better than a tender lamb."—To expect that strength will not manifest itself as strength, as the desire to overcome, to appropriate, to have enemies, obstacles, and triumphs, is every bit as absurd as to expect that weakness will manifest itself as strength. A quantum of strength is equivalent to a quantum of urge, will, activity, and it is only the snare of language (of the arch-fallacies of reason petrified in language), presenting all activity as conditioned by an agent—the "subject"—that blinds us to this fact. For, just as popular superstition divorces the lightning from its brilliance, viewing the latter as an activity whose subject is the lightning, so does popular morality divorce strength from its manifestations, as though there were behind the strong a neutral agent, free to manifest its strength or contain it. But no such agent exists; there is no "being" be-

hind the doing, acting, becoming; the "doer" has simply
been added to the deed by the imagination—the doing is
everything. The common man actually doubles the doing
by making the lightning flash; he states the same event
once as cause and then again as effect. The natural scientists are no better when they say that "energy *moves,*"
"energy *causes.*" For all its detachment and freedom from
emotion, our science is still the dupe of linguistic habits;
it has never yet got rid of those changelings called "subjects." The atom is one such changeling, another is the
Kantian "thing-in-itself." Small wonder, then, that the
repressed and smoldering emotions of vengeance and
hatred have taken advantage of this superstition and in
fact espouse no belief more ardently than that it is within
the discretion of the strong to be weak, of the bird of prey
to be a lamb. Thus they assume the right of calling the
bird of prey to account for being a bird of prey. We can
hear the oppressed, downtrodden, violated whispering
among themselves with the wily vengefulness of the impotent, "Let us be unlike those evil ones. Let us be good.
And the good shall be he who does not do violence, does
not attack or retaliate, who leaves vengeance to God, who,
like us, lives hidden, who shuns all that is evil, and altogether asks very little of life—like us, the patient, the
humble, the just ones." Read in cold blood, this means
nothing more than "We weak ones are, in fact, weak. It
is a good thing that we do nothing for which we are not
strong enough." But this plain fact, this basic prudence,
which even the insects have (who, in circumstances of
great danger, sham death in order not to have to "do" too
much) has tricked itself out in the garb of quiet, virtuous
resignation, thanks to the duplicity of impotence—as
though the weakness of the weak, which is after all his

essence, his natural way of being, his sole and inevitable reality, were a spontaneous act, a meritorious deed. This sort of person requires the belief in a "free subject" able to choose indifferently, out of that instinct of self-preservation which notoriously justifies every kind of lie. It may well be that to this day the subject, or in popular language the soul, has been the most viable of all articles of faith simply because it makes it possible for the majority of mankind—i.e., the weak and oppressed of every sort—to practice the sublime sleight of hand which gives weakness the appearance of free choice and one's natural disposition the distinction of merit.

XIV

Would anyone care to learn something about the way in which ideals are manufactured? Does anyone have the nerve? . . . Well then, go ahead! There's a chink through which you can peek into this murky shop. But wait just a moment, Mr. Foolhardy; your eyes must grow accustomed to the fickle light. . . . All right, tell me what's going on in there, audacious fellow; now I am the one who is listening.

"I can't see a thing, but I hear all the more. There's a low, cautious whispering in every nook and corner. I have a notion these people are lying. All the sounds are sugary and soft. No doubt you were right; they are transmuting weakness into merit."

"Go on."

"Impotence, which cannot retaliate, into kindness; pusillanimity into humility; submission before those one hates into obedience to One of whom they say that he has commanded this submission—they call him God. The inoffensiveness of the weak, his cowardice, his ineluctable standing and waiting at doors, are being given honorific titles such as patience; to be *unable* to avenge oneself is called to be *unwilling* to avenge oneself—even forgiveness ("for they know not what *they* do—we alone know what *they* do.") Also there's some talk of loving one's enemy—accompanied by much sweat."

"Go on."

"I'm sure they are quite miserable, all these whisperers and smalltime counterfeiters, even though they huddle close together for warmth. But they tell me that this very misery is the sign of their election by God, that one beats the dogs one loves best, that this misery is perhaps also a preparation, a test, a kind of training, perhaps even more than that: something for which eventually they will be compensated with tremendous interest—in gold? No, in happiness. They call this *bliss*."

"Go on."

"Now they tell me that not only are they better than the mighty of this earth, whose spittle they must lick (not from fear—by no means—but because God commands us to honor our superiors), but they are even better off, or at least they will be better off someday. But I've had all I can stand. The smell is too much for me. This shop where they manufacture ideals seems to me to stink of lies."

"But just a moment. You haven't told me anything about the greatest feat of these black magicians, who precipitate the white milk of loving-kindness out of every kind of blackness. Haven't you noticed their most consummate sleight of hand, their boldest, finest, most brilliant trick? Just watch! These vermin, full of vindictive hatred, what are they brewing out of their own poisons? Have you ever heard vengeance and hatred mentioned? Would you ever guess, if you only listened to their words, that these are men bursting with hatred?"

"I see what you mean. I'll open my ears again—and stop my nose. Now I can make out what they seem to have been saying all along: 'We, the good ones, are also the just ones.' They call the thing they seek not retribution but the triumph of justice; the thing they hate is not their enemy, by no means—they hate injustice, ungodliness; the thing they hope for and believe in is not vengeance, the sweet exultation of vengeance ('sweeter than honey' as Homer said) but 'the triumph of God, who is just, over the godless'; what remains to them to love on this earth is not their brothers in hatred, but what they call their 'brothers in love'—all who are good and just."

"And what do they call that which comforts them in all their sufferings—their phantasmagoria of future bliss?"

"Do I hear correctly? They call it Judgment Day, the coming of *their* kingdom, the 'Kingdom of God.' Meanwhile they live in 'faith,' in 'love,' in 'hope.'"

"Stop! I've heard enough."

XV

Faith in what? Love for what? Hope of what? There can be no doubt that these weaklings, too, want a chance to be strong, to have *their* kingdom come. They call it simply the Kingdom of God—what admirable humility! But in order to have that experience one must live a very long time, beyond death; one must have eternal life to indemnify oneself for that terrestrial life of faith, love, and hope. Indemnify for what and by what means? . . . It seems

to me that Dante committed a grave blunder when, with
disconcerting naïveté, he put over the gate of hell the inscription: "Me, too, eternal love created." At any rate, the
inscription over the gate of the Christian paradise, with
its "eternal bliss," would read more fittingly, "Me, too,
eternal hate created"—provided that it is fitting to place a
truth above the gateway to a lie. For in what, precisely,
does the bliss of that paradise consist?

We may have guessed by now, but still it is well to have
the thing certified for us by a competent authority in these
matters, Thomas Aquinas, the great teacher and saint. *Beati
in regno coelesti*, he says, meek as a lamb, *videbunt poenas
damnatorum, ut beatitudo illis magis complaceat.* Or, if
the reader prefers, here is the same sentiment more force-
fully expressed by a triumphant Father of the Church
(Tertullian) who wishes to dissuade his Christians from
the cruel debauch of public spectacles—on what grounds?
"Our faith offers us so much more," he writes in *De
spectaculis*, ch. 29 ff., "and something so much stronger.
Having been redeemed, joys of quite a different kind are
ours. We have martyrs instead of athletes. If we crave
blood, we have the blood of Christ. . . . But think what
awaits us on the day of his triumph!" And the rapt visionary continues: "Yes, and there are still to come other
spectacles—that last, that eternal Day of Judgment, that
Day which the Gentiles never believed would come, that
Day they laughed at, when this old world and all its generations shall be consumed in one fire. How vast the
spectacle that day, and how wide! What sight shall wake
my wonder, what my laughter, my joy and exultation as
I see all those kings, those great kings, welcomed (we are
told) in heaven, along with Jove, along with those who
told of their ascent, groaning in the depths of darkness!

And the magistrates who persecuted the name of Jesus, liquefying in fiercer flames than they kindled in their rage against the Christians! Those sages, too, the philosophers blushing before their disciples as they blaze together, the disciples whom they taught that God was concerned with nothing, that men have no souls at all, or that what souls they have shall never return to their former bodies! And, then, the poets trembling before the judgment seat, not of Rhadamanthus, not of Minos, but of Christ, whom they never looked to see! And then there will be the tragic actors to be heard, more vocal in their own tragedy; and the players to be seen, lither of limb by far in the fire; and then the charioteer to watch, red all over in the wheel of flame; and, next, the athletes to be gazed upon, not in their gymnasiums but hurled in the fire—unless it be that not even then would I wish to see them, in my desire rather to turn an insatiable gaze on them who vented their rage and fury on the Lord. 'This is he,' I shall say, 'the son of the carpenter or the harlot, (*Tertullian here mimics Jewish diatribe, as is shown by what immediately follows as well as by his term for the mother of Jesus, which occurs in the Talmud*) the Sabbath-breaker, the Samaritan, who had a devil. This is he whom you bought from Judas; this is he who was struck with reed and fist, defiled with spittle, given gall and vinegar to drink. This is he whom the disciples secretly stole away, that it might be said he had risen—unless it was the gardener who removed him, lest his lettuces should be trampled by the throng of visitors!' Such sights, such exultation—what praetor, consul, quaestor, priest, will ever give you of his bounty? And yet all these, in some sort, are ours, pictured through faith in the imagination of the spirit. But what are those things which eye hath not seen nor ear heard, nor ever entered into the heart of man (I Cor. 2:9)? Things of greater joy than circus, theater, or amphitheater, or any stadium, I believe."[1] *Per fidem:* so it is written.

XVI

Let us conclude. The two sets of valuations, good/bad and good/evil, have waged a terrible battle on this earth, lasting many millennia; and just as surely as the second set has for a long time now been in the ascendant, so surely are there still places where the battle goes on and the issue remains in suspension. It might even be claimed that by being raised to a higher plane the battle has become much more profound. Perhaps there is today not a single intellectual worth his salt who is not divided on that issue, a battleground for those opposites. The watchwords of the battle, written in characters which have remained legible throughout human history, read: "Rome vs. Israel, Israel vs. Rome." No battle has ever been more momentous than this one. Rome viewed Israel as a monstrosity; the Romans regarded the Jews as *convicted* of hatred against the whole of mankind—and rightly so if one is justified in associating the welfare of the human species with absolute supremacy of aristocratic values. But how did the Jews, on their part, feel about Rome? A thousand indications point to the answer. It is enough to read once more the Revelations of St. John, the most rabid outburst of vindictiveness in all recorded history. (We ought to acknowledge the profound consistency of the Christian instinct in assigning this book of hatred and the most extravagantly doting of the Gospels

[1] Translated by T. R. Glover.

to the same disciple. There is a piece of truth hidden here, no matter how much literary skulduggery may have gone on.) The Romans were the strongest and most noble people who ever lived. Every vestige of them, every least inscription, is a sheer delight, provided we are able to read the spirit behind the writing. The Jews, on the contrary, were the priestly, rancorous nation *par excellence,* though possessed of an unequaled ethical genius; we need only compare with them nations of comparable endowments, such as the Chinese or the Germans, to sense which occupies the first rank. Has the victory so far been gained by the Romans or by the Jews? But this is really an idle question. Remember who it is before whom one bows down, in Rome itself, as before the essence of all supreme values—and not only in Rome but over half the globe, wherever man has grown tame or desires to grow tame: before three Jews and one Jewess (Jesus of Nazareth, the fisherman Peter, the rug weaver Paul, and Maria, the mother of that Jesus). This is very curious: Rome, without a doubt, has capitulated. It is true that during the Renaissance men witnessed a strange and splendid awakening of the classical ideal; like one buried alive, Rome stirred under the weight of a new Judaic Rome that looked like an ecumenical synagogue and was called the Church. But presently Israel triumphed once again, thanks to the plebeian rancor of the German and English Reformation, together with its natural corollary, the restoration of the Church—which also meant the restoration of ancient Rome to the quiet of the tomb. In an even more decisive sense did Israel triumph over the classical ideal through the French Revolution. For then the last political nobleness Europe had known, that of seventeenth- and eighteenth-century France, collapsed under the weight of vindictive popular instincts. A wilder enthusiasm was never seen. And yet, in the midst of it all, something tremendous, something wholly unexpected happened: the ancient classical ideal appeared incarnate and in unprecedented splendor before the eyes and conscience of mankind. Once again, stronger, simpler, more insistent than ever, over against the lying shibboleth of the rights of the majority, against the furious tendency toward leveling out and debasement, sounded the terrible yet exhilarating shibboleth of the "prerogative of the few." Like a last signpost to an *alternative* route Napoleon appeared, most isolated and anachronistic of men, the embodiment of the noble ideal. It might be well to ponder what exactly Napoleon, that synthesis of the brutish with the more than human, did represent. . . .

XVII

Was it all over then? Had that greatest conflict of ideals been shelved for good? Or had it only been indefinitely adjourned? Might not the smoldering fire start up again one day, all the more terrible because longer and more secretly nourished? Moreover, should we not wish for this event with all our hearts, and even help to promote it? If the reader at this point begins to develop his own train of thought, he is not likely soon to come to the end of it. All the more reason why I should conclude, assuming that I have made sufficiently clear what I mean by the dangerous slogan on the title page of my last book, *Beyond Good and Evil*. At all events, I do not mean "beyond good and bad."

NOTE I want to take this opportunity to express publicly a wish which I have hitherto expressed only in occasional conversations with scholars: that the philosophy department of some leading university might offer a series of prizes for essays on the evolution of moral ideas. Perhaps my present book will help to encourage such a plan. I would propose the following question, which deserves the attention of philologists, historians, and philosophers alike, *What light does the science of linguistics, especially the study of etymology, throw on the evolution of moral ideas?* However, it would also be necessary for that purpose to enlist the assistance of physiologists and medical men. This can be most fittingly accomplished by the professional philosophers, who as a body have shown such remarkable skill in the past in bringing about amicable and productive relations between philosophy, on the one hand, and physiology and medicine, on the other. It should be stressed that all tables of values, all moral injunctions, with which history and anthropology concern themselves, require first and foremost a physiological investigation and interpretation and next a critique on the part of medical science. The question "What is this or that table of values really worth?" must be viewed under a variety of perspectives, for the question "valuable to what end?" is one of extraordinary complexity. For example, something obviously valuable in terms of the longest possible survival of a race (or of its best adaptation to a given climate, or of the preservation of its greatest numbers) would by no means have the same value if it were a question of developing a more powerful type. The welfare of the many and the welfare of the few are radically opposite ends. To consider the former *a priori* the higher value may be left to the naïveté of English biologists. All sciences are now under the obligation to prepare the ground for the future task of the philosopher, which is to solve the problem of value, to determine the true hierarchy of values.

Second Essay

"GUILT," "BAD CONSCIENCE," AND RELATED MATTERS

I

To breed an animal with the right to make promises—is not this the paradoxical problem nature has set itself with regard to man? and is it not man's true problem? That the problem has in fact been solved to a remarkable degree will seem all the more surprising if we do full justice to the strong opposing force, the faculty of oblivion. Oblivion is not merely a *vis inertiae,* as is often claimed, but an active screening device, responsible for the fact that what we experience and digest psychologically does not, in the stage of digestion, emerge into consciousness any more than what we ingest physically does. The role of this active oblivion is that of a concierge: to shut temporarily the doors and windows of consciousness; to protect us from the noise and agitation with which our lower organs work for or against one another; to introduce a little quiet into our consciousness so as to make room for the nobler functions and functionaries of our organism which do the governing and planning. This concierge maintains order and etiquette in the household of the psyche; which immediately suggests that there can be no happiness, no serenity, no hope, no pride, no *present,* without oblivion. A man in whom this screen is damaged and inoperative is like a dyspeptic (and not merely *like* one): he can't be done with anything. . . . Now this naturally forgetful animal, for whom oblivion represents a power, a form of strong health, has created for itself an opposite power, that of remembering, by whose aid, in certain cases, oblivion may be suspended—specifically in cases where it is a question of promises. By this I do not mean a purely passive succumbing to past impressions, the indigestion of being unable to be done with a pledge once made, but rather an active not wishing to be done with it, a continuing to will what has once been willed, a veritable "memory of the will"; so that, between the original determination and the actual performance of the thing willed, a whole world of new things, conditions, even volitional acts, can be interposed without snapping the long chain of the will. But how much all this presupposes! A man who wishes to dispose of his future in this manner must first have learned to separate necessary from accidental acts; to think causally; to see distant things as though they were near at hand; to distinguish means from ends. In short, he must have become not only calculating but himself calculable, regular even to his own perception, if he is to stand pledge for his own future as a guarantor does.

11

This brings us to the long story of the origin or genesis of responsibility. The task of breeding an animal entitled to make promises involves, as we have already seen, the preparatory task of rendering man up to a certain point regular, uniform, equal among equals, calculable. The tremendous achievement which I have referred to in *Daybreak* as "the custom character of morals," that labor man accomplished upon himself over a vast period of time, receives its meaning and justification here—even despite the brutality, tyranny, and stupidity associated with the process. With the help of custom and the social strait-jacket, man was, in fact, made calculable. However, if we place ourselves at the terminal point of this great process, where society and custom finally reveal their true aim, we shall find the ripest fruit of that tree to be the sovereign individual, equal only to himself, all moral custom left far behind. This autonomous, more than moral individual (the terms *autonomous* and *moral* are mutually exclusive) has developed his own, independent, long-range will, which dares to make promises; he has a proud and vigorous consciousness of what he has achieved, a sense of power and freedom, of absolute accomplishment. This fully emancipated man, master of his will, who dares make promises—how should he not be aware of his superiority over those who are unable to stand security for themselves? Think how much trust, fear, reverence he inspires (all three fully *deserved*), and how, having that sovereign rule over himself, he has mastery too over all weaker-willed and less reliable creatures! Being truly free and possessor of a long-range, pertinacious will, he also possesses a scale of values. Viewing others from the center of his own being, he either honors or disdains them. It is natural to him to honor his strong and reliable peers, all those who promise like sovereigns: rarely and reluctantly; who are chary of their trust; whose trust is a mark of distinction; whose promises are binding because they know that they will make them good in spite of all accidents, in spite of destiny itself. Yet he will inevitably reserve a kick for those paltry windbags who promise irresponsibly and a rod for those liars who break their word even in uttering it. His proud awareness of the extraordinary privilege responsibility confers has penetrated deeply and become a dominant instinct. What shall he call that dominant instinct, provided

he ever feels impelled to give it a name? Surely he will
call it his *conscience*.

III

His conscience? It seems a foregone conclusion that this
conscience, which we encounter here in its highest form,
has behind it a long history of transformations. The right
proudly to stand security for oneself, to approve oneself, is
a ripe but also a late fruit; how long did that fruit have
to hang green and tart on the tree! Over an even longer
period there was not the slightest sign of such a fruit; no
one had a right to predict it, although the tree was ready
for it, organized in every part to the end of bringing it
forth. "How does one create a memory for the human
animal? How does one go about to impress anything on
that partly dull, partly flighty human intelligence—that incarnation of forgetfulness—so as to make it stick?" As we
might well imagine, the means used in solving this age-
old problem have been far from delicate: in fact, there is
perhaps nothing more terrible in man's earliest history than
his mnemotechnics. "A thing is branded on the memory to
make it stay there; only what goes on hurting will stick"—
this is one of the oldest and, unfortunately, one of the
most enduring psychological axioms. In fact, one might
say that wherever on earth one still finds solemnity,
gravity, secrecy, somber hues in the life of an individual
or a nation, one also senses a residuum of that terror with
which men must formerly have promised, pledged,
vouched. It is the past—the longest, deepest, hardest of
pasts—that seems to surge up whenever we turn serious.
Whenever man has thought it necessary to create a mem-

ory for himself, his effort has been attended with torture, blood, sacrifice. The ghastliest sacrifices and pledges, including the sacrifice of the first-born; the most repulsive mutilations, such as castration; the cruelest rituals in every religious cult (and all religions are at bottom systems of cruelty)—all these have their origin in that instinct which divined pain to be the strongest aid to mnemonics. (All asceticism is really part of the same development: here too the object is to make a few ideas omnipresent, unforgettable, "fixed," to the end of hypnotizing the entire nervous and intellectual system; the ascetic procedures help to effect the dissociation of those ideas from all others.) The poorer the memory of mankind has been, the more terrible have been its customs. The severity of all primitive penal codes gives us some idea how difficult it must have been for man to overcome his forgetfulness and to drum into these slaves of momentary whims and desires a few basic requirements of communal living. Nobody can say that we Germans consider ourselves an especially cruel and brutal nation, much less a frivolous and thriftless one; but it needs only a glance at our ancient penal codes to impress on us what labor it takes to create a nation of thinkers. (I would even say that we are the one European nation among whom is still to be found a maximum of trust, seriousness, insipidity, and matter-of-factness, which should entitle us to breed a mandarin caste for all of Europe.) Germans have resorted to ghastly means in order to triumph over their plebeian instincts and brutal coarseness. We need only recount some of our ancient forms of punishment: stoning (even in earliest legend millstones are dropped on the heads of culprits); breaking on the wheel (Germany's own contribution to the techniques of punishment); piercing with stakes, drawing and quartering, trampling to death with horses, boiling in oil or wine (these were still in use in the fourteenth and fifteenth centuries), the popular flaying alive, cutting out of flesh from the chest, smearing the victim with honey and leaving him in the sun, a prey to flies. By such methods the individual was finally taught to remember five or six "I won'ts" which entitled him to participate in the benefits of society; and indeed, with the aid of this sort of memory, people eventually "came to their senses." What an enormous price man had to pay for reason, seriousness, control over his emotions—those grand human prerogatives and cultural showpieces! How much blood and horror lies behind all "good things"!

IV

But how about the origin of that other somber phenomenon, the consciousness of guilt, "bad conscience"? Would you turn to our genealogists of morals for illumination? Let me say once again, they are worthless. Completely absorbed in "modern" experience, with no real knowledge of the past, no desire even to understand it, no historical instinct whatever, they presume, all the same, to write the history of ethics! Such an undertaking must produce results which bear not the slightest relation to truth. Have these historians shown any awareness of the fact that the basic moral term *Schuld* (guilt) has its origin in the very material term *Schulden* (to be indebted)? Of the fact that punishment, being a *compensation*, has developed quite independently of any ideas about freedom of the will—indeed, that a very high level of humanization was necessary before even the much more primitive distinctions, "with intent," "through negligence," "by accident," *compos mentis,* and their opposites could be made and allowed to weigh in the judgments of cases? The pat and seemingly natural notion (so natural that it has often been used to account for the origin of the notion of justice itself) that the criminal deserves to be punished *because* he could have acted otherwise, is in fact a very late and refined form of human reasoning; whoever thinks it can be found in archaic law grossly misconstrues the psychology of uncivilized man. For an unconscionably long time culprits were not punished because they were felt to be responsible for their actions; not, that is, on the assumption that only the guilty were to be punished; rather, they were punished the way parents still punish their children, out of rage at some damage suffered, which the doer must pay for. Yet this rage was both moderated and modified by the notion that for every damage there could somehow be found an equivalent, by which that damage might be compensated —if necessary in the pain of the doer. To the question how did that ancient, deep-rooted, still firmly established notion of an equivalency between damage and pain arise, the answer is, briefly: it arose in the contractual relation between creditor and debtor, which is as old as the notion of "legal subjects" itself and which in its turn points back to the basic practices of purchase, sale, barter, and trade.

v

As we contemplate these contractual relationships we may readily feel both suspicion and repugnance toward the older civilizations which either created or permitted them. Since it was here that promises were made, since it was here that a memory had to be fashioned for the promiser, we must not be surprised to encounter every evidence of brutality, cruelty, pain. In order to inspire the creditor with confidence in his promise to repay, to give a guarantee for the stringency of his promise, but also to enjoin on his own conscience the duty of repayment, the debtor pledged by contract that in case of non-payment he would offer another of his possessions, such as his body, or his wife, or his freedom, or even his life (or, in certain theologically oriented cultures, even his salvation or the sanctity of his tomb; as in Egypt, where the debtor's corpse was not immune from his creditor even in the grave). The creditor, moreover, had the right to inflict all manner of indignity and pain on the body of the debtor. For example, he could cut out an amount of flesh proportionate to the amount of the debt, and we find, very early, quite detailed legal assessments of the value of individual parts of the body. I consider it already a progress, proof of a freer, more generous, more *Roman* conception of law, when the Twelve Tables decreed that it made no difference how much or little, in such a case, the creditor cut out—*si plus minusve secuerunt, ne fraude esto.* Let us try to understand the logic of this entire method of compensations; it is strange enough. An equivalence is provided by the creditor's receiving, in place of material compensation such as money, land, or other possessions, a kind of *pleasure.* That pleasure is induced by his being able to exercise his power freely upon one who is powerless, by the pleasure of *faire le mal pour le plaisir de le faire,* the pleasure of rape. That pleasure will be increased in proportion to the lowliness of the creditor's own station; it will appear to him as a delicious morsel, a foretaste of a higher rank. In "punishing" the debtor, the creditor shares a seignorial right. For once he is given a chance to bask in the glorious feeling of treating another human being as lower than himself—or, in case the actual punitive power has passed on to a legal "authority," of seeing him despised and mistreated. Thus compensation consists in a legal warrant entitling one man to exercise his cruelty on another.

VI

It is in the sphere of contracts and legal obligations that the moral universe of guilt, conscience, and duty, ("sacred" duty) took its inception. Those beginnings were liberally sprinkled with blood, as are the beginnings of everything great on earth. (And may we not say that ethics has never lost its reek of blood and torture—not even in Kant, whose categorical imperative smacks of cruelty?) It was then that the sinister knitting together of the two ideas *guilt* and *pain* first occurred, which by now have become quite inextricable. Let us ask once more: in what sense could pain constitute repayment of a debt? In the sense that to make someone suffer was a supreme pleasure. In exchange for the damage he had incurred, including his displeasure, the creditor received an extraordinary amount of pleasure; something which he prized the more highly the more it disaccorded with his social rank. I am merely throwing this out as a suggestion, for it is difficult, and embarrassing as well, to get to the bottom of such underground developments. To introduce crudely the concept of vengeance at this point would obscure matters rather than clarify them, since the idea of vengeance leads us straight back to our original problem: how can the infliction of pain provide satisfaction? The delicacy—even more, the *tartufferie*—of domestic animals like ourselves shrinks from imagining clearly to what extent cruelty constituted the collective delight of older mankind, how much it was an ingredient of all their joys, or how naïvely they manifested their cruelty, how they considered disinterested malevolence (Spinoza's *sympathia malevolens*) a normal trait, something to which one's conscience could assent heartily. Close observation will spot numerous survivals of this oldest and most thorough human delight in our own culture. In both *Daybreak* and *Beyond Good and Evil* I have pointed to that progressive sublimation and apotheosis of cruelty which not only characterizes the whole history of higher culture, but in a sense constitutes it. Not so very long ago, a royal wedding or great public celebration would have been incomplete without executions, tortures, or *autos da fé*; a noble household without some person whose office it was to serve as a butt for everyone's malice and cruel teasing. (Perhaps the reader will recall Don Quixote's sojourn at the court of the Duchess. *Don Quixote* leaves a bitter taste in our mouths today; we almost quail in reading it. This would have seemed very strange to Cervantes and to his contemporaries, who read the work with the clearest conscience in the world, thought it the funniest of books, and almost died laughing over it.) To behold suffering gives pleasure, but to cause another to suffer affords an even greater pleasure. This severe statement expresses an old, powerful, human, all too human sentiment—though the monkeys too might endorse it, for it is reported that they heralded and preluded man in the devising of bizarre cruelties. There is no feast without cruelty, as man's entire history attests. Punishment, too, has its festive features.

VII

These ideas, by the way, are not intended to add grist to the pessimist's mill of *taedium vitae*. On the contrary, it should be clearly understood that in the days when people were unashamed of their cruelty life was a great deal more enjoyable than it is now in the heyday of pessimism. The sky overhead has always grown darker in proportion as man has grown ashamed of his fellows. The tired, pessimistic look, discouragement in face of life's riddle, the icy *no* of the man who loathes life are none of them characteristic of mankind's evilest eras. These phenomena are like marsh plants; they presuppose a bog—the bog of morbid finickiness and moralistic drivel which has alienated man from his natural instincts. On his way to becoming an "angel" man has acquired that chronic indigestion and coated tongue which makes not only the naïve joy and innocence of the animal distasteful to him, but even life itself; so that at times he stops his nose against himself and recites with Pope Innocent III the catalogue of his unsavorinesses ("impure conception, loathsome feeding in the mother's womb, wretchedness of physical substance, vile stench, discharge of spittle, urine, and faeces"). Nowadays, when suffering is invariably quoted as the chief argument against existence, it might be well to recall the days when matters were judged from the opposite point of view; when people would not have missed for anything the pleasure of inflicting suffering, in which they saw a powerful agent, the principal inducement to living. By way of comfort to the milksops, I would also venture the suggestion that in those days pain did not hurt as much as it does today; at all events, such is the opinion of a doctor who has treated Negroes for complicated internal inflammations which would have driven the most stoical European to distraction—the assumption here being that the negro represents an earlier phase of human development. (It appears, in fact, that the curve of human susceptibility to pain drops abruptly the moment we go below the top layer of culture comprising ten thousand or ten million individuals. For my part, I am convinced that, compared with one night's pain endured by a hysterical bluestocking, all the suffering of all the animals that have been used to date for scientific experiments is as nothing.) Perhaps it is even legitimate to allow the possibility that pleasure in cruelty is not really extinct today; only, given our greater delicacy, that pleasure has had to undergo a certain sublimation and subtilization, to be translated into imaginative and psychological terms in order to pass muster before even the tenderest hypocritical conscience. ("Tragic empathy" is one such term; another is *les nostalgies de la croix*.) What makes people rebel against suffering is not really suffering itself but the senselessness of suffering; and yet neither the Christian, who projected a whole secret machinery of salvation into suffering, nor the naïve primitive, who interpreted all suffering from the standpoint of the spectator or the dispenser of suffering, would have conceived of it as senseless. In order to negate and dispose of the possibility of any secret, unwitnessed suffering, early man had to invent gods and a whole apparatus of intermediate spirits, invisible beings who could also see in the dark, and who would not readily let pass unseen any interesting spectacle of suffering. Such were the inventions with which life, in those days, performed its perennial trick of justifying itself, its "evil";

nowadays a different set of inventions would be needed, e.g., life as a riddle or an epistemological problem. According to the primitive logic of feeling (but is our own so very different?) any evil was justified whose spectacle proved edifying to the gods. We need only study Calvin and Luther to realize how far the ancient conception of the gods as frequenters of cruel spectacles has penetrated into our European humanism. But one thing is certain: the Greeks could offer their gods no more pleasant condiment than the joys of cruelty. With what eyes did Homer's gods regard the destinies of men? What, in the last analysis, was the meaning of the Trojan War and similar tragic atrocities? There can be no doubt that they were intended as festivals for the gods, and, insofar as poets in this respect are more "divine" than other men, as festivals for the poets. In much the same manner the moral philosophers of Greece, at a later date, let the eyes of God dwell on the moral struggles, the heroism, and the self-mortification of the virtuous man. The "Heracles" of stern virtue was on stage and was fully aware of it; to that nation of actors, unwitnessed virtue was inconceivable. Might not the audacious invention, by philosophers of that era, of man's free will, his absolute spontaneity in the doing of good or ill, have been made for the express purpose of insuring that the interest of the gods in the spectacle of human virtue could never be exhausted? This earthly stage must never be bare of truly novel, truly unprecedented suspense, complications, catastrophes. A truly deterministic world, whose movements the gods might readily foresee, must soon pall on them: reason enough why those friends of the gods, the philosophers, would not foist such a world on them. Ancient humanity, an essentially public and visual world, unable to conceive of happiness without spectacles and feasts, was full of tender regard for the "spectator." And, as we have said before, punishment too has its festive features.

VIII

We have observed that the feeling of guilt and personal obligation had its inception in the oldest and most primitive relationship between human beings, that of buyer and seller, creditor and debtor. Here, for the first time, individual stood and measured himself against individual. No phase of civilization, no matter how primitive, has been discovered in which that relation did not to some extent exist. The mind of early man was preoccupied to such an extent with price making, assessment of values, the devising and exchange of equivalents, that, in a certain sense, this may be said to have constituted his thinking. Here we find the oldest variety of human acuteness, as well as the first indication of human pride, of a superiority over other animals. Perhaps our word *man* (*manas*) still expresses something of that pride: man saw himself as the being that measures values, the "assaying" animal. Purchase and sale, together with their psychological trappings, antedate even the rudiments of social organization and covenants. From its rudimentary manifestation in interpersonal law, the incipient sense of barter, contract, guilt, right, obligation, compensation was projected into the crudest communal complexes (and their relations to other such complexes) together with the habit of measuring power against power. The eye had been entirely conditioned to that mode of vision; and with the awkward consistency of primitive thought, which moves with difficulty but, when it does move, moves inexorably in one direction, early mankind soon reached the grand generalization that everything has its price, everything can be paid for. Here we have the oldest and naïvest moral canon of justice, of all "fair play," "good will," and "objectivity." Justice, at this level, is good will operating among men of roughly equal power, their readiness to come to terms with one another, to strike a compromise—or, in the case of others less powerful, to *force* them to accept such a compromise.

IX

Keeping within the primeval frame of reference (which, after all, is not so very different from our own) we may say that the commonwealth stood to its members in the relation of creditor to debtor. People lived in a commonwealth, enjoying its privileges (which we are, perhaps, inclined to underestimate). They lived sheltered, protected, in peace and confidence, immune from injuries and hostilities to which the man "outside" was continually exposed, since they had pledged themselves to the community in respect of such injury and hostility. But supposing that pledge is violated? The disappointed creditor—the community—will get his money back as best he can, you may be sure. It is not so much a question of the actual damage done; primarily, the offender has broken his contract, his pledge to the group, thus forfeiting all the benefits and amenities of the community which he has hitherto enjoyed. The criminal is a debtor who not only refuses to repay the advantages and advances he has received but who even dares lay hands on his creditor. Hence he is not only stripped of his advantages, as is only just, but drastically reminded what these advantages were worth. The rage of the defrauded creditor, the community, returns him to the wild and outlawed condition from which heretofore he had been protected. It rejects him, and henceforth every kind of hostility may vent itself on him. Punishment, at this level of morality, simply mimics the normal attitude toward a hated enemy who has been conquered and disarmed, who forfeits not only every right and protection but all mercy as well. The offender is treated according to the laws of war and victory celebrations, brutally, without consideration; which may explain why war, including the martial custom of ritual sacrifice, has provided all the modes under which punishment appears in history.

X

As the commonwealth grew stronger, it no longer took the infractions of the individual quite so seriously. The individual no longer represented so grave a danger to the group as a whole. The offender was no longer outlawed and exposed to general fury. Rather, he was carefully shielded by the community against popular indignation, and especially against the indignation of the one he had injured. The attempt to moderate the rage of the offended party; to obviate a general disturbance by localizing the case; to find equivalents, "arrange things," (the Roman *compositio*); but most of all the attempt, ever more determined, to fix a price for every offense, and thus to dissociate, up to a certain point, the offender from his offense —these are the traits which characterize with increasing clarity the development of penal law. Whenever a community gains in power and pride, its penal code becomes more lenient, while the moment it is weakened or endangered the harsher methods of the past are revived. The humanity of creditors has always increased with their wealth; until finally the degree to which a creditor can tolerate impairment becomes the measure of his wealth. It is possible to imagine a society flushed with such a sense of power that it could afford to let its offenders go unpunished. What greater luxury is there for a society to indulge in? "Why should I bother about these parasites of mine?" such a society might ask. "Let them take all they want. I have plenty." Justice, which began by setting a price on everything and making everyone strictly accountable, ends by blinking at the defaulter and letting him go scot free. Like every good thing on earth, justice ends by suspending itself. The fine name this self-canceling justice has given itself is *mercy*. But mercy remains, as goes without saying, the prerogative of the strongest, his province beyond the law.

XI

A word should be said here against certain recent attempts to trace the notion of justice to a different source, namely rancor. But first of all, let me whisper something in the ear of psychologists, on the chance that they might want to study rancor at close range: that flower now blooms most profusely among anarchists and anti-Semites—unseen, like the violet, though with a different odor. And as the like spirit begets the like result, we must not be surprised if we see these recent attempts hark back to certain shady efforts, discussed earlier, to dignify vengeance by the name of justice (as though justice were simply an outgrowth of the sense of injury) and to honor the whole gamut of *reactive* emotions. I am the last person to object to the latter notion: in view of the long neglected relationship between our biological needs and our emotional reactions, it is a consideration of the utmost importance. Yet I want to draw attention to the fact that precisely out of the spirit of rancor has this new nuance of scientific "equity" sprung to the service of hatred, envy, malevolence, and distrust. For "scientific equity" ceases immediately, giving way to accents of mortal enmity and the crassest bias, the moment another group of emotions comes into play whose biological value seems to me even greater and for that reason even more deserving of scientific appraisal and esteem. I am speaking of the truly *active* emotions, such as thirst for power, avarice, and the like (*vide* E. Dühring, *The Value of Existence, A Course in Philosophy,* and elsewhere). So much for the general tendency. Against Dühring's specific proposition that the native soil of justice is in the reactive emotions, it must be urged that the exact opposite is the case: the soil of the reactive emotions is the very last to be conquered by the spirit of justice. Should it actually come to pass that the just man remains just even toward his despoiler (and not simply cool, moderate, distant, indifferent: to be just is a positive attitude), and that even under the stress of hurt, contumely, denigration the noble, penetrating yet mild objectivity of the just (the *judging*) eye does not become clouded, then we have before us an instance of the rarest accomplishment, something that, if we are wise, we will neither expect nor be too easily convinced of. It is generally true of even the most decent people that a small dose of insult, malice, insinuation is enough to send the blood to their eyes and equity out the window. The active man, the attacker and overreacher, is still a hundred steps closer to justice than the reactive one, and the reason is that he has no need to appraise his object falsely and prejudicially as the other must. It is an historical fact that the aggressive man, being stronger, bolder, and nobler, has at all times had the better view, the clearer conscience on his side. Conversely, one can readily guess who has the invention of "bad conscience" on his conscience: the vindictive man. Simply glance through history: in what sphere, thus far, has all legislation and, indeed, all true desire for laws, developed? In the sphere of "reactive" man? Not at all. Exclusively in the sphere of the active, strong, spontaneous, and aggressive. Historically speaking, all law—be it said to the dismay of that agitator (Dühring) who once confessed: "The doctrine of vengeance is the red thread that runs through my entire investigation of justice"—is a battle waged against the reactive emotions by the active and aggressive, who have employed part of their strength to curb the excesses of reactive pathos and bring about a compromise. Wherever justice is practiced and maintained, we see a stronger power intent on finding means to regulate the senseless raging of rancor among its weaker subordinates. This is accomplished by wresting the object of rancor from vengeful hands, or by substituting for vengeance the struggle against the enemies of peace and order, or by devising, proposing, and if necessary *enforcing* compromises, or by setting up a normative scale of equivalents for damages to which all future complaints may be referred. But above all, by the establishment of a code of laws which the superior power imposes upon the forces of hostility and resentment whenever it is strong enough to do so; by a categorical declaration of what it considers to be legitimate and right, or else forbidden and wrong. Once such a body of law has been established, all acts of highhandedness on the part of individuals or groups are seen as infractions of the law, as rebellion against the supreme power. Thus the rulers deflect the attention of their subjects from the particular injury and, in the long run, achieve the opposite end from that sought by vengeance, which tries to make the viewpoint of the injured person prevail exclusively. Henceforth the eye is trained to view the deed ever more impersonally—even the eye of the offended person, though this, as we have said, is the last to be affected. It follows that only after a corpus of laws has been established can there be any talk of "right" and "wrong" (and not, as Dühring maintains, after the act of injury). To speak of right and wrong *per se* makes no sense at all. No act of violence, rape, exploitation, destruction, is intrinsically "unjust," since life itself is violent, rapacious, exploitative, and destructive and cannot be conceived otherwise. Even more disturbingly, we have to admit that from the biological point of view legal conditions are necessarily exceptional conditions, since they limit the radical life-will bent on power and must finally subserve, as means, life's collective purpose, which is to create greater power constellations. To accept any legal system as sovereign and universal—to accept it, not merely as an instrument in the struggle of power complexes, but as a *weapon against struggle* (in the sense of Dühring's communist cliché that every will must regard every other will as its equal)—is an anti-vital principle which can only bring about man's utter demoralization and, indirectly, a reign of nothingness.

XII

One word should be added here about the *origin* and the *purpose* of punishment, two considerations radically distinct and yet too frequently confounded. How have our genealogists of morals treated these questions? Naïvely, as always. They would discover some kind of "purpose" in punishment, such as to avenge, or to deter, and would then naïvely place this purpose at the origin of punishment as its *causa fiendi*. And this is all. Yet the criterion of purpose is the last that should ever be applied to a study of legal evolution. There is no set of maxims more important for an historian than this: that the actual causes of a thing's origin and its eventual uses, the manner of its incorporation into a system of purposes, are worlds apart; that everything that exists, no matter what its origin, is periodically reinterpreted by those in power in terms of fresh intentions; that all processes in the organic world are processes of outstripping and overcoming, and that, in turn, all outstripping and overcoming means reinterpretation, rearrangement, in the course of which the earlier meaning and purpose are necessarily either obscured or lost. No matter how well we understand the utility of a certain physiological organ (or of a legal institution, a custom, a political convention, an artistic genre, a cultic trait) we do not thereby understand anything of its origin. I realize that this truth must distress the traditionalist, for, from time immemorial, the demonstrable purpose of a thing has been considered its *causa fiendi*—the eye is made for seeing, the hand for grasping. So likewise, punishment has been viewed as an invention for the purpose of punishing. But all pragmatic purposes are simply symbols of the fact that a will to power has implanted its own sense of function in those less powerful. Thus the whole history of a thing, an organ, a custom, becomes a continuous *chain* of reinterpretations and rearrangements, which need not be causally connected among themselves, which may simply follow one another. The "evolution" of a thing, a custom, an organ is not its *progressus* towards a goal, let alone the most logical and shortest *progressus,* requiring the least energy and expenditure. Rather, it is a sequence of more or less profound, more or less independent processes of appropriation, including the resistances used in each instance, the attempted transformations for purposes of defense or reaction, as well as the results of successful counterattacks. While forms are fluid, their "meaning" is even more so. The same process takes place in every individual organism. As the whole organism develops in essential ways, the meaning of the individual organs too is altered. In some cases their partial atrophy or numerical diminution spells the increased strength and perfection of the whole. This amounts to saying that partial desuetude, atrophy and degeneration, the loss of meaning and purpose —in short, death—must be numbered among the conditions of any true *progressus,* which latter appears always in the form of the will and means to greater power and is achieved at the expense of numerous lesser powers. The scope of any "progress" is measured by all that must be sacrificed for its sake. To sacrifice humanity as mass to the welfare of a single stronger human species would indeed constitute progress. . . .

I have emphasized this point of historical method all the more strongly because it runs counter to our current instincts and fashions, which would rather come to terms

with the absolute haphazardness or the mechanistic mean-
inglessness of event than with the theory of a will to power
mirrored in all process. The democratic bias against anything that dominates or wishes to dominate, our modern
misarchism (to coin a bad word for a bad thing) has
gradually so sublimated and disguised itself that nowadays
it can invade the strictest, most objective sciences without
anyone's raising a word of protest. In fact it seems to me
that this prejudice now dominates all of physiology and
the other life sciences, to their detriment, naturally, since
it has conjured away one of their most fundamental concepts, that of *activity*, and put in its place the concept of
adaptation—a kind of second-rate activity, mere reactivity.
Quite in keeping with that bias, Herbert Spencer has defined life itself as an ever more purposeful inner adaptation
to external circumstances. But such a view misjudges the
very essence of life; it overlooks the intrinsic superiority of
the spontaneous, aggressive, overreaching, reinterpreting
and re-establishing forces, on whose action adaptation
gradually supervenes. It denies, even in the organism itself, the dominant role of the higher functions in which
the vital will appears active and shaping. The reader will
recall that Huxley strongly objected to Spencer's "admin-
istrative nihilism." But here it is a question of much more
than simply "administration."

XIII

To return to the issue of punishment, we must distinguish
in it two separate aspects: first its relatively permanent
features: custom, the act, the *drama*, a certain strict sequence of procedures; and second, all that is fluid in it:

its meaning, its purpose, the expectations attending on the execution of such procedures. In keeping with the views I have stated earlier, I presuppose here that the procedure itself antedates its use for purposes of punishment and that the latter has only been projected into the procedure, which had existed all along, though in a different framework. In short, I absolutely part company with the naïve view which would see the procedure as having been invented for punitive purposes, as earlier the hand for prehensile purposes. Concerning that other, fluid, "meaning" aspect of punishment, I would say that in a very late culture such as our present-day European culture the notion "punishment" has not one but a great many meanings. The whole history of punishment and of its adaptation to the most various uses has finally crystallized into a kind of complex which it is difficult to break down and quite impossible to define. (It is impossible to say with certainty today *why* people are punished. All terms which semiotically condense a whole process elude definition; only that which has no history can be defined.) However, at an earlier stage that synthesis of "meanings" must have been more easily soluble, its components more easily disassociated. We can still see how, from one situation to the next, the elements of the synthesis changed their valence and reorganized themselves in such a way that now this element, now that predominated at the expense of the others. It might even happen that in certain situations a single element (the purpose of *deterring*, for example) absorbed the rest. To give the reader some idea how uncertain, secondary, and accidental the "meaning" of punishment really is, and how one and the same procedure may be used for totally different ends, I shall furnish him with a schema abstracted from the relatively small and random body of material at my disposal.

1. Punishment administered with the view of rendering the offender harmless and preventing his doing further damage.

2. Punishment consisting of the payment of damages to the injured party, including affect compensation.

3. Punishment as the isolation of a disequilibrating agent, in order to keep the disturbance from spreading further.

4. Punishment as a means of inspiring fear of those who determine and execute it.

5. Punishment as cancellation of the advantages the culprit has hitherto enjoyed (as when he is put to work in the mines).

6. Punishment as the elimination of a degenerate element (or, as in Chinese law, a whole stock; a means of keeping the race pure, or of maintaining a social type).

7. Punishment as a "triumph," the violating and deriding of an enemy finally subdued.

8. Punishment as a means of creating memory, either for the one who suffers it—so-called "improvement"—or for the witnesses.

9. Punishment as the payment of a fee, exacted by the authority which protects the evil-doer from the excesses of vengeance.

10. Punishment as a compromise with the tradition of vendetta, to the extent that this is still maintained and invoked as a privilege by powerful clans.

11. Punishment as a declaration of war, a warlike measure, against an enemy of peace, order and authority.

However incomplete, this list will serve to show that punishment is rife with utilitarian purposes of every kind. All the more reason why we should delete from it a fictitious usefulness which looms very large in popular thought these days, and which reckless writers are using freely to buttress our tottering belief in punishment. Punishment, these men claim, is valuable because it awakens a sense of guilt in the culprit; we should therefore view it as the true instrument of the psychological reaction called "remorse," "pangs of conscience." But this is a blunder, even as far as modern man and his psychology are concerned; applied to early man the notion becomes wholly absurd. True remorse is rarest among criminals and convicts: prisons and penitentiaries are not the breeding places of this gnawer. All conscientious observers are agreed here, though the fact may disappoint their innermost hopes and wishes. By and large, punishment hardens and freezes; it concentrates; it sharpens the sense of alienation; it strengthens resistance. If it should happen that now and again it breaks the will and brings about a miserable prostration and self-abasement, we find that psychological effect even less gratifying than the one which is most common, i.e., a dry, self-absorbed gloom. But if we stop to consider the millennia of prehistory, we may say with some assurance that it is precisely punishment that has most effectively retarded the development of guilt feeling, at any rate in the hearts of the victims of punitive authority. For we must not underestimate the extent to which the criminal is prevented, by the very witnessing of the legal process, from regarding his deed as intrinsically evil. He sees the very same actions performed in the service of justice with perfectly clear conscience and general approbation: spying, setting traps, outsmarting, bribing, the whole tricky, cunning system which chiefs of police, prosecutors, and informers have developed among themselves; not to mention the cold-blooded legal practices of despoiling, insulting, torturing, murdering the victim. Obviously none of these practices is rejected and condemned *per se* by his judges, but only under certain conditions. "Bad conscience," that most uncanny and interesting plant of our vegetation, has definitely not sprung from this soil, indeed for a very long time the notion that he was punishing a "culprit" never entered a judge's mind. He thought he had to do with a mischief-maker, an unaccountable piece of misfortune. And in his turn the man whose lot it was to be punished considered his punishment a misfortune. He no more felt a moral pang than if some terrible unforeseen disaster had occurred, if a rock had fallen and crushed him.

XV

Spinoza once, with some embarrassment, perceived this fact (to the annoyance of some of his commentators, like Kuno Fischer, who have gone out of their way to misconstrue his meaning). Teased one afternoon by heaven knows what memory, he was pondering the question of what really remained to him of that famous *morsus conscientiae*. Had he not relegated both good and evil to the realm of figments and grimly defended the honor of his "free" God against those blasphemers who would have God invariably act *sub ratione boni* ("But this would mean subordinating God to fate, and result in the worst absurdity")? The world for Spinoza had returned to that state of innocence which it had known before the invention of bad conscience—but what, in the process, had become of the sting of conscience? "It is the opposite of joy," he says finally, "a sadness attended by the memory of some past event which disappointed our expectations," (*Ethics* III, Propos. 18, Schol. 1. 2.). In much the same way for thousands of years, all evil-doers overtaken by punishment would think, "Something has unexpectedly gone wrong here," and not, "I should never have done that." They would undergo punishment as one undergoes sickness or misfortune or death, with that stout, unrebellious fatalism which still gives the Russians an advantage over us Westerners in the management of their lives. If actions were "judged" at all in those days, it was solely from the prudential point of view. There can be no doubt that we must look for the real effect of punishment in a sharpening of man's wits, an extension of his memory, a determination to proceed henceforth more prudently, suspiciously, secretly, a realization that the individual is simply too weak to accomplish certain things; in brief, an increase of self-knowledge. What punishment is able to achieve, both for man and beast, is increase of fear, circumspection, control over the instincts. Thus man is *tamed* by punishment, but by no means *improved;* rather the opposite. (It is said that misfortune sharpens our wits, but to the extent that it sharpens our wits it makes us worse; fortunately it often simply dulls them.)

XVI

I can no longer postpone giving tentative expression to my own hypothesis concerning the origin of "bad conscience." It is one that may fall rather strangely on our ears and that requires close meditation. I take bad conscience to be a deep-seated malady to which man succumbed under the pressure of the most profound transformation he ever underwent—the one that made him once and for all a sociable and pacific creature. Just as happened in the case of those sea creatures who were forced to become land animals in order to survive, these semi-animals, happily adapted to the wilderness, to war, free roaming, and adventure, were forced to change their nature. Of a sudden they found all their instincts devalued, unhinged. They must walk on legs and carry themselves, where before the water had carried them: a terrible heaviness weighed upon them. They felt inapt for the simplest manipulations, for in this new, unknown world they could no longer count on the guidance of their unconscious drives. They were forced to think, deduce, calculate, weigh cause and effect—unhappy people, reduced to their weakest, most fallible organ, their consciousness! I doubt that there has ever been on earth such a feeling of misery, such a leaden discomfort. It was not that those old instincts had abruptly ceased making their demands; but now their satisfaction was rare and difficult. For the most part they had to depend on new, covert satisfactions. All instincts that are not allowed free play turn inward. This is what I call man's interiorization; it alone provides the soil for the growth of what is later called man's *soul*. Man's interior world, originally meager and tenuous, was expanding in every dimension, in proportion as the outward discharge of his feelings was curtailed. The formidable bulwarks by means of which the polity protected itself against the ancient instincts of freedom (punishment was one of the strongest of these bulwarks) caused those wild, extravagant instincts to turn in upon man. Hostility, cruelty, the delight in persecution, raids, excitement, destruction all turned against their begetter. Lacking external enemies and resistances, and confined within an oppressive narrowness and regularity, man began rending, persecuting, terrifying himself, like a wild beast hurling itself against the bars of its cage. This languisher, devoured by nostalgia for the desert, who had to turn *himself* into an adventure, a torture chamber, an insecure and dangerous wilderness—this fool, this pining and desperate prisoner, became the inventor of "bad conscience." Also the generator of the greatest and most disastrous of maladies, of which humanity has not to this day been cured: his sickness of himself, brought on by the violent severance from his animal past, by his sudden leap and fall into new layers and conditions of existence, by his declaration of war against the old instincts that had hitherto been the foundation of his power, his joy, and his awesomeness. Let me hasten to add that the phenomenon of an animal soul turning in upon itself, taking arms against itself, was so novel, profound, mysterious, contradictory, and pregnant with possibility, that the whole complexion of the universe was changed thereby. This spectacle (and the end of it is not yet in sight) required a divine audience to do it justice. It was a spectacle too sublime and paradoxical to pass unnoticed on some trivial planet. Henceforth man was to figure among the most unexpected and breathtaking throws in the game of dice played by Heracleitus' great "child," be he called Zeus or Chance. Man now aroused an interest, a suspense, a hope, almost a conviction—as though in him something were heralded, as though he were not a goal but a way, an interlude, a bridge, a great promise. . . .

XVII

My hypothesis concerning the origin of bad conscience presupposes that this change was neither gradual nor voluntary, that it was not an organic growing into new conditions but rather an abrupt break, a leap, a thing compelled, an ineluctable disaster, which could neither be struggled against nor even resented. It further presupposes that the fitting of a hitherto unrestrained and shapeless populace into a tight mold, as it had begun with an act of violence, had to be brought to conclusion by a series of violent acts; that the earliest commonwealth constituted a terrible despotism, a ruthless, oppressive machinery for not only kneading and suppling a brutish populace but actually shaping it. I have used the word "commonwealth," but it should be clearly understood what I mean: a pack of savages, a race of conquerors, themselves organized for war and able to organize others, fiercely dominating a population perhaps vastly superior in numbers yet amorphous and nomadic. Such was the beginning of the human polity; I take it we have got over that sentimentalism that would have it begin with a contract. What do men who can command, who are born rulers, who evince power in act and deportment, have to do with contracts? Such beings are unaccountable; they come like destiny, without rhyme or reason, ruthlessly, bare of pretext. Suddenly they are here, like a stroke of lightning, too terrible, convincing, and "different" for hatred even. Their work is an instinctive imposing of forms. They are the most spontaneous, most unconscious artists that exist. They appear, and presently something entirely new has arisen, a live dominion whose parts and functions are delimited and interrelated, in which there is room for nothing that has not previously received its meaning from the whole. Being natural organizers, these men know nothing of guilt, responsibility, consideration. They are actuated by the terrible egotism of the artist, which is justified by the work he must do, as the mother by the child she will bear. Bad conscience certainly did not originate with these men, yet, on the other hand, that unseemly growth could not have developed *without* them, without their hammer blows, their artist's violence, which drove a great quantity of freedom out of sight and made it latent. In its earliest phase bad conscience is nothing other than the instinct of freedom forced to become latent, driven underground, and forced to vent its energy upon itself.

XVIII

We should guard against taking too dim a view of this phenomenon simply because it is both ugly and painful. After all, the same will to power which in those violent artists and organizers created polities, in the "labyrinth of the heart"—more pettily, to be sure, and in inverse direction —created negative ideals and humanity's bad conscience. Except that now the material upon which this great natural force was employed was man himself, his old animal self—and not, as in that grander and more spectacular phenomenon—his fellow man. This secret violation of the self, this artist's cruelty, this urge to impose on recalcitrant matter a form, a will, a distinction, a feeling of contradiction and contempt, this sinister task of a soul divided against itself, which makes itself suffer for the pleasure of suffering, this most energetic "bad conscience"—has it not given birth to a wealth of strange beauty and affirmation? Has it not given birth to beauty itself? Would beauty exist if ugliness had not first taken cognizance of itself, not said to itself, "I am ugly"? This hint will serve, at any rate, to solve the riddle of why contradictory terms such as *selflessness, self-denial, self-sacrifice* may intimate an ideal, a beauty. Nor will the reader doubt henceforth that the *joy* felt by the self-denying, self-sacrificing, selfless person was from the very start a *cruel* joy. —So much for the origin of altruism as a moral value. Bad conscience, the desire for self-mortification, is the wellspring of all altruistic values.

XIX

There can be no doubt that bad conscience is a sickness, but so, in a sense, is pregnancy. We shall presently describe the conditions which carried that "sickness" to its highest and most terrible peak. But first let us return for a moment to an earlier consideration. The civil-law relationship of debtor to creditor has been projected into yet another context, where we find it even more difficult to understand today, namely into the relationship between living men and their forebears. Among primitive tribes, each new generation feels toward the preceding ones, and especially toward the original founders of the tribe, a *juridical* obligation (rather than an *emotional* obligation, which seems to be of relatively recent origin). Early societies were convinced that their continuance was guaranteed solely by the sacrifices and achievements of their ancestors and that these sacrifices and achievements required to be paid back. Thus a debt was acknowledged which continued to increase, since the ancestors, surviving as powerful spirits, did not cease to provide the tribe with new benefits out of their store. Gratuitously? But nothing was gratuitous in those crude and "insensitive" times. Then how could they be repaid? By burnt offerings (to provide them with food), by rituals, shrines, customs, but above all, by obedience—for all rites, having been established by the forebears, were also permanently enjoined by them. But could they ever be *fully* repaid? An anxious doubt remained and grew steadily, and every so often there occurred some major act of "redemption," some gigantic repayment of the creditor (the famous sacrifice of the first-born, for example; in any case blood, human blood). Given this primitive logic, the fear of the ancestor and his power and the consciousness of indebtedness increase in direct proportion as the power of the tribe itself increases, as it becomes more successful in battle, independent, respected and feared. Never the other way round. Every step leading to the degeneration of the tribe, every setback, every sign of imminent dissolution, tends to diminish the fear of the ancestral spirits, to make them seem of less account, less wise, less provident, less powerful. Following this kind of logic to its natural term, we arrive at a situation in which the ancestors of the most powerful tribes have become so fearful to the imagination that they have receded at last into a numinous shadow: the ancestor becomes a god. Perhaps this is the way all gods have arisen, out of *fear*. . . . And if anyone should find it necessary to add, "But also out of piety," his claim would scarcely be justified for the longest and earliest period of the human race. But it would certainly hold true for that intermediate period during which the noble clans emerged, of whom it may justly be said that they paid back their ancestors (heroes or gods) with interest all those noble properties which had since come to reside abundantly in themselves. We shall have an opportunity later on of dealing with this "ennoblement" of the ancestral spirits (which is not the same thing as their "consecration"), but first, let us bring to a conclusion the story of man's consciousness of guilt.

XX

Man's firm belief that he was indebted to the gods did not cease with the decline of tribal organization. Just as man has inherited from the blood aristocracies the concepts *good* and *bad,* together with the psychological penchant for hierarchies, so he has inherited from the tribes, together with the tribal gods, a burden of outstanding debt and the desire to make final restitution. (The bridge is provided by those large populations of slaves and serfs, who, either perforce or through servile mimicry, had adopted the cults of their overlords. The heritage spreads out from them in all directions.) The sense of indebtedness to the gods continued to grow through the centuries, keeping pace with the evolution of man's concept of the deity. (The endless tale of ethnic struggle, triumph, reconciliation, and fusion, in short, whatever precedes the final hierarchy of racial strains in some great synthesis, is mirrored in the welter of divine genealogies and legends dealing with divine battles, victories, and reconciliations. Every progress toward universal empire has also been a progress toward a universal pantheon. Despotism, by overcoming the independent nobles, always prepares the way for some form of monotheism.) The advent of the Christian god, the "highest potency" god yet conceived by man, has been accompanied by the widest dissemination of the sense of indebtedness, guilt. If we are right in assuming that we have now entered upon the inverse development, it stands to reason that the steady decline of belief in a Christian god should entail a commensurate decline in man's guilt consciousness. It also stands to reason—doesn't it?—that a complete and definitive victory of atheism might deliver mankind altogether from its feeling of being indebted to its beginnings, its *causa prima*. Atheism and a kind of "second innocence" go together.

XXI

So much, for the moment, about the connection of "guilt" and "duty" with religious presuppositions. I have deliberately left on one side the "moralization" of these terms (their pushing back into conscience, the association of the notion of bad conscience with a deity), and even wrote at the end of the last paragraph as though such a moralization had never taken place; as though with the notion of a divine creditor falling into disuse those notions too were doomed. Unfortunately this is far from being the case. The modern moralization of the ideas of guilt and duty—their relegation to a purely subjective "bad conscience"—represents a determined attempt to invert the normal order of development, or at least to stop it in its tracks. The object now is to close the prospect of final deliverance and make man's gaze rebound from an iron barrier; to force the ideas of guilt and duty to face about and fiercely turn on—whom? Obviously on the "debtor," first of all, who, infested and eaten away by bad conscience, which spreads like a polyp, comes to view his debt as unredeemable by any act of atonement (the notion of "eternal penance"). But eventually the "creditor" too is turned on in the same fashion. Now the curse falls upon man's *causa prima* ("Adam," "original sin," the "bondage of the will"); or upon nature, which gave birth to man and which is now made the repository of the evil principle (nature as the instrument of the devil); or upon universal existence, which now appears as absolute non-value (nihilistic turning away from life, a longing for nothingness or for life's "opposite," for a different sort of "being"— Buddhism, etc.). Then suddenly we come face to face with that paradoxical and ghastly expedient which brought temporary relief to tortured humanity, that most brilliant stroke of Christianity: God's sacrifice of himself for man. God makes himself the ransom for what could not otherwise be ransomed; God alone has power to absolve us of a debt we can no longer discharge; the creditor offers himself as a sacrifice for his debtor out of sheer love (can you believe it?), out of love for his debtor. . . .

XXII

By now the reader will have guessed what has really been happening behind all these façades. Man, with his need for self-torture, his sublimated cruelty resulting from the cooping up of his animal nature within a polity, invented bad conscience in order to hurt himself, after the blocking of the more natural outlet of his cruelty. Then this guilt-ridden man seized upon religion in order to exacerbate his self-torment to the utmost. The thought of being in God's debt became his new instrument of torture. He focused in God the last of the opposites he could find to his true and inveterate animal instincts, making these a sin against God (hostility, rebellion against the "Lord," the "Father," the "Creator"). He stretched himself upon the contradiction "God" and "Devil" as on a rack. He projected all his denials of self, nature, naturalness out of himself as affirmations, as true being, embodiment, reality, as God (the divine Judge and Executioner), as transcendence, as eternity, as endless torture, as hell, as the infinitude of guilt and punishment. In such psychological cruelty we see an insanity of the *will* that is without parallel: man's will to find himself guilty, and unredeemably so; his will to believe that he might be punished to all eternity without ever expunging his guilt; his will to poison the very foundation of things with the problem of guilt and punishment and thus to cut off once and for all his escape from this labyrinth of obsession; his will to erect an ideal (God's holiness) in order to assure himself of his own absolute unworthiness. What a mad, unhappy animal is man! What strange notions occur to him; what perversities, what paroxysms of nonsense, what bestialities of idea burst from him, the moment he is prevented ever so little from being a beast of action! . . . All this is exceedingly curious and interesting, but dyed with such a dark, somber, enervating sadness that one must resolutely tear away one's gaze. Here, no doubt, is sickness, the most terrible sickness that has wasted man thus far. And if one is still able to hear—but how few these days have ears to hear it!—in this night of torment and absurdity the cry *love* ring out, the cry of rapt longing, of redemption in love, he must turn away with a shudder of invincible horror. . . . Man harbors too much horror; the earth has been a lunatic asylum for too long.

XXIII

This should take care, once for all, of the origin of "Our Holy Lord."—A single look at the Greek gods will convince us that a belief in gods need not result in morbid imaginations, that there are nobler ways of creating divine figments—ways which do not lead to the kind of self-crucifixion and self-punishment in which Europe, for millennia now, has excelled. The Hellenic gods reflected a race of noble and proud beings, in whom man's animal self had divine status and hence no need to lacerate and rage against itself. For a very long time the Greeks used their gods precisely to keep bad conscience at a distance, in order to enjoy their inner freedom undisturbed; in other words, they made the opposite use of them that Christianity has made of *its* god. They went very far in that direction, these splendid and lionhearted children, and no less an authority than the Homeric Zeus gives them to understand, now and again, that they make things a little too easy for themselves. "How strange," he says once (the case is that of Aegisthus, a *very* bad case indeed): "How strange that the mortals complain so loudly of us gods! They claim that we are responsible for all their evils. But they are the ones who create their own misery, by their folly, even in the teeth of fate." Yet the reader notices at once that even this Olympian spectator and judge is far from holding a grudge against them or thinking ill of them therefore.

"How foolish they are!" he thinks as he watches the misdeeds of mortals; and the Greeks, even during the heyday of their prosperity and strength, allowed that foolishness, lack of discretion, slight mental aberrations might be the source of much evil and disaster. Foolishness, not sin. . . . But even those mental aberrations were a problem. "How can such a thing happen to people like us, nobly bred, happy, virtuous, well educated?" For many centuries noble Greeks would ask themselves this question whenever one of their number had defiled himself by one of those incomprehensible crimes. "Well, he must have been deluded by a god," they would finally say, shaking their heads. This was a typically Greek solution. It was the office of the gods to justify, up to a certain point, the ill ways of man, to serve as "sources" of evil. In those days they were not agents of punishment but, what is nobler, repositories of guilt.

XXIV

It is clear that I am concluding this essay with three unanswered questions. It may occur to some reader to ask me, "Are you constructing an ideal or destroying one?" I would ask him, in turn, whether he ever reflected upon the price that had to be paid for the introduction of every new ideal on earth? On how much of reality, in each instance, had to be slandered and misconceived, how much of falsehood ennobled, how many consciences disturbed, how many gods sacrificed? For the raising of an altar requires the breaking of an altar: this is a law—let anyone who can prove me wrong. We moderns have a millennial heritage of conscience-vivisection and cruelty to the animals in our-

selves. This is our most ancient habit, our most consummate artistry perhaps, in any case our greatest refinement,
our special fare. Man has looked for so long with an evil
eye upon his natural inclinations that they have finally
become inseparable from "bad conscience." A converse
effort can be imagined, but who has the strength for it?
It would consist of associating all the *unnatural* inclinations—the longing for what is unworldly, opposed to the
senses, to instinct, to nature, to the animal in us, all the
anti-biological and earth-calumniating ideals—with bad
conscience. To whom, today, may such hopes and pretensions address themselves? The *good* men, in particular,
would be on the other side; and of course all the comfortable, resigned, vain, moony, weary people. Does anything
give greater offense and separate one more thoroughly
from others than to betray something of the strictness and
dignity with which one treats oneself? But how kind and
accommodating the world becomes the moment we act
like all the rest and let ourselves go! To accomplish that
aim, different minds are needed than are likely to appear
in this age of ours: minds strengthened by struggles and
victories, for whom conquest, adventure, danger, even
pain, have become second nature. Minds accustomed to
the keen atmosphere of high altitudes, to wintry walks,
to ice and mountains in every sense. Minds possessed of a
sublime kind of malice, of that self-assured recklessness
which is a sign of strong health. What is needed, in short,
is just superb health. Is such health still possible today?

But at some future time, a time stronger than our effete,
self-doubting present, the true Redeemer will come, whose
surging creativity will not let him rest in any shelter or
hiding place, whose solitude will be misinterpreted as a
flight from reality, whereas it will in fact be a dwelling

on, a dwelling *in* reality—so that when he comes forth into the light he may bring with him the redemption of that reality from the curse placed upon it by a lapsed ideal. This man of the future, who will deliver us both from a lapsed ideal and from all that this ideal has spawned— violent loathing, the will to extinction, nihilism—this great and decisive stroke of midday, who will make the will free once more and restore to the earth its aim, and to man his hope; this anti-Christ and anti-nihilist, conqueror of both God and Unbeing—*one day he must come.* . . .

XXV

But why go on? I've reached the term of my speech; to continue here would be to usurp the right of one younger, stronger, more pregnant with future than I am —the right of Zarathustra, *impious* Zarathustra. . . .

Third Essay

WHAT DO ASCETIC IDEALS MEAN?

"Wisdom likes men who are reckless,
scornful and violent; being a woman,
her heart goes out to a soldier."

Zarathustra

I

What do ascetic ideals betoken?—In artists, nothing or too
many things; in scholars and philosophers, something like
a flair for the conditions most favorable to intellectual distinction; in women, at best, one more seductive charm, a
touch of *morbidezza* added to fair flesh, the angelic look
of a plump, pretty animal; in men who are physiologically
maladjusted or unstrung (the vast majority), an attempt to
see themselves as "too good" for this world, a pious de-
bauchery, their strongest weapon against slow pain and
tedium; in priests, the basic priestly creed, the main instrument of priestcraft, the supreme guarantee of their
power; in saints, an excuse to hibernate, their *novissima
gloriae cupido*, their repose in nothingness ("God"), their
own brand of madness. The fact that the ascetic ideal can
mean so many things to man is indicative of a basic trait
of the human will, its fear of the void. Our will requires
an aim; it would sooner have the void for its purpose than
be void of purpose. Have I made myself clear? . . . "Not
at all, my dear sir!" Well, then, let us start again from the
beginning.

II

What do ascetic ideals betoken?—Or, to take a special case which I have often been asked about: what, for instance, does it mean when an artist like Richard Wagner pays homage to chastity in his later years? Or perhaps it would be truer to say that he has done this all along, but only latterly in a spirit of asceticism. What does this violent ascetic revulsion signify? For Wagner has actually made a complete about-face. What does it mean when an artist faces about completely? . . . Here we are forcibly reminded of what was probably the best, happiest, most reckless period of Wagner's life, the period when his mind was profoundly exercised by the story of Luther's wedding. Who knows what chance events brought it about that we have, today, in place of this wedding music, *Die Meistersinger?* And who knows how much of the former still echoes in the latter? At all events there can be no doubt that *Luther's Wedding* too would have been a praise of chastity. But at the same time a praise of the life of the senses; and it would have seemed right to me that way, and Wagnerian as well. There is no inherent contradiction between chastity and sensual pleasure: every good marriage, every real love affair transcends these opposites. It seems to me that Wagner would have done well to impress this pleasant fact on his Germans once more, through the vehicle of a comedy on Luther, at once bold and lovely. Detractors of the flesh have always abounded among the Germans, and perhaps Luther's greatest merit was to have had the courage of his sensuality (in those days one spoke, delicately enough, of "evangelical freedom"). But even in cases where a real conflict exists between the sexual urge and chastity, the issue, fortunately, need not be tragic. At least this holds for all those happy, soundly constituted mortals who are far from regarding their precarious balance between beast and angel as an argument against existence. The finest and most luminous among them, such as Goethe and Hafiz, have even seen in this conflict one more enticement to life. . . . On the other hand, it is obvious that, once those pigs who have failed as pigs (and there are such) come round to the worship of chastity, they will view it simply as their own opposite and will worship it with the most tragic grunting zeal. It was that embarrassing and quite gratuitous conflict which the aging Wagner meant to set to music and present on the stage. Why? we may fairly ask. What were pigs to him? What are they to us?

III

This brings us directly to another question: what could that country simpleton, that poor devil and child of nature, Parsifal, have meant to him? Parsifal, converted in the end to Catholicism by such shady means—was he really meant *seriously?* One might be tempted to think, or wish, that the opposite were true, that Wagner's Parsifal was meant as a jest, as the satyr play with which the tragedian Wagner took leave of us, of himself, and especially of tragedy, in a manner befitting his greatness. That he wished to take leave of us with the most extravagant parody of the tragic spirit itself, of the whole grisly sadness and somberness of his earlier work, of the ascetic ideal in its crassest form. Such an act would have befitted a master tragedian, for the great artist reaches the peak of his greatness only when he has learned to see himself and his art beneath him, when he is able to laugh about them. Is Wagner's *Parsifal* such a secret, exultant laugh, signalizing the artist's final freedom? One would certainly wish that it were, for what becomes of Parsifal if we take him seriously? Must we really see him, as someone once put it to me, as "the product of an insane hatred of knowledge, spirit, and sensuality"? A curse pronounced in the same breath on the mind and the senses? An apostasy and return to Christian morbidity and obscurantism? In the last analysis, a denial and cancellation of himself by an artist who all his life had worked for the opposite end, to create an art combining the greatest spiritual and sensual power? Who, furthermore, had applied the same principles in his life as in his art? We need only remember how enthusiastically the young Wagner followed the footsteps of the philosopher Feuerbach. Feuerbach's war cry of "healthy sensuality," sounded during the thirties and forties, seemed to Wagner as to so many other Germans (they called themselves "Young Germany") to be the new gospel. Did he finally come to think otherwise in these matters? At least it seems that toward the end he was determined to preach otherwise. And not only from the stage, in the trumpets of *Parsifal*. The murky writings of his last years are full of passages betraying a secret desire, timid, unsure, unacknowledged, to preach quite literally conversion, self-mortification, Christianity, medievalism, and to tell his disciples, "There is nothing here: you must seek salvation elsewhere." In one place he even invokes the blood of the Redeemer. . . .

IV

Since a case of this sort—a very typical case, by the way—
is attended with so much embarrassment, let me say one
thing at the start: it is always well to divorce an artist from
his work, and to take *him* less seriously than *it*. He is,
after all, only a condition of the work, the soil from which
it grows, perhaps only the manure on that soil. Thus he is,
in most cases, something that must be forgotten if one
wants to enter into the full enjoyment of the work. To in-
vestigate the origins of a work belongs to the physiologists and vivisectionists of the mind, never to men endowed
with esthetic sensibility. The creator of *Parsifal* could not
avoid identification or at least deep familiarity with medieval psychological conflicts—a domain obnoxious to all that
is lofty or disciplined, a kind of intellectual perversity—
any more than a pregnant woman can avoid the queasy
details of pregnancy, which must be forgotten in order to
enjoy the child. An artist must resist the temptation to
"analogy by contiguity," which would persuade him that
he, himself, *is* what he imagines and expresses. The truth
of the matter is that if he *were* that thing, he would be
unable to imagine or express it: Homer would not have
created Achilles, nor Goethe Faust, if Homer had been
an Achilles or Goethe a Faust. An artist worth his salt is
permanently separated from ordinary reality. On the other
hand, we all know that the constant unrealness of his innermost being will sometimes fill him with despair, and
that he will then attempt what is strictly forbidden him,
to trespass upon actuality, to be like other men. With what
success? The reader can easily guess. . . . Here we have

the typical velleity of the artist, the velleity to which the aging Wagner too succumbed and for which he had to pay so dearly, so disastrously (it cost him his most valuable friends). But quite apart from that velleity, who would not wish for Wagner's own sake that he had taken leave of us and his art in a different fashion; not with *Parsifal* but more triumphantly, with more assurance, and less misleadingly and ambiguously in terms of his total commitment, less in the spirit of Schopenhauer's nihilism?

v

What, then, do ascetic ideals betoken? As regards the artist we may now say: nothing at all. Or else such a variety of things that the result is the same. But, after all, what does it matter? Artists have never stood sufficiently proudly and independently in (or against) the world for their changes of attitude to be deserving of notice. They have ever been in the service of some ethics or philosophy or religion, and all too often they have been tools in the hands of a clique, smooth sycophants either of vested interests or of forces newly come to power. In any case they have always needed protection, security, a force to back them up. Artists never stand resolutely for themselves; standing alone goes against their deepest instincts. For example, Richard Wagner used Schopenhauer as his moral support, once the latter had been accepted. Who can imagine that he would have had the courage for the ascetic ideal without the authority of Schopenhauer's philosophy, without Schopenhauer's prestige, which in the seventies was very great all over Europe? (I leave out of account here the question whether in the new German Empire an artist could have succeeded who lacked the milk of pious—Empire-pious—sentiments.) This brings us to the more important question: what does it mean when a true philosopher pays homage to the ascetic ideal, a sturdy, independent mind like Schopenhauer, who has the courage of his convictions and need not wait for precedents and encouragement from above? Consider in this connection Schopenhauer's curious, and to some of us most fascinating, attitude to art. It was doubtless that which first converted Wagner to Schopenhauer (at the instance, as every one knows, of the poet Herwegh) to such a degree that his later esthetic views completely contradict his earlier ones. As an example of the earlier view, we may take the treatise *Opera and Drama,* of the latter, his articles from 1870 onwards. What most impresses one is the radical change in his notion of the position of music itself. What did it now matter to him that he had once conceived of music as a means, a "woman," which required an end, a "man," *drama* for its completion? It suddenly dawned on him that Schopenhauer's theory was much more favorable to the sovereignty of music: music seen as apart from all the other arts, the triumphant culmination of all art, not concerned like the others with images of the phenomenal world but, rather, speaking the language of the will directly from the deep source of Being, its most elementary manifestation. There corresponded to this extraordinary rise in the value of music an equally amazing increase in the prestige of the musician: he now became an oracle, a priest, or more than a priest—a kind of mouthpiece of the absolute, a telephone line of Transcendence. God's ventriloquist, he would talk not only music but metaphysics. Small wonder, then, that one day he should talk ascetic ideals.

VI

Schopenhauer made use of the Kantian version of the esthetic problem, though he certainly did not look upon it with the eyes of Kant. Kant had thought he was doing an honor to art when, among the predicates of beauty, he gave prominence to those which flatter the intellect, i.e., impersonality and universality. This is not the place to inquire whether Kant did not attack the whole problem in the wrong way; all I wish to point out here is that Kant, like all philosophers, instead of viewing the esthetic issue from the side of the artist, envisaged art and beauty solely from the "spectator's" point of view, and so, without himself realizing it, smuggled the "spectator" into the concept of beauty. This would not have mattered too much had that "spectator" been sufficiently familiar to the philosophers of beauty, as a strong personal experience, a wealth of powerful impressions, aspirations, surprises, and transports in the esthetic realm. But I am afraid the opposite has always been the case, and so we have got from these philosophers of beauty definitions which, like Kant's famous definition of beauty, are marred by a complete lack of esthetic sensibility. "That is beautiful," Kant proclaims, "which gives us disinterested pleasure." Disinterested! Compare with this definition that other one, framed by a real spectator and artist, Stendhal, who speaks of beauty as "a promise of happiness." Here we find the very thing which Kant stresses exclusively in the esthetic condition rejected and canceled. Which is right, Kant or Stendhal?— When our estheticians tirelessly rehearse, in support of Kant's view, that the spell of beauty enables us to view even *nude* female statues "disinterestedly" we may be allowed to laugh a little at their expense. The experiences of artists in this delicate matter are rather more "interesting"; certainly Pygmalion was not entirely devoid of esthetic feeling. Let us honor our estheticians all the more for the innocence reflected in such arguments—Kant, for example, when he descants on the peculiar character of the sense of touch with the ingenuousness of a country parson! To come back to Schopenhauer, who was so much closer to the arts than Kant but who yet could not escape from the spell of Kant's definition—how are we to account for his view?

Schopenhauer interpreted the term "disinterested" in a wholly personal way, basing it on an experience which he must have had quite regularly. There are few things about which he speaks with such assurance as the effect of esthetic contemplation. He claims that it counteracts the sexual "interest" (like lupulin and camphor), and he never tires of glorifying this release from the will as the great boon of the esthetic condition. One might even be tempted to ask whether he did not derive his basic conception of Will vs. Idea (the notion that only the Idea can deliver us from the Will) from a generalization of that sexual interest. (In all questions pertaining to Schopenhauer's philosophy we must never leave out of account that it was conceived by a young man of twenty-six; so that it partakes not only of the specific character of Schopenhauer but of the specific traits of that period of life.) Listen, for instance, to one of the most explicit of all the countless passages he has written extolling the esthetic condition (*The World as Will and Idea, I*), and you will hear the suffering, the happiness, the gratitude behind the words. "This is the painless condition which Epicurus praised as the highest good and the condition of the gods. For a moment we are delivered from the wretched urgency of the will; we celebrate the day of rest in the treadmill of volition; the wheel of Ixion stands still. . . ." What vehemence in these words, what images of pain and endless disgust! What an almost pathological time confrontation in the terms, "the moment" as against the "wheel of Ixion," the "treadmill of volition," the "wretched urgency of the will"! But assuming that Schopenhauer was one hundred per cent right in his own case, we might still ask what has really been gained for our understanding of the nature of beauty? Schopenhauer has described one effect of beauty, that it acts as a sedative of the will, but can it even be claimed that this is a regular effect? As I have pointed out, Stendhal, no less sensual a man than Schopenhauer but more happily constituted, stresses a very different effect of beauty: "it promises happiness." For him it is precisely the excitement of the will, of "interest," through beauty that matters. And might one not urge against Schopenhauer himself that he was quite wrong in seeing himself as a Kantian, that he had failed to understand Kant's definition as its author intended it? That he too responded to beauty from an interested motive, even out of the strongest, most personal interest, that of the tortured man seeking release from his torment? If we now return to our original question, "What does it mean when a philosopher pays homage to the ascetic ideal?" we receive our first clue: he craves release from a torture.

VII

Let us not immediately pull a long face at the word *torture*; there is plenty to offset it, to mitigate it—there will even be something left over to laugh about. We must take account of the fact that Schopenhauer, who treated sexuality (including woman, that *instrumentum diaboli*) as a personal enemy, absolutely required enemies to keep him in good spirits; that he loved atrabilious words, that he fulminated for the sake of fulminating, out of passion; that he would have sickened, become a *pessimist* (which he was not, much as he would have liked to be) had he been deprived of his enemies, of Hegel, of woman, of sensuality, of the human will to survival. You may be certain that without these Schopenhauer would not have stayed, he would have run away. It was his enemies who kept him alive. Just as with the ancient Cynics, his rage was his balm, his recreation, his compensation, his specific against tedium, in short, his happiness. This much in regard to what is most personal in the case of Schopenhauer; but there is, on the other hand, something typical about it too, and this brings us back to our main issue. Wherever there have been philosophers, from India to England (to indicate the opposite extremes of speculative orientation), there has prevailed a special philosopher's resentment against sensuality; Schopenhauer is only the most eloquent, and, for him who has ears to hear, the most delightful exponent of that resentment. There likewise exists a properly philosophical prejudice in favor of the ascetic ideal, let us make no mistake about it. Both dispositions, as I have said, are *typical*; if a philosopher lacks them, we may be sure that he is spurious. What does that *mean?* For it is our duty to interpret such a state of affairs, which in itself simply stands there stupidly to all eternity, like every thing-in-itself. Every animal, including *la bête philosophe*, strives instinctively for the optimum conditions under which it may release its powers. Every animal, instinctively and with a subtle flair that leaves reason far behind, abhors all interference that might conceivably block its path to that optimum. (The path I am speaking of does not lead to "happiness" but to power, to the most energetic activity, and in a majority of cases to actual unhappiness.) Thus the philosopher abhors marriage and all that would persuade him to marriage, for he sees the married state as an obstacle to fulfillment. What great philosopher has ever been married? Heracleitus, Plato, Descartes, Spinoza, Leibniz, Kant, Schopenhauer—not one of them was married; moreover, it is impossible to imagine any of them married. I maintain that a married philosopher belongs in comedy, and as for that great exception, Socrates, it would almost seem that the malicious Socrates got married in a spirit of irony, precisely in order to prove that contention. Every philosopher would speak as Buddha spoke when he was told that a son had been born to him: "Rāhula has been born to me; a fetter has been forged for me" (Rāhula means "little daemon"). Every free spirit would be set thinking, provided he had ever stopped thinking, just as it once happened to Buddha: " 'Close and oppressive is life in a house, a place of impurity; to leave the house is freedom' and, thus meditating, he left the house." The ascetic ideal suggests so many bridges to independence that a philosopher cannot help rejoicing as he listens to the story of all those resolute men who one day made up their minds to say "no" to every form of servitude and went forth into a desert—even if they were really only strong mules, and as far as possible from being strong spirits. What, then, does the ascetic ideal betoken in a philosopher? The reader will have guessed my answer before now. Asceticism provides him with the condition most favorable to the exercise of his intelligence. Far from denying "existence," he affirms his existence, and his alone, perhaps even to the point of *hubris: pereat mundus, fiat philosophia, fiat philosophus, fiam!*

VIII

It is clear: these philosophers are by no means unprejudiced witnesses and judges of the value of the ascetic ideal. They think only of themselves; what are saints to them? They think of the things they cannot do without: freedom from constraint, interference, noise, business, duties, worries; a clear head, the free, joyous play of the mind; a bracing air, thin, clear, free, dry as mountain air, in which all animal being becomes sublimated and takes wing; peace in all the basements; all the dogs well chained, no baying of enmity and bushy rancor; no pangs of frustrated ambition; modest and submissive bowels, industrious as mill wheels, but remote; a heart estranged, distant, turned to the future, posthumous. In short, theirs is the serene asceticism of a divinely winged animal that soars above life but does not alight on it. We all know the three mighty slogans of the ascetic ideal: poverty, humility, chastity, and when we examine the lives of the great productive spirits closely, we are bound to find all three present in some degree. Not, to be sure, as their "virtues"— what have such men to do with virtue?—but as the most natural conditions of their optimum existence, their strongest productivity. It might very well be that their dominant intellectual discipline had first to curb a boundless and sensitive pride, or a reckless sensuality, or that they found it difficult at first to maintain their will to seclusion in the face of a taste for luxury and refinement, or a prodigality of heart and hand. But, being their dominant instinct, that sense of discipline will always prevail in the end and succeed in controlling all other instincts. There is nothing "virtuous" about all this. By the way, that "desert" into which strong, independent minds like to withdraw is very different from the image our pseudo-intellectuals have of it; in fact, often enough our pseudo-intellectuals *are* themselves that desert. And it is a foregone conclusion that mere mimes of the intellect could not endure it for a moment, for it is not romantic or Syrian enough for them, not sufficiently stagey. (Though there is no lack of camels in it, to be sure.) A deliberate obscurity; a side-stepping of fame; a backing away from noise, adulation, accolades, influence; a modest position, a quotidian existence, something which hides more than it reveals; occasional intercourse with harmless and gay birds and beasts, the sight of which refreshes; a mountainside for company, not a blind one but one with lakes for eyes; sometimes even a room at a crowded inn where one is sure of being mistaken for somebody else and may securely speak to anyone: such is our desert, and believe me, it is lonely enough. I admit that when Heracleitus retired into the courtyards and colonnades of the vast Temple of Artemis he dwelt in a nobler kind of desert—why don't we have such temples? (But perhaps we do not lack them altogether; I just happen to remember the handsomest study I ever had, on the Piazza di San Marco, given spring and the time of day between ten o'clock and noon.) Yet the things which Heracleitus fled from were the very same things we are still anxious to avoid: the democratic chatter of the Ephesians, their politics, the latest news of the "empire" (Persia, mind you), their up-to-date penny-arcade trumpery. For philosophers need peace above all, today more than ever. We reverence all that is quiet, cold, distinguished, distant and past, whatever does not, as we look at it, make us taut and put us on the defensive, whatever we can converse with without having to shout. It is only necessary to listen to the tone of a mind as it speaks; every mind has its special timbre, and is fond of that timbre. The man over there, for example, must be an agitator, that is to say a nincompoop: whatever enters his head comes out dull and thick, fraught with the echo of great hollow spaces. That other one always sounds hoarse; is it possible that he has *thought* himself hoarse? It is indeed possible—ask the physiologists. But whoever thinks *words* is an orator, not a thinker; he betrays that he does not think *things* but only in respect of things; he really thinks only of himself and his listeners. And there is a third one who speaks importunately, buttonholes us, breathes on us (we automatically shut our mouths, even though he addresses us through a book: the timbre of his style gives him away) telling us that he is pressed for time, that he finds it difficult to believe in himself, that he must speak now or never. Yet a mind sure of itself speaks quietly, seeks out hidden places, is in no hurry. It is easy to tell a philosopher: he avoids three shiny, loud things—fame, princes, and women; which is not to say that they won't seek him out. He avoids glare, and for this reason he avoids his own time and the "light" of its day. In this he is like a shadow: the more the sun goes down, the larger he grows. As regards his "humility," he can tolerate a certain dependency and eclipse as he can tolerate darkness. What is more, he is fearful of being disturbed by lightning: he shies at the condition of a tree that is too isolated and unprotected, on which every storm can vent its caprice, and every caprice its storm. His "maternal" instinct, that secret love for what is growing in him, recommends to the philosopher conditions that dispense him from thinking about himself, much as woman's maternal instinct has fostered her dependent condition. He really asks for very little. His motto is "We are owned by the things we own"—again, not from virtue, from a meritorious sense of frugality and simplicity, but rather because the power that rules him wisely and inexorably demands it. That power is concerned with only one thing, and it dedicates its time, energy, love, interest to that one sole end. The philosopher hates to be disturbed by either enmities or friendships; he easily forgets or despises. He considers martyrdom in bad taste; to "suffer for the truth" he leaves to ambitious and histrionic persons or to any others who have time on their hands (he is obliged to *do something* for the truth). Big words he uses sparingly, and it is said that even the word "truth" goes against his grain: it has a vainglorious ring. . . . Finally, regarding the "chastity" of the philosopher, it should be clear that his fruitfulness does not lie in begetting children. The perpetuation of his name, his small immortality, must come through other means. (The philosophers of ancient India expressed it rather more haughtily: "Why should he have progeny, whose soul is the world?") All this has nothing to do with chastity, in the sense of ascetic scruple or hatred of the flesh, any more than it is chastity when an athlete or jockey practices sexual continence. It is simply the mandate of his dominant instinct, at least during the great periods of pregnancy. Every artist is familiar with the adverse effect which sexual intercourse has during times of great intellectual tension and preparation. The strongest and instinctually surest among them do not need to learn this by experience, since their "maternal" instinct has from the start made its strict dispositions, putting all animal instincts at the service of that one great end, so that the lesser energy is absorbed by the greater.

The case of Schopenhauer should be viewed in the light of this interpretation. Contact with beauty released the central energy of his nature (i.e. his profound speculative energy), making it explode and thus, at a stroke, assume mastery of his consciousness. Yet I do not mean by this to exclude the possibility that the peculiar sweetness and richness proper to the esthetic condition may stem from its sensual ingredient—just as the "idealism" of nubile girls may be traced to the same source. It may well be that the emergence of the esthetic condition does not suspend sensuality, as Schopenhauer believed, but merely transmutes it in such a way that it is no longer experienced as a sexual incentive. I shall return to this notion another time, in connection with even more delicate problems of the "physiology" of esthetics, an area that to this day has scarcely been touched.

IX

We have seen that a certain asceticism, that is to say a strict yet high-spirited continence, is among the necessary conditions of strenuous intellectual activity as well as one of its natural consequences. So it cannot surprise us to find that philosophers have always treated the ascetic ideal with a certain fondness. Careful historical analysis will show an even closer tie between the ascetic ideal and philosophy. It might be claimed that philosophy took its first steps with the help of the leading strings of that ideal—awkwardly indeed, and reluctantly, always on the verge of losing its balance and falling on its face. It was the case with the first philosophers, as with all good things at their inception, that they were continually looking around for someone to help them and at the same time were afraid of all onlookers. It is enough to rehearse the traditional motivations and virtues of the philosopher: his bent toward scepticism, toward negation, toward suspension of judgment, toward analysis, toward neutrality and objectivity. Has it ever been fully realized that for the longest time all these tendencies ran counter to the requirements of accepted ethics (not to mention *reason* in this connection, which even Luther in his day called "Madame Sophistry, the clever whore")? That if a philosopher had taken cognizance of himself, he would have had to recognize himself as a trespasser on forbidden ground, and that in consequence he was at the greatest pains to avoid such cognizance? But the same has been true of all the good things upon which we pride ourselves these days. Even measured by the Greek standard, our whole modern existence, insofar as it is not weakness but power and the consciousness of power, looks like sheer *hubris* and impiety: things exactly contrary to the ones we reverence today had for the longest time conscience on their side and God for their guardian. Our whole attitude toward nature, our violation of nature with the help of machines and the heedless ingenuity of technicians and engineers, is *hubris*; so is our attitude to God as some putative spider weaving purposes and ethics behind a vast web of causation (we might say what Charles the Bold said of his fight with Louis XI, *"Je combats l'universelle araignée"*); so is our attitude toward ourselves, upon whom we perform experiments which we would never perform on any animal, cheerfully and curiously splitting open the soul, while the body still breathes. What do we care any longer for the "salvation" of the soul? And afterwards we cure ourselves. We have no doubt today that sickness is instructive, much more instructive than health, and seem to require "contaminators" even more than we do medicine men or saviours. We violate ourselves, nutcrackers of the soul, questionable questioners, as though life were nothing but a cracking of nuts. Does this not make us every day more questionable but also more worth questioning, perhaps more worthy to be alive? All good things have at one time been considered evil; every original sin has, at some point, turned into an original virtue. Marriage, for example, was looked upon for a long time as an infraction of the rights of the community: a man so presumptuous as to want a wife to himself had to atone for his presumption by paying a penalty. (Another example of the same development is the *jus primae noctis,* which in Cambodia is still the prerogative of the priests, those guardians of the "old tradition.") The gentle, benevolent, indulgent, compassionate feelings, whose value has latterly risen so high that they have almost become absolutes, for centuries brought self-contempt in their train: men were ashamed of their meekness, even as today they are ashamed of their severity (cf. my remarks on that subject in *Beyond Good and Evil*). As for man's submission to the *law,* we all know how men's consciences all over the world rebelled against a law that would wrest from them the right of vendetta. For a long time the "law" continued to be a *vetitum,* a heinous and radical innovation, a force in submitting to which one felt shamed before one's own conscience. Every step taken on this earth by our ancestors has been paid for with the greatest torments of body and mind. In *Daybreak* I wrote: "Not progress alone but simple change, simple movement, has had its countless martyrs." Nothing could be more alien to us today than this point of view. "Nothing was ever bought more dearly than the small portion of human reason and freedom that is now our pride. And it is that pride which makes it almost impossible for us today to imagine the vast tracts of ritual ethics which, as the truly determining history, precede our world history; those times when suffering, cruelty, dissimulation, vengeance, irrationality were all seen as virtues; well-being, intellectual curiosity, peace, and compassion as dangers; to be pitied and to labor as disgraces; madness as something divine, and change as immoral and a herald of disaster."

x

In that same book I have explained under what pressures the earliest inquirers had to live; how, when they were not feared, they were despised. Speculation made its first appearance on this earth under disguise, with an ambiguous look, an evil heart, and often a frightened head. There was something inactive, brooding, unaggressive about these sages which inspired profound distrust. They had no other resource against this distrust than to inspire fear themselves. (The old Brahmans excelled at this as much as any.) Our ancient philosophers knew how to endow their existence with a solidity and depth of meaning which made them feared; but on closer inspection we discover that they were concerned with something even more fundamental, with inspiring an awe of themselves in their own hearts. As men of a heroic age, they did this by heroic means. Self-inflicted cruelty, ingenious self-castigation, was the principal instrument of these power-hungry anchorites and innovators, who had first of all to subdue tradition and the gods in themselves in order to be able to *believe* in their new departure. I wish to refer the reader here to the famous story of King Vishvamitra, who, after millennia of self-torture, acquired such a sense of power and confidence in himself that he undertook to build a new heaven. Here we have a majestic parable of the most ancient as well as the most modern philosopher's development. Whoever, at any time, has undertaken to build a new heaven has found the strength for it in his own hell. . . . To formulate this whole state of affairs briefly, we may say that, in order to be able to function at all, philosophers have always had to present themselves in the guise of some accepted type of sage, preferably religious—as priest, warlock, soothsayer, and the like. For a very long time the ascetic ideal served the philosopher as the sole phenomenal guise under which he could exist *qua* philosopher: he had to *represent* that ideal in order to assert himself as philosopher; but in order to represent it he had to believe in it. The peculiarly withdrawn, anti-sensual, austere attitude of philosophers, which has persisted to this day and has actually come to be seen as the philosophical attitude *par excellence,* is really the product of the emergency in which philosophy found itself at its inception. That is to say, for an unconscionably long time philosophy would not have been possible without an ascetic disguise, an ascetic misinterpretation of motive. Until quite recent times the ascetic priesthood continued to furnish the larval form, repulsive and somber, under which alone philosophy could survive and crawl about. Have things really changed? Has the glittering and dangerous insect hidden in the larva really been released from its prison, thanks to a sunnier, warmer, brighter ambience? Is there really enough pride, courage, self-assurance, intellectual energy, responsibility, *freedom of the will,* to make philosophy possible in our world today?

XI

Only now that we have focused on the role of the ascetic priest can we really come to grips with our original problem. Only now that we are face to face with the classical representative of "seriousness" can we talk seriously. "What does seriousness really mean?" we may be tempted to ask at this point. This is a question properly within the province of the moral physiologist, but we must pass it over for the time being. The ascetic priest derived from his ideal not only his faith but also his determination, his power, his interest. His *raison d'être* stands or falls with the ascetic ideal. Should it surprise us, then, that those of us who oppose that ideal come up against a powerful enemy, an enemy willing to fight to the bitter end against all who would discount it? On the other hand, it does not seem likely that such a prejudiced view of our problem will give us much help toward solving it. The ascetic priest will scarcely succeed even in vindicating his ideal, for the same reason that a woman is not likely to succeed in vindicating femininity; much less can we expect to find in him an objective judge of the question mooted here. Rather than having to fear that he will brilliantly controvert us, we will probably need to furnish him with arguments against us. . . . The moot point is the value which the ascetic priest places on existence. He confronts existence (comprising all of "nature," our whole transitory terrestrial world) with a differently constituted kind of Being, which it must oppose and exclude—unless it wishes to turn against itself; in which case our earthly existence may be viewed as a bridge to transcendence. The ascetic treats life as a maze in which we must retrace our steps to the point at which we entered or as an error which only a resolute act can correct, and he further *insists* that we conduct our lives conformably to his ideal. This appalling code of ethics is by no means a curious, isolated incident in the history of mankind; rather it is one of its broadest and longest traditions. An observer viewing our terrestrial existence from another planet might easily be persuaded that this earth is strictly an ascetic star, the habitation of disgruntled, proud, repulsive creatures, unable to rid themselves of self-loathing, hatred of the earth and of all living things, who inflict as much pain as possible on themselves, solely out of pleasure in giving pain—perhaps the only kind of pleasure they know. Simply consider how worldwide and regular is the occurrence of the ascetic priest. The type is not confined to a single race: he thrives everywhere; all classes of society produce him. Not that he propagates his code of ethics through biological reproduction—quite the contrary, a profound instinct deters him from reproducing his kind. Surely it must be a necessity of the first rank that makes this anti-biological species emerge and thrive again and again; if such a contradiction in terms does not die out, it must surely be in the interest of life itself. For an ascetic life is indeed a contradiction in terms. Here we find rancor without parallel, the rancor of an insatiable power-drive which would dominate, not a single aspect of life, but life itself, its deepest and strongest foundations. Here we witness an attempt to use energy to block the very sources of energy. Here the eye looks enviously and malevolently on all biological growth and on its principal expressions, beauty and joy, while it gazes with delight on all that is misshapen or stunted, on pain, disaster, ugliness, on gratuitous sacrifice, on unselving and self-castigation. All this is paradoxical to the highest degree. We are face to face with a deliberate split, which gloats on its own discomfiture and grows more self-assured and triumphant the more its biological energy decreases. The ascetic ideal has always fought under a banner bearing the motto, "triumph in agony." This tempting riddle, this image of rapturous pain, has always been its source of illumination, its pledge of final victory. *Crux, nux, lux*— for the ascetic these three invariably go together.

XII

What will such perversity vent itself on, once it begins to philosophize? Obviously on whatever is generally felt to be most sure and most real. It will look for error precisely in those places where the normal life instinct has proclaimed truth most authoritatively. For example, like the ascetics of the *Vedas,* it will declare that body, pain, multiplicity, the subject/object dichotomy, are illusions. What a triumph to be able to deny reality to the ego—what a triumph over the senses, over appearance, what a great and cruel triumph when finally even reason is humbled! The height of sadistic pleasure is reached when reason in its self-contempt and self-mockery decrees that the realm of truth does indeed exist but that reason is debarred from it. (In the Kantian concept of the "noumenal" character of things we may discern a vestige of this prurient ascetic split which enjoys turning reason against itself. For the noumenal character, to Kant, signifies that aspect of things about which the intellect knows only that it can never comprehend it.)—Yet precisely in our capacity as philosophers we must not be ungrateful for such radical inversions of customary perspectives and valuations, by means of which the human mind has all too long raged against itself, to all appearances recklessly and fruitlessly. It is no small discipline and preparation of the intellect on its road to final "objectivity" to see things for once through the wrong end of the telescope; and "objectivity" is not meant here to stand for "disinterested contemplation" (which is a rank absurdity) but for an ability to have one's pros and cons within one's command and to use them or not, as one chooses. It is of the greatest importance to know how to put the most diverse perspectives and psychological interpretations at the service of intellection. Let us, from now on, be on our guard against the hallowed philosophers' myth of a "pure, will-less, painless, timeless knower"; let us beware of the tentacles of such contradictory notions as "pure reason," "absolute knowledge," "absolute intelligence." All these concepts presuppose an eye such as no living being can imagine, an eye required to have no direction, to abrogate its active and interpretative powers—precisely those powers that alone make of seeing, seeing *something*. All seeing is essentially perspective, and so is all knowing. The more emotions we allow to speak in a given matter, the more different eyes we can put on in order to view a given spectacle, the more complete will be our conception of it, the greater our "objectivity." But to eliminate the will, to suspend the emotions altogether, provided it could be done—surely this would be to castrate the intellect, would it not?

XIII

But let us return to our argument. The kind of inner split we have found in the ascetic, who pits "life against life," is nonsense, not only in psychological terms, but also physiologically speaking. Such a split can only be *apparent*; it must be a kind of provisional expression, a formula, an adaptation, a psychological misunderstanding of something for which terms have been lacking to designate its true nature. A mere stopgap to fill a hiatus in human understanding. Let me state what I consider to be the actual situation. The ascetic ideal arises from the protective and curative instinct of a life that is degenerating and yet fighting tooth and nail for its preservation. It points to a partial physiological blocking and exhaustion, against which the deepest vital instincts, still intact, are battling doggedly and resourcefully. The ascetic ideal is one of their weapons. The situation, then, is exactly the opposite from what the worshipers of that ideal believe it to be. Life employs asceticism in its desperate struggle against death; the ascetic ideal is a dodge for the preservation of life. The ubiquitousness and power of that ideal, especially wherever men have adopted civilized forms of life, should impress upon us one great, palpable fact: the persistent morbidity of civilized man, his biological struggle against death, or to put it more exactly, against *taedium vitae*, exhaustion, the longing for "the end." The ascetic priest is an incarnation of the wish to be different, to be elsewhere; he *is* that wish, raised to its highest power, its most passionate intensity. And it is precisely the intensity of his wishing that forges the fetter binding him to this earth. At the same time he becomes an instrument for bettering the human condition, since by this intensity he is enabled to maintain in life the vast flock of defeated, disgruntled sufferers and self-tormentors, whom he leads instinctively like a shepherd. In other words, the ascetic priest, seemingly life's enemy and great negator, is in truth one of the major conserving and affirmative forces. . . . But what about the sources of man's morbidity? For certainly man is sicker, less secure, less stable, less firmly anchored than any other animal; he is the *sick* animal. But has he not also been more daring, more defiant, more inventive than all the other animals together?—man, the great experimenter on himself, eternally unsatisfied, vying with the gods, the beasts, and with nature for final supremacy; man, unconquered to this day, still unrealized, so agitated by his own teeming energy that his future digs like spurs into the flesh of every present moment. . . . How could such a brave and resourceful animal but be the most precarious, the most profoundly sick of all the sick beasts of the earth? There have been many times when man has clearly had enough; there have been whole epidemics of "fed-upness" (for example, around 1348, the time of the Dance of Death) but even this tedium, this weariness, this satiety breaks from him with such vehemence that at once it forges a new fetter to existence. As if by magic, his negations produce a wealth of tenderer affirmations. When this master of destruction, of self-destruction, wounds himself, it is that very wound that forces him to live.

XIV

The more regular morbidity becomes among the members of the human race, the more grateful we should be for the rare "windfalls"—men fortunate enough to combine a sound physical organization with intellectual authority. We should do our best to protect such men from the noxious air of the sickroom. It is the sick who are the greatest threat to the well; it is the weaklings, and not their own peers, who visit disaster upon the strong. But who, today, knows this, who acts on it? We try constantly to diminish man's fear of man; forgetting that it is the fear they inspire which forces the strong to be strong and, if need be, terrible. We should encourage that fear in every possible way, for it alone fosters a sound breed of men. The real danger lies in our loathing of man and our pity of him. If these two emotions should one day join forces, they would beget the most sinister thing ever witnessed on earth: man's *ultimate* will, his will to nothingness, nihilism. And indeed, preparations for that event are already well under way. One who smells not only with his nose but also with his eyes and ears will notice everywhere these days an air as of a lunatic asylum or sanatorium. (I am thinking of all the current cultural enterprises of man, of every kind of Europe now existing.) It is the diseased who imperil mankind, and not the "beasts of prey." It is the predestined failures and victims who undermine the social structure, who poison our faith in life and our fellow men. Is there anyone who has not encountered the veiled, shuttered gaze of the born misfit, that introverted gaze which saddens us and makes us imagine how such a man must speak to himself? "If only I could be someone else," the look seems to sigh, "but there's no hope of that. I am what I am; how could I get rid of myself? Nevertheless, I'm fed up." In the marshy soil of such self-contempt every poisonous plant will grow, yet all of it so paltry, so stealthy, so dishonest, so sickly-sweet! Here the worms of vindictiveness and *arrière-pensée* teem, the air stinks of secretiveness and pent-up emotion; here a perennial net of malicious conspiracy is woven—the conspiracy of the sufferers against the happy and successful; here victory is held in abomination. And what dissimulation, in order not to betray that this is hatred! What a display of grand attitudes and grandiose words! what an art of "honest calumny!" What noble eloquence flows from the lips of these ill-begotten creatures! What sugary, slimy, humble submissiveness swims in their eyes! What are they after, really? The ambition of these most abject invalids is to at least *mime* justice, love, wisdom, superiority. And how clever such an ambition makes them! For we cannot withhold a certain admiration for the counterfeiter's skill with which they imitate the coinage of virtue, even its golden ring. They have by now entirely monopolized virtue; "We alone," they say, "are the good, the just, we alone the Men of Good Will." They walk among us as warnings and reprimands incarnate, as though to say that health, soundness, strength, and pride are vicious things for which we shall one day pay dearly; and how eager they are, at bottom, to be the ones to make us pay! How they long to be the executioners! Among them are vindictive characters aplenty, disguised as judges, who carry the word *justice* in their mouths like a poisonous spittle and go always with pursed lips, ready to spit on all who do not look discontent, on all who go cheerfully about their business. Nor are there lacking among them those most unspeakably vain and loathsome frauds who are bent on parading as innocents, those moral masturbators who bring their stunted sensuality to the market swathed in rhymes and other swaddling clothes and labeled "one hundred per cent pure." Is there any place today where the sick do not wish to exhibit some form of superiority and to exercise their tyranny over the strong? Especially the sick females, who have unrivaled resources for dominating, oppressing, tyrannizing. The sick woman spares nothing dead or alive; she digs up the longest-buried things. (The Abyssinian Bogos say "Woman is a hyena.") One look into the background of every family, every institution, every commonwealth is enough to convince us that the battle of the sick against the well is raging on all sides; for the most part a quiet battle, conducted with small doses of poison, with pin-pricks, the insidious long-suffering look, but quite often too with the loud pharisaical gesture simulating noble indignation. The indignant barking of these sick dogs can be heard even in the sacred halls of science. (I need only remind the reader once more of that Prussian apostle of vindictiveness, Eugen Dühring, who today makes the most indecent and offensive use of moralistic claptrap. He stands out, even among his own crew of anti-Semites, by the vehemence of his moralistic drivel.) What would these men, so tireless in their masquerades, so insatiable in their thirst for vengeance, require in order to see themselves as triumphant? Nothing less than to succeed in implanting their own misery, and all misery, in the consciences of the happy, so as to make the happy one day say to one another, "It is a disgrace to be happy! *There is too much misery in the world!*" But no greater and more disastrous

misunderstanding could be imagined than for the strong
and happy to begin doubting their right to happiness. Let
us have done with such topsy-turviness, with such dreadful emasculation of feeling! Our first rule on this earth
should be that the sick must not contaminate the healthy.
But this requires that the healthy be isolated from the sick,
be spared even the sight of the sick, lest they mistake that
foreign sickness for their own. Or is it their task, perhaps,
to be medical attendants and doctors? There could be no
worse way for them to misjudge their role. The higher
must not be made an instrument of the lower; the "pathos
of distance" must to all eternity keep separate tasks separate. The right to exist of the full-toned bell is a thousand
times greater than that of the cracked, miscast one: it alone
heralds in the future of all mankind. What the healthy
can and should do must never be demanded of the sick,
or placed within their power; but how should the former
be able to do what they alone can do, and at the same
time act the part of physicians, comforters, saviors of the
sick? . . . Then let us have fresh air, and at any rate get
far away from all lunatic asylums and nursing homes of
culture! And let us have good company, our own company!
Or solitude, if need be. But let us get far away, at any
rate, from the evil vapor of internal corruption and dry
rot. In order, my friends, that we may, at least for a while
yet, guard ourselves against the two worst plagues which
perhaps lie in store for us more than anyone—unrelieved
loathing of man and unrelieved pity of him!

XV

If the reader has thoroughly grasped—and I demand that here especially he dig down deeply—that it cannot be the task of the healthy to wait on the sick, or to make them well, he will also have grasped another important thing: that for physicians and medical attendants we require men who are themselves sick. I believe that we have here the key to the meaning of the ascetic priest. We must look upon the ascetic priest as the predestined advocate and savior of a sick flock if we are to comprehend his tremendous historical mission. His dominion is over sufferers; he is instinctively propelled toward this empire, in which he can display his own peculiar gifts and even find a kind of happiness. He must be sick himself, he must be deeply akin to all the shipwrecked and diseased, if he is to understand them and be understood by them; yet he must also be strong, master over himself even more than over others, with a will to power that is intact, if he is to be their support, overlord, disciplinarian, tyrant, god. They are his flock, and he must defend them—against whom? Against the healthy, obviously, but also against their envy of the healthy; he must be the natural antagonist and *contemner* of all rude, violent, savage health and power. The priest is the earliest version of that delicate animal which contemns more readily than it hates. He would not be spared the task of warring with the beasts of prey, but his war will be a war of cunning ("intellect") rather than of brute force, as goes without saying. He might even be obliged to develop out of himself a new type of savage animal, or at least to adumbrate a new kind of ferocity in which the polar bear, the smooth, cold, patient tiger, and the fox would combine to form a new species, at once attractive and awe-inspiring. If the occasion should arise he might even step, with ursine dignity and calculated superiority, among the other wild animal species: herald and mouthpiece of even more mysterious powers, determined to sow in their midst pain, inner division, self-contradiction—confident of his rule over all sufferers. To be sure, he carries with him balms and ointments, but in order to cure he must first create patients. And even as he alleviates the pain of his patients he pours poison into their wounds. Such, then, is the supreme accomplishment of this magician and animal tamer, in whose orbit all that is sound becomes sick and all that is sick, tame. This strange shepherd actually succeeds very well in defending his sick flock. He defends them even against themselves, against all the wickedness and malice smoldering within the herd and whatever other troubles are bred among the sick. He fights a clever, hard, secret battle against anarchy and disintegration, always aware of the piling-up of rancor, that most dangerous of dynamites. His essential task is to set off the dynamite in such a way that the blast will injure neither himself nor the herd. In other words, it is up to the priest to redirect resentment toward a new object. For is it not true that every sufferer instinctively seeks a cause for his suffering; more specifically, an agent, a "guilty" agent who is susceptible to pain—in short some living being or other on whom he can vent his feelings directly or in effigy, under some pretext or other? The release of aggression is the best palliative for any kind of affliction. The wish to alleviate pain through strong emotional excitation is, to my mind, the true physiological motive behind all manifestations of resentment. I strongly disagree with those who would see here a mere defensive or prophylactic reaction to sudden injury or jeopardy, a mere reflex, such as a headless frog makes to throw off an acid. There is a fundamental difference between the two processes: in the one case the effort is simply to prevent further injury, in the other to *dull* by means of some violent emotion a secret, tormenting pain that is gradually becoming intolerable—to banish it momentarily from consciousness. For that purpose an emotion of maximum violence is required, and any pretext that comes to hand will serve. "*Somebody* must be responsible for my discomfort." This sort of reasoning is universal among sick people and holds all the more sway over them the more obscure the real physiological cause of their discomfort is to them. (That cause may lie in an affection of the sympathetic nerve, or an excessive secretion of bile, or a deficiency of alkaline sulphates and phosphates in the blood, or an abdominal obstruction which impedes the circulation of the blood, or a disorder of the ovaries, etc.) All sufferers alike excel in finding imaginary pretexts for their suffering. They revel in suspicion and gloat over imaginary injuries and slights; they ransack the bowels of their past and present for obscure and dubious incidents which give free rein to their torturous suspicions; they intoxicate themselves with the poison of their own minds. They tear open the most ancient wounds, fasten the guilt on friend, wife, child—whatever is closest to them. Every suffering sheep says to himself, "I suffer; it must be somebody's fault." But his shepherd, the ascetic priest, says to him, "You are quite right, my sheep, somebody must be at fault here, but that somebody is yourself. You alone are to blame—you alone are to blame for yourself." This is not only very bold but also abundantly false.

But one thing, at least, has been accomplished: resentment has found a new target.

By now the reader should perceive what life's curative instinct, through the agency of the ascetic priest, has at least *tried* to accomplish, and what end is served by the temporary tyranny of such paradoxical and sophistical concepts as *guilt, sin* or *sinfulness, perdition, damnation.* The end is always to render the sick, up to a certain point, harmless, to make the incurable destroy themselves and to introvert the resentment of the less severely afflicted. In other words, the goal is to utilize the evil instincts of all sufferers for the purposes of self-discipline, self-surveillance, self-conquest. It goes without saying that a "medication" of this sort can never result in a physiologically effective cure, nor can it even be claimed that the vital instinct has really been tapped for the rehabilitation of the personality. All that this method achieved for a long time was the organization and concentration of the sick on one side (the word *church* is the popular term for this grouping), and a kind of provisional sequestration of the sounder and more fully "achieved" on the other; in short, the opening up of a chasm between sickness and health. And yet this was a great deal. (I proceed in this essay on an assumption which, addressing the kind of reader I do, I need not laboriously justify. I assume that sinfulness is not a basic human condition but merely the ethico-religious interpretation of physiological distemper.—The fact that a person thinks himself "guilty" or "sinful" is no proof that he *is* so, any more than the fact that a person feels healthy is a proof of his health. Take, for example, the famous witch trials. In those days even the most acute and humane judges had not the faintest doubt that the witches were guilty. The "witches" themselves had no doubt, and yet there was no guilt.—To state my assumption somewhat more broadly: "psychological pain" is not a fact but merely a causal interpretation of a set of facts which so far have eluded exact formulation—really no more than a fat word taking the place of a vague question mark. If anyone is unable to get rid of a psychological pain, the fault lies not in his "psyche" but, more likely, in his belly [to put it crudely, which does not mean that it should be understood crudely]. . . . The strong, healthy person digests his experiences [including every deed and misdeed] as he does his meals, even though he may have swallowed a tough morsel. If he can't get rid of an experience, then this kind of indigestion is every bit as physical as the other, and often, in fact, merely one of the consequences of the other. Let me add that one may hold such notions and yet be an enemy of all materialism.)

XVII

But is our ascetic priest really a physician?—We have already seen that it is scarcely correct to call him a physician, much as he likes to see himself venerated as a savior. What he combats is only the discomfort of the sufferer, not the cause of his suffering, not even the condition of illness itself. This must always be our principal objection to priestly cures. But once we place ourselves in the position of the priest and adopt his perspective, we cannot fail to admire the great variety of things he has discovered and thought about. His genius will then be found to reside in his endless ability to alleviate and comfort. How resourcefully he has conceived his solacing task, how bold and unscrupulous he has been in his choice of methods! Christianity has been the richest treasure house of ingenious nostrums. Never have so many restoratives, palliatives, narcotics been gathered together in one place, never has so much been risked for that end, never has so much subtlety been employed in guessing what stimulants will relieve the deep depression, the leaden fatigue, the black melancholy of the physiologically incapacitated. For, to put it quite generally, the main object of all great religions has been to counteract a certain epidemic malaise due to unreleased tension. It may safely be assumed that large masses of the earth's population periodically suffer from physiological anxiety which, however, from lack of adequate physiological knowledge is not understood as such; whereupon religion steps in with its staple of psychological and moral remedies. This anxiety or distemper may be due to a variety of causes. It may result from a crossing of races too dissimilar (or of classes too dissimilar. Class distinctions are always indicative of genetic and racial differences: the European *Weltschmerz* and the pessimism of the nineteenth century were both essentially the results of an abrupt and senseless mixing of classes); or from an unsuccessful emigration, from a race finding itself in a climate to which it is not entirely adapted (the case of the Hindu in India); or from the senescence of a race (the Parisian brand of pessimism from 1850 onward); or from faulty diet (the alcoholism of the middle ages, or the vegetarian absurdity); or from bad blood, malaria, syphilis (the great depression after the Thirty Years' War, which infected one half of Germany with disease and thus pre-

pared the ground for German servility and pusillanimity).
In each of these cases a battle had to be waged against
anxiety.—Let us now briefly review the main forms and
practices of that battle. (I shall leave on one side here, as
is only fair, the traditional philosophers' battle against
anxiety, which is always synchronous with that other.
This battle, though by no means devoid of interest, is too
abstruse, too remote from practical life, too tangential and
finespun—as when, for example, philosophers try to prove
that pain is an error, under the illusion that the pain will
vanish once the error is recognized; yet lo and behold! it
refuses to vanish. . . .) The first of the means used is to
reduce the vital energy to its lowest point. If possible,
there should be no willing, no wishing at all; nothing that
would excite the blood (no salt, the hygiene of the fakir);
no love; no hate; equanimity; no retaliation; no acquisi-
tion of riches; no work; mendicancy; preferably no woman,
or as little woman as possible; in intellectual matters,
Pascal's maxim, "We must stultify ourselves." The result,
in psychological and moral terms, is self-abrogation, sancti-
fication. In physiological terms, it is hypnosis—the attempt
to achieve for man something approximating the hiberna-
tion of certain animal species or the estivation of many
plants in tropical climates; a minimum of energetic processes, a state in which the vital functions persist without,
however, emerging into consciousness. To this end an extraordinary amount of human resourcefulness has been
employed—and not altogether in vain. There can be no
doubt that those "sportsmen" of sanctity, in whom all nations and cultures have abounded, have in fact found true
deliverance from the thing they combatted with such rig-
orous training. Their cabinet of hypnotic drugs has actually helped them, in countless instances, to overcome their

profound physiological depression, and for this reason their methods cannot be discounted by the anthropologist. Nor are we justified in viewing any intention to starve the body and emotions as a symptom of madness, as some beef-eating freethinkers and Christopher Slys would have us do. Yet it is certainly true that a regimen of this kind may lead to all kinds of mental disorders, to the "mystic and ethereal light" of the Hesychasts on Mount Athos, to visual and auditory hallucinations, to voluptuous inundations and ecstasies (St. Theresa). Though it goes without saying that the subjects' own explanations of these phenomena have always been extravagantly false, we cannot fail to notice the sincere gratitude that makes them *want* to give explanations of this kind. Redemption itself, that final, complete hypnosis and tranquillity, appears as the supreme mystery in all such accounts, which even the highest symbols cannot fully express. It is viewed as a return to the ground of being, a deliverance from all illusion, as "knowledge," "truth," as a release from all objects, desires and acts, a state beyond good and evil. "Good and evil," says the Buddhist, "are both fetters; the Awakened One has triumphed over both." "Neither the done nor the undone," says the Vedic Brahmin, "gives him (the sage) pain; his dominion is no longer marred by any action; he has left both good and evil behind." Clearly the notion is common to Buddhism and Brahmanism. Neither the Hindu nor the Christian believes that such redemption can be reached by the path of virtue, of moral improvement, no matter how highly both regard the hypnotic value of virtue. The fact that they have been staunchly realistic in this regard is much to the credit of the three greatest religions, otherwise so thoroughly riddled with moralizing. "There is no such thing as duty for him who has knowledge. . . . Redemption is not achieved through the adding of virtues, for it consists in union with Brahma, to whose perfection nothing can be added; nor yet through the discarding of faults, for Brahma, with whom to be united spells redemption, is pure forever." (Both these passages are taken from Shankara's *Commentaries,* cited by the first European expert on Indian philosophy, my friend Paul Deussen.) Let us then give due honor to the concept of redemption in the great religions. On the other hand we might find it difficult to suppress a smile when we see how extravagantly these weary souls, too weary even for dreaming, prize deep sleep—deep sleep standing for the entry of the soul into Brahma, the accomplished mystical union. "When he is fast asleep," the oldest and most venerable scripture tells us, "and so completely at rest that he no longer sees any dream image, then, O my Beloved, he is at one with Him Who Is, he has returned to himself. Enwrapped by the cognitive self, he no longer has any consciousness of what is inner and what is outer. Over this bridge neither day nor night comes, neither age nor death, neither suffering nor good or ill deed." "In profound sleep the soul is lifted out of the body, enters the highest sphere of light, and thus puts on its true identity. It becomes the Supreme Spirit, who walks about, dallies, plays and amuses himself, whether with women, or chariots, or friends. The soul no longer thinks of its appendage, the body, to which the prāna (the breath of life) is harnessed like a draught animal to a cart." Yet we must not forget that we find here, under the sumptuous robe of oriental extravagance, the same kind of appraisal as in Epicurus, that classically cool, limpid, but suffering Greek. No person who suffers deeply and is deeply out of tune can help viewing the hypnotic nirvana, the peace of profound sleep, as the greatest of goods, as the positive value *par excellence*. (Following the same emotional logic, all pessimistic religions bestow upon nothingness the title of God.)

XVIII

Such hypnotic damping of the sensibilities, of the sense of pain, presupposes rather exceptional aptitudes, notably courage, contempt for public opinion, intellectual stoicism. Much more common, because much easier, is another regimen for combatting depression: mechanical activity. There is no doubt that such activity can appreciably alleviate man's suffering. Nowadays it is spoken of rather dishonestly as "the blessing of labor." It brings relief by turning the attention of the sufferer away from his suffering. Since he is constantly preoccupied with doing, there is little room left in his mind for suffering—the chamber of man's consciousness is pretty narrow, after all. Mechanical activity, with its numerous implications (regular performance, punctual and automatic obedience, unvarying routine, a sanctioning, even an enjoining of impersonality, self-oblivion)—how thoroughly and subtly has the ascetic priest made use of it in his battle against pain! All he has had to do, especially when dealing with sufferers of the lower classes, slaves or prisoners (or women, who as a rule are both things), has been to exercise a little art of name changing in order to make them see as blessings things which hitherto they had abominated. The dissatisfaction of the slave with his lot has not, at any rate, been an invention of the priest.—An even more highly prized specific against depression has been the ministration of small pleasures, which are readily accessible and can be made routine. This form of medication is frequently associated with the preceding one. The most common form of curative pleasure is the pleasure of "giving pleasure" (i.e. charity, the alleviation of stress, comforting, praise, friendly advice). In prescribing love of one's neighbor, the ascetic priest really prescribes an excitation of the strongest, most affirmative urge there is (the will to power), albeit in most cautious doses. The satisfaction of "minimum superiority," which is provided by all charitable, helpful, encouraging acts, is the best tonic for the physiologically incapacitated, so long as it be well administered; otherwise the same fundamental instinct causes them to hurt one another. In the documents of early Christianity we find mention of mutual-aid societies, organizations to assist the poor and the sick and for the burial of the dead, all sprung from the lowest social stratum, and all using, advisedly, the small pleasure, the doing of mutual good, as a specific against depression. Perhaps in those days it was something new, a real discovery? Inevitably such a will to mutual aid, such a movement to form organizations and congregations, must gradually develop the will to power far beyond its original narrow scope; the creation of *masses* is an important step in the battle against depression. With the development of the congregation, the individual too is given a new interest, which often lifts him beyond his private ill-humor, his distaste for himself (Geulincx's *despectio sui*). All sick and morbid persons instinctively long to be organized, out of a desire to shake off their feeling of weakness and tedium. The ascetic priest divines that instinct and promotes it. Wherever mass congregations arise we may be sure that they have been demanded by the instinct of weakness and organized by the shrewdness of priests. For there is one thing we must not leave out of account: it is every bit as natural for the strong to disaggregate as for the weak to congregate. Whenever the former join forces, it is done solely in view of some concerted aggressive action, some gratification of the will to power, and invariably against the resistance of individual consciences. The latter, on the other hand, derive delight from the very fact of organization. Their gregarious instinct is deeply gratified thereby, just as the instinct of the born ruler is profoundly disturbed and irritated by any demand for organization. The entire course of history bears out the fact that every oligarchy conceals a desire for tyranny. Every oligarchy vibrates with the tension which each individual member must maintain in order to master that desire. (So it was in Greece, for example, as Plato bears witness in a hundred places, Plato who knew his own kind, as well as himself. . . .)

XIX

The ascetic specifics which we have dealt with so far (the damping of the vital spirits; mechanical activity; the "small pleasure" and especially the "love of one's fellow"; mass organization; the dawn of power in the congregation, which enabled the individual to forget his troubles in the joy he felt at the success of the group) seem all, by modern standards, quite harmless remedies for corporate doldrums. Let us now turn our attention to the more interesting deleterious drugs. They all have one characteristic in common: extravagance of feeling, the strongest anodyne for a long, dull, enervating pain. Endless priestly ingenuity has been exercised on the question, "How can we produce extravagance of feeling?" This may sound rather severe; it would obviously sound pleasanter if I said, for instance: "The ascetic priest has at all times tried to make use of the element of *enthusiasm* present in any strong emotion." But why should I caress further the ears of our modern milk-sops, who are already effeminate enough? Why should *we* give an inch to their verbal hypocrisy? For a psychologist this would amount to a flagrant *act* of hypocrisy, quite apart from the fact that it would sicken us. For the "good taste" of a psychologist—others may call it his integrity—resides today in his determination to resist the wretched moralizing jargon which has covered all modern judg-ments of men and affairs with its slime. Let us not deceive ourselves: the essential characteristic of modern minds and modern books is not that they lie, but rather that they show a dogged *innocence* in their moralistic hypocrisy. To have to unearth everywhere this kind of innocence is perhaps the most distasteful of all the present-day psy-chologist's painful labors, for precisely here lies one of our own great perils: the source of a vast loathing. . . . I have no doubt what use posterity will make of all modern books and other cultural products (provided they last, of which there is however no danger, and further provided that a generation will arise one day whose taste is stricter, harder, sounder): it will use them as emetics, because of their mawkishness, their deep-dyed feminism under the mask of "idealism." Our educated men and women are "too good" to lie; that much is true, but it is certainly not a point in their favor. The honest-to-goodness "lie" (whose value is fully discussed in Plato) would be something far too strict and strong for them; it would demand of them something that must not be demanded, namely that they take a good look at their own egos, that they try to distinguish between the true and false in themselves. Their province is the "dishonest" lie. The "good" of today are, to a man, determined to treat every issue in a spirit of profound hypocrisy—innocent, straightforward, true-blue hypocrisy. These "good" people are so totally bemoralized and lost to all honesty that none of them could withstand a truth concerning man. Or, to put it more palpably, not one of them could face a *true* biography. Here are a few proofs: Lord Byron noted down a very few personal things about himself, but Thomas Moore was too "good" for them; he burned his friend's papers. The same has been said of Dr. Gwinner, for Schopenhauer too had jotted down something about himself, possibly against himself. Beethoven's biographer, the solid American Thayer, abruptly stopped in the middle of his work; having arrived at a certain point in this noble and naïve life, he couldn't take it any longer. Should we be surprised, then, that no intelligent person today cares to say an honest word about himself, unless he is bent on asking for trouble? There has been some talk of a forthcoming autobiography of Richard Wagner: who can doubt that it will be a very *cautious* autobiography? Finally, let us remember the ridiculous outcry which the Catholic priest Jansenius aroused throughout Protestant Germany with his incredibly simplistic and innocuous account of the Reformation. What would people say if someone suddenly decided to treat that whole movement in a different spirit? If one day an authentic psychologist decided to tell the story of the real Luther, no longer with the moralistic simplicity of a country parson, nor with the mawkishness and excessive discretion of our Protestant historians, but with the intrepidity of a Taine: in the spirit of strength, and not in the cautious and opportunistic spirit of connivance? (Incidentally, it is the Germans who have produced the perfect exemplar of the latter—indeed a thing to be proud of—Leopold Ranke, that classical advocate of every "stronger cause," that smartest of all the smart *Realpolitiker*.)

xx

Does not all this suggest good reasons why we psychologists should keep an alert and suspicious eye on ourselves? The chances are that we are much too "good" for our trade, that we too are *infected*, the victims of a fashionable moralistic taste, no matter how much contempt we may feel for such a taste. I am reminded of the diplomat who said to his colleagues, "Gentlemen, let us distrust our first reactions, they are invariably much too favorable. . . ." This is how a psychologist today should address his colleagues, for the issue we are dealing with demands, in fact, a great strictness toward ourselves, a considerable distrust of immediate reactions. The issue, as the reader of the preceding essay will remember, is the use of the ascetic ideal as a safety valve for pent-up emotion. The object is to pry the human soul loose from its joints, to sink it deep in terror, frost, fire, and transports until it suddenly rids itself of all its dullness, anxiety, gloom. What are the roads leading to this goal? What are the most infallible roads? . . . Any strong emotion will do—rage, fear, lust, vengeance, hope, triumph, despair, cruelty—provided it has sudden release. And the ascetic priest has, in fact, employed the whole pack of hounds that reside in man, releasing now one, now another, always to the end of awakening him from his dull melancholy, of putting his lingering misery to flight, at least temporarily. And he has always done it under the aegis of some religious interpretation and "justification." Every such emotional debauch has to be paid for in the end, so much goes without saying. That is why, by modern standards, remedies of this kind are highly objectionable. Yet, in fairness, we must allow that they have been employed in good faith, that in prescribing them the ascetic priest was deeply convinced that they were useful, even indispensable (the priest himself, in many instances, being shattered by the misery he had to inflict); and, further, that the physiological ravages (including serious mental disturbances) attendant upon such excess are consonant with the spirit of the medication, which does not aim to cure but simply to relieve depression, to palliate, to drug. Certainly that aim may be accomplished in this way. In order to make a ravishing music sound in the human soul, the ascetic priest has to play upon the sense of guilt. In the preceding essay I have briefly touched on the origin of that sense, treating it as an aspect of animal psychology; guilt was viewed there in its raw state. I may now add that to take shape it needed the hands of the ascetic priest, that virtuoso of guilt. "Sin," the priestly version of that animal "bad conscience" (characterized earlier as introverted cruelty) constituted the greatest event in the entire history of the sick soul, the most dangerous sleight of hand of religious interpretation. At odds with himself for one physiological reason or another, rather like a caged animal, unable to comprehend his plight, avid for reasons (reasons are always comforting) and for narcotics, man must finally have recourse to one who knows the hidden causes. Behold, he is given a hint by his magician, the very *first* hint as to the cause of his suffering: he is told to look at himself, to search his own soul for a guilt, a piece of his personal past; to view his suffering as a penance. . . . The sufferer takes the hint, he has *understood,* and from now on he is like a hen about whom a circle has been drawn. Now he will never escape from that confining circle; the patient has been transformed into a "sinner." This new "sinner" aspect of the patient has been with us for millennia; who knows whether we will ever expunge it from our consciousness? Wherever we look we meet the hypnotic stare of the sinner, fixed on the same identical thing—his "guilt," the sole cause of his suffering. Everywhere guilty conscience, Luther's "gruesome beast"; everywhere the hashing over of the past, the distortion of fact, the jaundiced look; everywhere a deliberate misinterpretation of suffering as guilt, terror, and punishment; everywhere the flagellant's lash, the hair shirt, the sinner stretching himself on the rack of his sadistic conscience; everywhere dumb torment, agonizing fear, the spasms of an unknown bliss, the cry for redemption. No doubt such a system of procedures, once instituted, made short work of the ancient depression and tedium. Life became once again a highly interesting business. Initiated into these mysteries, the sinner became wide-awake, eternally wide-awake, aglow yet burned out, exhausted yet far from weary. The ascetic priest, that grand old magician and warrior against depression, had conquered at last; his kingdom had come. People no longer complained of pain but were insatiable for it. Every hurtful debauch of feeling, all that shatters, bowls over, crushes, and transports, every secret of the torture chamber, the ingenuity of hell itself, had finally been discovered and exploited. All was at the service of the magician, at the service of the ascetic ideal. He continued to repeat, as he had done all along, "My kingdom is not of this earth." But had he still a right to say this?

. . . Goethe once remarked that he could think of only thirty-six tragic situations. One might guess from this, if one didn't already know it, that Goethe was no ascetic priest, for the latter knows many more.

XXI

To criticize this whole method of medication would be a waste of breath. Who would seriously maintain that the kind of emotional debauch prescribed by the ascetic priest (under the most sacred names, of course, and with the highest sense of the sacredness of his mission) has ever really benefited anyone? Let us, at least, come to an agreement on the meaning of the word "benefit." If all it means is "improve," then I have no quarrel with its use in this context, except that I would add that for me to "improve" means to tame, to weaken, to discourage, to effeminate, emasculate, sophisticate—in short, to "make worse." If it is a question of ailing and depressed people, such a regimen makes them sicker even if it does make them better. Simply ask the alienists what happens when the human system is constantly subjected to the cruel teasings of penance, to paroxysms of contrition, to an obsession with being saved. Likewise consult history, and you will find that wherever the ascetic priest has been able to enforce his treatment, the sickness has increased alarmingly, both in breadth and depth. What has its "success" consisted of? A shattered nervous system on top of all the pre-existing ailments; and this on the largest as well as on the smallest scale. In the wake of every collective penance-workout we find huge epileptic epidemics, such as the St. Vitus' and St. John's dances of the Middle Ages;

terrible paralyses and permanent depressions resulting, in some cases, in the complete change of temperament of an entire people or city (Geneva, Basel); phenomena like the witch craze and a kind of mass somnambulism (of which latter we find eight great epidemics in the short span between 1564 and 1605). We also find those agonized mass deliriums whose ghastly cry *"Evviva la morte!"* once echoed through large parts of Europe, interrupted now by voluptuous idiosyncrasies, now by destructive ones. We find that same erratic change of affect, with its odd calms between storms and its mad moments of *volte-face*, even today, whenever the ascetic doctrine of sin scores a signal victory. (Religious neurosis *appears* to be a form of evil, I have no doubt. But what *is* it, really?) The ascetic ideal, with its sublime moral cult, with its brilliant and irresponsible use of the emotions for holy purposes, has etched itself on the memory of mankind terribly and unforgettably. I can think of no development that has had a more pernicious effect upon the health of the race, and especially the European race, than this. It may be called, without exaggeration, the supreme disaster in the history of European man's health. The only other development that can hold a candle to it has been specifically Teutonic: I refer to the poisoning of Europe with alcohol, which has kept pace with the political and racial ascendancy of the Germanic tribes. (Wherever they instilled their blood they also instilled their characteristic vice.) Syphilis might be mentioned third, though a considerable distance below the other two in importance.

XXII

Just as the ascetic priest has corrupted man's mental health wherever he has held sway, so he has corrupted his esthetic taste. And he continues to corrupt it. *"Ergo?"* I hope the reader will simply grant me that *ergo,* as I am in no mood to explain it. A single hint may suffice: it has to do with the central document of Christian literature, the book *par excellence,* the paradigm of all the rest. In the very heart of Graeco-Roman splendor, which was also a splendor of books, in the heart of a literature not yet atrophied and dispersed, when it was still possible to read a few books for which we would now trade half of all that is printed, the simple-minded presumption of the Christian agitators known as the Fathers of the Church dared to decree: "We have our own classical literature. We don't need that of the Greeks." And they pointed proudly to certain collections of legends, apostolic epistles, and apologetic penny tracts—the same kind of literature with which the English Salvation Army wages its war against Shakespeare and other pagans. The reader may have guessed already that I have no fondness for the New Testament. I admit that I am somewhat ill at ease to stand so entirely alone in my judgment of this most esteemed, overesteemed, document (the taste of two millennia is against me), but what can I do? This is the way I am, and I have the courage to stand up for my faulty taste. The Old Testament is another story. I have the highest respect for that book. I find in it great men, a heroic landscape, and one of the rarest things on earth, the naïveté of a strong heart. What is more, I find a *people.* In the New Testament, on the other hand, I find nothing but petty sectarianism, a rococo of the spirit, abounding in curious scrollwork and intricate geometries and breathing the air of the conventicle; to say nothing of that occasional whiff of bucolic mawkishness which is characteristic of the epoch (and the locale) and which is not so much Jewish as Hellenistic. Here humility and braggadocio are bedfellows; here we find a stupendous volubility of feeling; the trappings of passion without real passion; an embarrassing amount of gesturing: obviously there is a lack of good breeding all the way through. Think of the tremendous fuss these pious little people make over their little trespasses! Who cares? Certainly God least of all. In the end all these petty provincials even demand the crown of eternal life—on the strength of what? and what do they want with it? Can presumption be carried farther? Just imagine an *immortal Peter!* . . . These little men are fired with the most ridiculous of ambitions: chewing the cud of their private grievances and misfortunes, they try to attract the attention of the Great Demiurge, to force him to *care!* And then, the horrible chumminess with which they address their Maker! That Jewish (but by no means exclusively Jewish) nuzzling and pawing of God! . . . In eastern Asia are found small, inconsequential pagan tribes which might have taught these early Christians a lesson or two in tact; those tribes, as Christian missionaries have told us, do not permit themselves to use the name of God at all. Such conduct, it seems to me, shows a great deal of delicacy; but it is altogether too delicate, not for the primitive Christians only, but for many who came after. To get a clear sense of the contrast, think of Luther, the most eloquent and presumptuous of German peasants; think of his manner of speaking, especially when he held converse with God! Luther's militant attitude toward the mediating saints of the church (especially "that Devil's sow, the Pope") was, in the last analysis, the truculence of a lout toward the Church's etiquette, that reverent etiquette of a hieratic taste, which would admit only the discreet and consecrated into the holy of holies, and would exclude the louts. The latter must never be allowed to speak there. But the peasant Luther would have it otherwise; the traditional practice was not German enough for him. He wanted to be able to speak directly, in his own voice, "informally" with his God. . . . Well, that's what he did.—Obviously the ascetic ideal was at no time a school of good taste, much less of good manners. At best it has been a school of hieratic manners. The reason is that there is something about it which is the deadly enemy of good manners: a lack of restraint, dislike for restraint. It wants to be, and always will be, a *ne plus ultra*.

XXIII

The ascetic ideal has corrupted not only health and taste, but a good many things besides—if I were to try to enumerate them all there would never be an end. But my purpose here is not to show what the ideal has effected but only what it signifies, suggests, what lies behind it, beneath it, and hidden within it; the things it has expressed, however vaguely and provisionally. It was only with this purpose in view that I afforded my reader a rapid view of its tremendous consequences, some of which have been disastrous. I wanted to prepare him for the last and, to me, most terrible aspect of the question "What does the ascetic ideal signify? What is the meaning of its incredible *power*? Why have people yielded to it to such an extent?

Why have they not resisted it more firmly?" The ascetic ideal expresses a *will:* where do we find a contrary ideal expressing a contrary will? The goal of the ascetic ideal is so universal that, compared with it, all other human interests appear narrow and petty. It orients epochs, nations, individuals inexorably toward that one goal, permitting no alternative interpretation or goal. It rejects, denies, affirms, confirms exclusively in terms of its own interpretation— and has there ever been a system of interpretations more consistently reasoned out? It submits to no other power but believes in its absolute superiority, convinced that no power exists on earth but receives meaning and value from it. . . . Where do we find the antithesis to this closed system? Why are we unable to find it? . . . People say to me that such a counterideal exists, that not only has it waged a long, successful battle against asceticism but to all intents and purposes triumphed over it. The whole body of modern scholarship is cited in support of this— that modern scholarship which, as a truly realistic philosophy, clearly believes only in itself, has the courage of its convictions, and has managed splendidly thus far to get along without God, transcendence and restrictive virtues. But such noisy propaganda talk quite fails to impress me. These trumpeters of the "real" are poor musicians. Their voices do not arise out of any authentic depths, the depths of a scholarly conscience—for the scholarly conscience today is an abyss. In the mouths of such trumpeters the word *scholarship* is impudence, indeed blasphemy. The case is exactly the opposite of what is claimed here: scholarship today has neither faith in itself nor an ideal beyond itself, and wherever it is still passion, love, ardor, suffering, it represents not the opposite of the ascetic ideal but, in fact, its noblest and latest form. Does this sound strange to you? There are plenty of decent, modest, hard-working scholars amongst us, who seem perfectly content with their little niche and for this reason proclaim, rather immodestly, that everyone should be content with things as they are these days—especially in the humanities and in science, where so much that is useful remains to be done. I quite agree. I would be the last to want to spoil the pleasure these honest workers take in their work, for I like what they are doing. And yet the fact that people work very hard at their disciplines and are content in their work in no way proves that learning as a whole today has an aim, an ideal, a passionate belief. As I have just said, the reverse is true. Wherever it is not simply the most recent manifestation of the ascetic ideal (and those are rare, noble, special cases, much too special to affect the general verdict), learning today is a hiding place for all manner of maladjustment, lukewarmness, self-depreciation, guilty conscience. Its restless activity thinly veils a lack of ideals, the want of a great love, dissatisfaction with a continence imposed on it from without. How much does learning hide these days, or, at least, how much does it wish to hide! The solidity of our best scholars, their automatic industry, their heads smoking night and day, their very skill and competence: all these qualities betoken more often than not a desire to hide and suppress something. Haven't we all grown familiar with learning as a drug? Scholars are naturally pained by such a view, as everyone knows to his cost who has had close contact with them. A chance remark will hurt them to the quick. We exasperate our learned friends at the very moment we try to honor them; we unleash their fury merely because we are too insensitive to guess that we have before us sufferers unwilling to admit their suffering to themselves, stupefied and unconscious men, mortally afraid of regaining their consciousness. . . .

XXIV

Let us now look at those special cases I mentioned a moment ago, those few idealists still surviving among the philosophers, scholars, and scientists of today. Is it perhaps among them that we must look for the effective antagonists of the ascetic ideal? This is, in fact, what these "unbelievers" (for they are agnostics, all of them) believe themselves to be. Such faith as remains to them is invested in their conviction that they oppose the ascetic ideal. Whenever that issue arises they turn solemn, and their words and gestures become impassioned. But does that prove that what they believe is true? We whose business it is to *inquire* have gradually grown suspicious of all believers. Our mistrust has trained us to reason in a way diametrically opposed to the traditional one: wherever we find strength of faith too prominent, we are led to infer a lack of demonstrability, even something improbable, in the matter to be believed. We have no intention of denying that man is saved by faith, but for this very reason we deny that faith proves anything. A strong, saving faith casts suspicion on the object of that faith; so far from establishing its "truth," it establishes a certain probability —of deception. How does all this apply to our case?— These proud solitaries, absolutely intransigent in their insistence on intellectual precision, these hard, strict, continent, heroic minds, all these wan atheists, Antichrists, immoralists, nihilists, sceptics, suspenders of judgment, embodying whatever remains of intellectual conscience today—are they really as free from the ascetic ideal as they imagine themselves to be? I would tell them something which they cannot see because they are too close to themselves: it is they, precisely, who today represent the ascetic ideal; it is they who are its most subtle exponents, its scouts and advance guard, its most dangerous and elusive *temptation*. If I have ever solved a riddle aright, I would wager that this is a sound guess! These men are a long way from being *free* spirits, because they still believe in truth. . . . When the Christian crusaders in the East happened upon the invincible Society of Assassins, that order of free spirits *par excellence*, whose lower ranks observed an obedience stricter than that of any monastic order, they must have got some hint of the slogan reserved for the highest ranks, which ran, "Nothing is true; everything is permitted." Here we have real freedom, for the notion of truth itself has been disposed of. Has any Christian freethinker ever dared to follow out the labyrinthine consequences of this slogan? Has any of them ever truly experienced the Minotaur inhabiting that maze? I have my doubts. In fact I know none has. Nothing could be more foreign to our intransigents than true freedom and detachment; they are securely tied to their belief in truth—more securely than anyone else. I know all these things only too well: the venerable "philosopher's continence" which such a faith imposes, the intellectual stoicism which in the end renounces denial quite as strictly as it does affirmation, the desire to stop short at the brute fact, the fatalism of *petits faits* (with which French scholarship nowadays tries to gain an advantage over German), the renunciation of all exegesis (that is to say of all those violations, adjustments, abridgments, omissions, substitutions, which among them constitute the business of interpretation). These things, taken together, spell asceticism every bit as much as does the renunciation of sensuality; they are, in fact, but a special mode of such renunciation. As for the absolute will to truth which begets such abstinence, it is nothing other than a belief in the ascetic ideal in its most radical form, though an unconscious one. It is the belief in a metaphysical value, in that absolute value of "the true" which stems from the ascetic ideal and stands or falls with it. Strictly speaking, there is no such thing as a science without assumptions; the very notion of such a science is unthinkable, absurd. A philosophy, a "faith" is always needed to give science a direction, a meaning, a limit, a *raison d'être*. (Whoever wants to invert the procedure, that is, put philosophy on a "strictly scientific basis" must first stand not only philosophy but truth itself on its head: the worst breach of etiquette imaginable in the case of two such venerable females.) To quote from a book of my own, *The Gay Science:* "The truthful man (using "truth" in that audacious sense science presupposes) is led to assume a world which is totally other than that of life, nature and history. Does this not mean that he is forced to deny this world of ours? . . . The faith on which our belief in science rests is still a metaphysical faith. Even we students of today, who are atheists and anti-metaphysicians, light our torches at the flame of a millennial faith: the Christian faith, which was also the faith of Plato, that God is truth, and truth divine. . . . But what if this equation becomes less and less credible, if the only things that may still be viewed as divine are error, blindness, and lies; if God himself turns out to be our *longest* lie?" Here let us pause and take thought. It appears that today inquiry itself stands in need of justification (by which I do not mean to say that such justification can be found). In this connection let us glance at both the oldest and the most recent philosophers: to a man they lack all awareness that the will to truth itself needs to be justified. There is a gap here in every philosophy—how are we to explain it? By the fact that the ascetic ideal has so far governed all philosophy; that truth was premised as Being, as God, as supreme sanction; that truth was not allowed to be called in question. But once we withhold our faith from the God of the ascetic ideal a new problem poses itself, the problem of the value of truth. The will to truth must be scrutinized; our business now is tentatively to question the will to truth. (If any reader thinks I have treated the subject too summarily, I refer him to the section entitled "To What Extent Do We Still Believe?" in my book *The Gay Science*. The whole fifth chapter of that book might be consulted with profit, as well as the preface of *Daybreak*.)

XXV

No, let no one cite the scientist or scholar when I ask for the natural antagonist of the ascetic ideal, when I ask, "Where do we find an antithetical will enforcing an antithetical ideal?" Science is far too dependent for that, it always requires a normative value outside itself in order to operate securely. Learning and inquiry are far from antagonistic to the ascetic ideal; indeed we may say that this ideal is their motive force. Whenever they oppose it, their opposition is not really to the ideal itself but only to certain external aspects of it, to some temporary deadness or dogmatism. By denying its exoteric features, they bring the ideal to life once more. As I have already indicated, inquiry and the ascetic ideal have grown from the same soil; they are at one in their overestimation of truth, in their belief that truth is incommensurate and not susceptible of criticism. This shared belief makes them inevitably allies, so that whoever opposes or questions one must oppose or question the other. Any depreciation of the ascetic ideal entails as a necessary consequence a depreciation of scientific research—and it is high time we woke up to this fact. (As for art, which I hope to discuss more fully at another time, it is far more radically opposed to the ascetic ideal than is science. In art the lie becomes consecrated, the will to deception has good conscience at its back. Plato felt this instinctively—the greatest enemy of art Europe has thus far produced. Plato vs. Homer: here we have the whole, authentic antagonism; on the one hand the deliberate transcendentalist and detractor of life, on the other, life's instinctive panegyrist. An artist who enlists under the banner of the ascetic ideal corrupts his artistic conscience. And yet we see this happen quite regularly: there is no creature on earth more corruptible than the artist.) In the physiological sense, too, science is closely allied with the ascetic ideal: a certain biological impoverishment is necessary to both. It is necessary that the emotions be cooled, the tempo slowed down, that dialectic be put in place of instinct, that seriousness set its stamp on face and gesture—seriousness, which always bespeaks a system working under great physiological strain. Simply examine all those epochs in a nation's history when the scholar assumes a prominent position: those are always the crepuscular times of fatigue and decline; the times of reckless health, instinctual security, confidence in the future, are over. It does not augur well for a culture when the mandarins are in the saddle, any more than does the advent of democracy, of arbitration courts in place of wars, of equal rights for women, of a religion of pity—to mention but a few of the symptoms of declining vitality. (Inquiry seen as a problem; what does inquiry signify: cf. my preface to *The Birth of Tragedy*.) Let us honestly face the fact that inquiry is the best ally of the ascetic ideal, precisely because it is the least conscious, least spontaneous, most secret of allies. All through history the "poor in spirit" and the scholarly antagonists of the ideal have played the same game (one must beware of viewing the latter as the "spiritually rich." This they are not, rather they are the hectic comsumptives of the spirit.) As for their famous victories, there have doubtless been such—but victories over what? The ascetic ideal has always emerged unscathed. The only thing inquiry has accomplished has been to raze wall after wall of outer fortifications which the ascetic ideal had succeeded in building around itself, to the detriment of its looks. Or does anyone seriously believe that the defeat of, say, theological astronomy spelled the defeat of the ideal? Does anyone believe that man has grown less hungry for a transcendental solution to life's riddle simply because life has become more casual, peripheral, expendable, in the visible order of things? Has not man's determination to belittle himself developed apace precisely since Copernicus? Alas, his belief that he was unique and irreplaceable in the hierarchy of beings had been shattered for good: he had become an animal, quite literally and without reservations; he who, according to his earlier belief, had been almost God ("child of God," "God's own image"). Ever since Copernicus man has been rolling down an incline, faster and faster, away from the center—whither? Into the void? Into the "piercing sense of his emptiness"? But has not this been precisely the most direct route to his old ideal? All science (and by no means astronomy alone, concerning whose humiliating and discrediting effect Kant has left us a remarkable confession—"It destroys my importance") all science, natural as well as *unnatural* (by which I mean the self-scrutiny of the "knower") is now determined to talk man out of his former respect for himself, as though that respect had been nothing but a bizarre presumption. We might even say that man's hard-won self-contempt has brought with it its own special brand of pride, an austere form of stoic *ataraxia,* his last and most serious claim to a sense of respect (for in disrespecting we show that we still maintain a *sense* of respect). Can this really be called opposition to the ascetic ideal? Does anyone seriously maintain today (as theologians did for a while) that Kant's "victory" over the conceptual apparatus of dogmatic theology (God, soul, freedom, immortality) has hurt that ideal? (I leave out of account the question whether Kant himself intended anything of the sort.) But it is certainly true that, since Kant, transcendentalists of every persuasion have had *carte blanche;* they have become emancipated from theology; Kant has indicated to them the secret path whereon, without interference and in keeping with scholarly decorum, they may gratify their hearts' desires. Similarly, does anybody now hold it against the agnostics, those admirers of mystery and the unknown, that they worship the question mark itself as their god? (Xaver Doudan once wrote of the ravages worked by *"l'habitude d'admirer l'inintelligible au lieu de rester tout simplement dans l'inconnu."* He thought that the ancients were innocent of that habit.) Assuming that whatever man apprehends not only fails to satisfy his wishes but, indeed, contradicts and confounds them, what a divine expedient to make our intellect, rather than our appetites, responsible for this state of affairs! "There is no true intellection; consequently there must be a God"—what a newfangled syllogistic refinement! what a triumph of the ascetic ideal!

XXVI

Do, perhaps, our modern writers on history reflect a sounder attitude, and one that inspires greater confidence? Their major claim is to be a mirror of events; they reject teleology; they no longer want to "prove" anything; they disdain to act the part of judges (and in this they show a measure of good taste); they neither affirm nor deny, they simply ascertain, describe. . . . All this is very ascetic but even more nihilistic, let us be frank about it! The modern historian has a sad, hard, but determined stare, a stare that looks *beyond,* like that of a lonely arctic explorer (so as not to have to look into the matter, perhaps, or not to have to look back?) There is nothing here but snow; all life is hushed. The last crows whose voices are still heard are "What for?", "In vain," and *"nada."* Nothing thrives any longer except, perhaps, Czarist metapolitics and Tolstoian *pity*. But there is another kind of historian today, perhaps even more modern—an epicurean, philandering kind, who ogles life as much as he does the ascetic ideal, who wears the word "artist" like a kid glove, and who has entirely engrossed the praise of contemplation. How we regret even ascetics and wintry landscapes once these clever fops come in view! No thank you! The devil take that whole contemplative tribe! I would much rather roam with the historical nihilists through their cold, gloomy fogs. In fact, if I were put to the choice, I might even prefer to listen to an entirely a-historical, anti-historical fellow, like that Dühring, whose music now intoxicates a newly emerging group of "simple souls," the anarchic fringe of our educated proletariat. Our calm, contemplative historians are a hundred times worse than that. I can think of nothing as nauseating as such an "objective" armchair, such a perfumed epicure of history, half priest, half satyr, *à la Renan*, who by his falsetto voice betrays what is missing, in what place the cruel Fates have applied their surgical shears. This outrages my taste, and my patience as well. Let him keep his patience who has nothing to lose here. As for me, such a sight makes me furious, such "spectators" embitter me against the spectacle more than the spectacle itself—meaning history, of course—and put me willy-nilly into an anacreontic mood. Nature, who gave the bull his horns, the lion his fangs, gave me a foot—for what? . . . For crushing, by Anacreon, and not simply for running away! For crushing the rotten armchairs, the craven complacency, the prurient eunuchdom that paws over history, the ogling of ascetic ideals, the hypocritical "fairness" of impotence. I have great respect for the ascetic ideal so long as it really believes in itself and is not merely a masquerade. But I have no patience with those coquettish dung beetles who are so eager to smell of the infinite that, before long, the infinite comes to smell of dung. I have no patience with mummies who try to mimic life, with worn-out, used-up people who swathe themselves in wisdom so as to appear "objective," with histrionic agitators who wear magic hoods on their straw heads, with ambitious artists who try to pass for ascetics and priests yet are, at bottom, only tragic buffoons. And I am equally out of patience with those newest speculators in idealism called anti-Semites, who parade as Christian-Aryan worthies and endeavor to stir up all the asinine elements of the nation by that cheapest of propaganda tricks, a moral attitude. (The ease with which any wretched imposture succeeds in present-day Germany may be attributed to the progressive stultification of the German mind. The reason for this general spread of inanity may be found in a diet composed entirely of newspapers, politics, beer, and Wagner's music. Our national vanity and hemmed-in situation and the shaking palsy of current ideas have each done their bit to prepare us for such a diet.) Europe today is extremely rich and inventive in stimulants; in fact, it depends entirely on stimulants and distilled spirits. This may explain the prevalence of counterfeit ideals, those most rarefied distillations of the spirit, as well as the stale quasi-alcoholic fumes one breathes wherever one goes. I wonder how many cargoes of fake idealism, fake heroism, and fake eloquence, how many tons of compassion liqueur (brand: *La Religion de la Souffrance*), how many stilts of "virtuous indignation" for the use of the intellectually flat-footed, how many comedians of Christian morality Europe would have to export today in order to clear its atmosphere. . . . Obviously such overproduction opens up splendid commercial possibilities: a good business could be done in small ideal-idols and the "idealists" that go with them—I hope someone sufficiently enterprising will take up the suggestion. The opportunity to "idealize" the entire globe is in our hands! But why speak of enterprise here at all? The only things needed are the hands, ingenuous, very ingenuous hands. . . .

XXVII

But enough of this. Let's have done with these curiosities and complexities of the modern mind, which inspire as much laughter as they do chagrin. Our particular issue can dispense with them; what does the significance of the ascetic ideal have to do with yesterday and today? I intend to treat those other matters more thoroughly and exactly in another book (*The Will to Power: a Study in the Transvaluation of All Values*) under the chapter heading, "Concerning the History of European Nihilism." The one thing I hope I have made clear here is that even at the highest intellectual level the ascetic ideal is still being subverted. Great is the number of those who travesty or counterfeit it—let us be on our guard against them; whilst in all places where a strict, potent, scrupulous spirit still survives every trace of idealism seems to have vanished. The popular term for such abstinence is *atheism*—but the term does scant justice to the will to truth which motivates its votaries. Yet that will, that *residual* ideal, constitutes, believe me, the ideal itself in its strictest and most sublimated form, absolutely esoteric, divested of all trappings: the essence, not the residue. Honest and intransigent atheism (the only air breathed today by the elite of this world) is thus not opposed to asceticism, all appearances to the contrary. Rather it is one of the last evolutionary phases of that ideal, one of its natural and logical consequences. It is the catastrophe, inspiring of respect, of a discipline in truth that has lasted for two millennia and which now prohibits the lie implicit in monotheistic belief. (The same evolution has gone on in India, quite independently of our own, thus affording substantiating proof. There the identical ideal has compelled the identical conclusion. The decisive phase was reached five centuries before the Christian era, with Buddha or, more accurately, with the Sankhya philosophy, later popularized by the Buddha and codified into a religion.) What is it, in truth, that has triumphed over the Christian god? The answer may be found in my *Gay Science:* "The Christian ethics with its key notion, ever more strictly applied, of truthfulness; the casuistic finesse of the Christian conscience, translated and sublimated into the scholarly conscience, into intellectual integrity to be maintained at all costs; the interpretation of nature as a proof of God's beneficent care; the interpretation of history to the glory of divine providence, as perpetual testimony of a moral order and moral ends; the interpretation of individual experience as preordained, purposely arranged for the salvation of the soul—all these are now things of the past: they revolt our consciences as being indecent, dishonest, cowardly, effeminate. It is this rigor, if anything, that makes us good Europeans and the heirs of Europe's longest, most courageous self-conquest." All great things perish of their own accord, by an act of self-cancellation: so the law of life decrees. In the end it is always the legislator himself who must heed the command *patere legem, quam ipse tulisti.* Thus Christianity as dogma perished by its own ethics, and in the same way Christianity as ethics must perish; we are standing on the threshold of this event. After drawing a whole series of conclusions, Christian truthfulness must now draw its strongest conclusion, the one by which it shall do away with itself. This will be accomplished by Christianity's asking itself, "What does all will to truth signify?" Here I touch once more on my problem, on *our* problem, my unknown friends (for I do not yet know whether I have any friends among you): what would our existence amount to were it not for this, that the will to truth has been forced to examine itself? It is by this dawning self-consciousness of the will to truth that ethics must now perish. This is the great spectacle of a hundred acts that will occupy Europe for the next two centuries, the most terrible and problematical but also the most hopeful of spectacles. . . .

XXVIII

Until the advent of the ascetic ideal, man, the animal *man*, had no meaning at all on this earth. His existence was aimless; the question, "Why is there such a thing as man?" could not have been answered; man willed neither himself nor the world. Behind every great human destiny there rang, like a refrain, an even greater "In vain!" Man knew that something was lacking; a great vacuum surrounded him. He did not know how to justify, to explain, to affirm himself. His own meaning was an unsolved problem and made him suffer. He also suffered in other respects, being altogether an ailing animal, yet what bothered him was not his suffering but his inability to answer the question "What is the meaning of my trouble?" Man, the most courageous animal, and the most inured to trouble, does not deny suffering *per se*: he wants it, he seeks it out, provided that it can be given a meaning. Finally the ascetic ideal arose to give it meaning—its only meaning, so far. But any meaning is better than none and, in fact, the ascetic ideal has been the best stopgap that ever existed. Suffering had been interpreted, the door to all suicidal nihilism slammed shut. No doubt that interpretation brought new suffering in its wake, deeper, more inward, more poisonous suffering: it placed all suffering under the perspective of *guilt*. . . . All the same, man had saved himself, he had achieved a meaning, he was no longer a leaf in the wind, a plaything of circumstance, of "crass casualty": he was now able to will something—no matter the object or the instrument of his willing; the will itself had been saved. We can no longer conceal from ourselves what exactly it is that this whole process of willing, inspired by the ascetic ideal, signifies—this hatred of humanity, of animality, of inert matter; this loathing of the senses, of reason even; this fear of beauty and happiness; this longing to escape from illusion, change, becoming, death, and from longing itself. It signifies, let us have the courage to face it, a will to nothingness, a revulsion from life, a rebellion against the principal conditions of living. And yet, despite everything, it is and remains a *will*. Let me repeat, now that I have reached the end, what I said at the beginning: man would sooner have the void for his purpose than be void of purpose. . . .

ANCHOR BOOKS

PHILOSOPHY AND RELIGION

ALBRIGHT, WILLIAM FOXWELL From the Stone Age to Christianity, A100

ARENDT, HANNAH The Human Condition, A182

BARRETT, WILLIAM Irrational Man, A321

BARTH, KARL Community, State and Church, A221

BENZ, ERNST The Eastern Orthodox Church—Its Thought and Life, trans. Winston, A332

BERENSON, BERNARD Aesthetics and History, A36

BERGSON, HENRI *Laughter* (with Meredith's *Essay on Comedy*) in Comedy, A87

—— Matter and Memory, A172

—— The Two Sources of Morality and Religion, A28

BROWN, ROBERT MCAFEE, & WEIGEL, GUSTAVE, S.J. An American Dialogue, A257

BURKE, EDMUND Edmund Burke: Selected Writings and Speeches, ed. Stanlis, A334

BURTT, E. A. The Metaphysical Foundations of Modern Science, A41

CARY, JOYCE Art and Reality, A260

CROSS, FRANK MOORE, JR. The Ancient Library of Qumran, A272

FORSTER, E. M. Alexandria: A History and a Guide, A231

FREUD, SIGMUND The Future of an Illusion, A99

GALILEO Discoveries and Opinions of Galileo, trans. Drake, A94

GASTER, THEODOR H. The Dead Sea Scriptures, A92

HEIDEGGER, MARTIN An Introduction to Metaphysics, A251

HERBERG, WILL, ed. Four Existentialist Theologians, A141

—— Protestant-Catholic-Jew, A195

JASPERS, KARL Man in the Modern Age, A101

KAUFMANN, WALTER Critique of Religion and Philosophy, A252

—— The Faith of a Heretic, A336

—— From Shakespeare to Existentialism, A213

KIERKEGAARD, S. Either/Or: 2 vols., A181a, A181b

—— Fear and Trembling *and* The Sickness unto Death, A30

KRAMER, SAMUEL NOAH, ed. Mythologies of the Ancient World, A229

LEITH, JOHN H., ed. Creeds of the Churches: A Reader in Christian Doctrine from the Bible to the Present, A312

LENSKI, GERHARD The Religious Factor, A337

LITTELL, FRANKLIN H. From State Church to Pluralism, A294

LOWRIE, WALTER A Short Life of Kierkegaard, A273

LUTHER, MARTIN Martin Luther: Selections from His Writings, ed. Dillenberger, A271

MARX, KARL, & ENGELS, FRIEDRICH Basic Writings on Politics and Philosophy, A185

MEREDITH, GEORGE Essay on Comedy (with Bergson's *Laughter*) in Comedy, A87

MEYERHOFF, HANS, ed. The Philosophy of History in Our Time, A164

MURRAY, GILBERT Five Stages of Greek Religion, A51

NEWMAN, JAMES R. Science and Sensibility, A357

NIETZSCHE, FRIEDRICH The Birth of Tragedy and The Genealogy of Morals, A81

ORTEGA Y GASSET, JOSE The Dehumanization of Art and Other Writings on Art and Culture, A72

PAOLUCCI, HENRY & ANNE, eds. Hegel on Tragedy, A276

PEIRCE, CHARLES S. Values in a Universe of Chance, A126

RATHMELL, J. C. A., ed. The Psalms of Sir Philip Sidney and the Countess of Pembroke, A311

REPS, PAUL, ed. Zen Flesh, Zen Bones, A233

ROSE, MARTIAL, ed. The Wakefield Mystery Plays, A371

RUSSELL, BERTRAND Mysticism and Logic, A104

SANTAYANA, GEORGE Three Philosophical Poets: Lucretius, Dante, Goethe, A17

ANCHOR BOOKS

PSYCHOLOGY

ALLPORT, GORDON W. The Nature of Prejudice, A149

BETTELHEIM, BRUNO Paul and Mary: Two Case Histories from *Truants from Life*, A237

BRENNER, CHARLES An Elementary Textbook of Psychoanalysis, A102

FREUD, SIGMUND The Future of an Illusion, A99

—— A General Selection from the Works of Sigmund Freud, ed. Rickman, A115

FROMM, ERICH May Man Prevail?, A275

GOFFMAN, ERVING Asylums: Essays on the Social Situation of Mental Patients and Other Inmates, A277

—— The Presentation of Self in Everyday Life, A174

JONES, ERNEST Hamlet and Oedipus, A31

—— The Life and Work of Sigmund Freud, ed. & abr. in 1 vol. Trilling & Marcus, A340

JUNG, C. G. Psyche and Symbol, A136

RIEFF, PHILIP Freud: The Mind of the Moralist, A278

VICO, GIAMBATTISTA The New Science of Giambattista Vico, trans. Bergin & Fisch, A254

WHYTE, LANCELOT LAW The Unconscious Before Freud, A286

WIENER, NORBERT The Human Use of Human Beings, A34

ANCHOR BOOKS

BIOGRAPHY, AUTOBIOGRAPHY AND LETTERS

LINGUISTICS AND LANGUAGE

ESSAYS, BELLES LETTRES & LITERARY CRITICISM